At the Crossroads of Post-Communist Modernisation

At the Crossroads of Post-Communist Modernisation

Russia and China in Comparative Perspective

Edited by

Christer Pursiainen

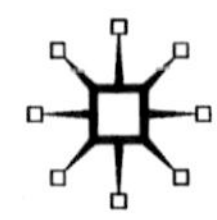

First published 2012 by
PALGRAVE MACMILLAN

Palgrave Macmillan in the UK is an imprint of Macmillan Publishers Limited, registered in England, company number 785998, of Houndmills, Basingstoke, Hampshire RG21 6XS.

Palgrave Macmillan in the US is a division of St Martin's Press LLC, 175 Fifth Avenue, New York, NY 10010.

Palgrave Macmillan is the global academic imprint of the above companies and has companies and representatives throughout the world.

Palgrave® and Macmillan® are registered trademarks in the United States, the United Kingdom, Europe and other countries

ISBN: 978–0–230–36392–2

This book is printed on paper suitable for recycling and made from fully managed and sustained forest sources. Logging, pulping and manufacturing processes are expected to conform to the environmental regulations of the country of origin.

A catalogue record for this book is available from the British Library.

A catalog record for this book is available from the Library of Congress.

10 9 8 7 6 5 4 3 2 1
21 20 19 18 17 16 15 14 13 12

Printed and bound in the United States of America

Contents

Tables

Figures

Preface and Acknowledgements

This book is the result of a three-year project by a team of six researchers from China, Finland, Russia and the United States, all of whom have extensive careers in the social sciences, specialising in the study of either Russian or Chinese societies, or both. The idea to bring these researchers together took shape in 2006, during a visit to Beijing by a delegation of the Aleksanteri Institute – the Finnish Centre for Russian and East European Studies at the University of Helsinki. Naturally, in discussions during this visit, comparative perspectives on developments in Russia and China were often raised. Indeed, it was concluded that a structured comparison of the developments in these two major post-communist countries would be a most interesting project, particularly because at that time there seemed to be no other such books in English on the market.

The idea received a favourable response from the Academy of Finland and with its kind financial support the project was started with a kick-off seminar in March 2008 under the auspices of the Aleksanteri Institute, which became the administrative host of the project. From the very beginning, the plan was to proceed through specifically tailored small-scale workshops with external and critical discussants in order to develop the research team's own draft papers and ideas on how to compare these two countries, as well as to facilitate a wider debate on the theme at large. The first workshop was organised in Moscow in November 2008 at the Higher School of Economics, Faculty of Political Science. The next workshop took place in Beijing in September 2009 at Tsinghua University, Institute of Strategic Studies, School of Public Policy and Management. This was followed by the final workshop in San Francisco in April 2010 at Stanford University, Center on Democracy, Development and the Rule of Law, Institute of International Studies.

Our sincere thanks go to the above-mentioned distinguished institutions. The three workshops helped structure the work of the research team; in addition, we very much benefited from the often challenging comments from our Russian, Chinese and US colleagues, who represent the highest level of scholarship: Kevin O'Brien, Chu Shulong, Dong Xiaoyang, Tom Fingar, Steven Fish, Li Bo, Alexander Lomanov, Fedor

Lukyanov, Kathryn Stoner-Weiss, Nancy Tuma, Mark Urnov, Andrew Walder, Wu Yongping, Igor Zevelev and Zhao Huasheng.

We are also most thankful to Linda Cook and Chris Lanzit for their very useful comments on the final draft of the manuscript, as well as to the three anonymous reviewers who, at different stages of the manuscript, provided us with their constructive but critical evaluations. There are many other people to thank. We owe much to our excellent assistants at different phases of the project: Ira Jänis-Isokangas, Markus Kainu, Ming Tang and Igor Tomashov. We are also especially grateful to the Aleksanteri Institute staff: Marja Riikonen, who so professionally and patiently took care of the financial administration; Essi Lindroos and Anna Salonsalmi, who were most helpful in all practical matters; and Timo Hellenberg, for what could be called the overall inspiration in initiating this project during our trip to western China in September 2006. Thanks also to Toby Archer, who did the final checking of the language and made useful comments on the text. Jingchao Peng from the Swedish Peace Research Institute's Beijing office provided very important logistical support during our workshop in Tshingua University, as did Desirée Gibson from the Keck Center for International and Strategic Studies at Claremont McKenna College during our Stanford University visit. Finally, we express our great appreciation to Ambassador Matti Anttonen, who found time to host a most inspiring evening at the Embassy of Finland during our workshop in Moscow.

You are now holding the result of our adventure of more than three years. It goes without saying that one book cannot be comprehensive enough to cover the most important aspects of socio-political change over the last twenty or thirty years in countries such as Russia and China. Yet we believe that while each of the aspects discussed in this work deserves a book of its own – and in fact, a lot of such books do exist – the novelty of our approach is that we draw a concise but holistic picture that focuses on, to our mind, the essence of the transformations in Russia and China. Unlike many books dealing with Russia and China simultaneously, we are not focusing on their bilateral relations. These two countries appear in many ways to be on the same side of an emerging new ideological and global competition, representing an alternative modernisation model to that of the West. Yet there are also naturally crucial differences between these countries' strategies and conditions. We are confident that our approach enables a structured comparison of these two countries in spite of the multiple sub-themes and different empirical conditions. While the overall approach represents a minimum consensus by the authors, the breadth of theoretical and empirical themes involved in this kind of a study makes it impossible to agree on each and every issue and interpretation. We have therefore chosen to follow the traditional form of an edited compilation, showing clearly under each chapter, and sometimes in the footnotes, who is responsible for which chapter and section. Still, this book can be regarded as a whole, and it is much more coherent than many edited volumes.

While the book draws a long-term and general picture of its theme, some of the issues deal with contemporary daily politics. It should therefore be mentioned that the individual chapters were mostly completed in the summer of 2011 and the whole manuscript assembled in September 2011. However, some figures and developments relate to the December 2011 State Duma elections in Russia and were updated after that event in the respective chapter.

An offshoot of the project was the XI Aleksanteri Conference, which was held in Helsinki in November 2011 on the very same theme as this book. The high-level keynote speakers, over one hundred papers, and the overall enthusiasm of the participants proved that our comparative Russia–China theme is perhaps more than a question for a specific moment, but rather part of an emerging research programme dealing with the results of post-communism and other societal and political transformation processes. Questions such as 'is the transition over?', 'are the hybrid regimes here to stay?' and 'what is this so-called new authoritarianism?' seem to be challenging enough to justify further investigation and new theoretical openings.

Contributors

Li Chunling is Professor of Sociology at the Institute of Sociology, Chinese Academy of Social Sciences (CASS). She received her Master's in History from Beijing University (1987) and her PhD in Sociology from CASS (1998).

Linda Jakobson is Program Director of East Asian studies at the Lowy Institute for International Policy, Sydney. She was the Programme Director and Senior Researcher for the China and Global Security Programme at the Stockholm International Peace Research Institute (SIPRI) whilst based in Beijing, as well as Programme Director on China at the Finnish Institute of International Affairs.

Markku Kivinen is Director of the Aleksanteri Institute, Finnish Centre for Russian and Eastern European Studies, University of Helsinki. He was Professor of Sociology at the University of Lapland, Finland (1991–96) and a visiting professor at the University of Michigan (2001). He received his MA, Licentiate's degree, and PhD in Sociology from the University of Helsinki.

Sergei Medvedev is Professor and Associate Dean at the State University – Higher School of Economics in Moscow. He studied at the universities of Moscow, Prague and New York City, and holds a PhD in History. Over the past 15 years, he has held research positions and professorships in Russia, Germany, Italy and Finland.

Minxin Pei is the Tom and Margot Pritzker '72 Professor of Government and the Director of the Keck Center for International and Strategic Studies at Claremont McKenna College. From 1999 to 2009 he was a senior associate at the Carnegie Endowment for International Peace and directed its China Program from 2004 to 2009. He was on the faculty of the Politics Department at Princeton University from 1992 to 1998. He received his MA and PhD in Political Science from Harvard University.

Christer Pursiainen is Senior Advisor at the Secretariat of the Council of the Baltic Sea States, Stockholm. He has worked in institutions such as Nordregio, Nordic Centre for Spatial Development in Stockholm; Russian-European Centre for Economic Policy, Moscow; Aleksanteri

Institute, Finnish Centre for Russian and East European Studies at the University of Helsinki; and the Finnish Institute of International Affairs, Helsinki. He is Doctor of Political Science and Docent in International Relations at the University of Helsinki. It should be noted that all the arguments he proposes in this book are his responsibility alone and do not reflect the opinions of his current employer.

1
Introduction

Christer Pursiainen

In the two decades that have followed the 1989–1991 collapse of communism in the former Soviet bloc and the June 1989 crackdown on the pro-democracy movement in Tiananmen Square in Beijing, the former communist states have traversed diverse paths away from communist rule. Some former Soviet satellite states in Eastern and Central Europe – amongst them Hungary, the Czech Republic, Poland, and Slovakia, and the three Baltic states previously part of the Soviet Union – have made relatively successful transitions to consolidated democracies and market economies. A small number of former Soviet republics, such as Ukraine and Georgia, continue to struggle in their transformation process and face uncertain futures. The former Soviet republics in Central Asia and Belarus have degenerated into autocratic regimes that have successfully preserved the power of the previous ruling elites despite adopting ostensibly democratic, but heavily manipulated, electoral institutions.

Two countries, Russia and China, being great powers in their own right, provide a particularly interesting comparison in the context of post-communist societal and political change. This book will take a closer look at these two countries' transformations in three interconnected dimensions: socioeconomic development, political system change, and international relations.

Anomaly or alternative?

This book is a comparative case study of the modernisation paths and strategies of Russia and China. However, first it is useful to put the theme into the context of the more general debate about whether a new global ideological competition is taking shape in the aftermath of post-communist transition. Is it so that instead of the communism versus capitalism juxtaposition, 'hybrid regimes' or 'new authoritarianism', represented by countries such as Russia and China, challenge the Western type of liberal–democratic modernisation strategy?

There was a time when the socialist or communist model of modernisation appeared to a large part of the world's population, or at least to their ruling elites, not only as an inevitable next step after capitalism, but also as the most effective one in terms of socioeconomic development. The leaders of the two communist great powers quite often made big promises to this effect. We may remember the Soviet leader Nikita Khrushchev's claim in late 1950s of the Soviet Union surpassing the economic power of the US within about five years. And we can recall Mao Zedong's envisaged scenario during the catastrophic years of the Great Leap Forward, according to which China, within a few years, would catch up and then surpass first British industrial capacity and, soon after that, the capacity of the other great powers. This optimism also looked plausible for many non-communist observers. In social science literature, the German scholar Wilhelm Fucks presented his widely debated study in 1965, which forecast that by about 1978 China would become the most powerful economy in the world, and by 1992 China's economic might alone would surpass the total combined economic capacity of the US, the Soviet Union, and what he called the 'Western European Union'.[1]

These forecasts failed, and the reason for this is simple – wrong indicators. Fucks' rather sophisticated calculations were based on the production of steel and coal, as were Khrushchev's and Mao's, too. These seemed to be the right indicators of economic development and, in a wider sense, of modernisation, at that time when such more general indicators as GNP – today's somewhat outdated but still dominant economic measurement tool – were still new. In any case, this approach completely overlooked the major socioeconomic and scientific–technological developments which were already in progress. In the capitalist West, a post-industrial information and service society was rapidly developing, and partially replacing traditional industrial society. True, the previously underdeveloped communist countries such as the Soviet Union and China felt that they had managed to catch up with the capitalist world in the early phase of modernisation. They did this via forced industrialisation, enabled by the concentrated power of their totalitarian systems. This led to them celebrating their optimism, but by the late 1970s it was clear that the liberal–capitalist model was superior when the new modernisation phase started to dominate global economic developments. The development of post-industrial economies seemed to take place only within the liberal–capitalist ever-globalising system, due to the fact that, at least domestically, it allowed bottom-up initiatives to flourish. On the other hand, the totalitarian planned economies seemed not to be able to deal with the challenges of the new era.

When the Soviet Union's system, along with those of almost all other communist countries, collapsed between the end of the 1980s and the beginning of the 1990s, it seemed to confirm the power of the Western model. The argument was quickly put forward that the world was witnessing "not just the end of the Cold War, or the passing of a particular period of postwar history, but the end of history as such: that is, the end point of mankind's ideological evolution and the universalisation of Western liberal democracy as the final form of human government."[2] Today, it is obvious that this argument was, at the very least, an overestimation; the crucial question is whether it missed even the main direction of the global development that was already going on at that time, in the same way as the earlier forecasts that celebrated communist victory missed the reality. Around twenty years after the 'end of history', it is noticeable that the history has 'returned' and the dreams are over.[3] More and more books are coming onto the market which claim that it is instead the experience of particularly China's seemingly very efficient modernisation, which will inspire and dominate the current century as a reference model for many non-Western countries. Instead of becoming more like the West and emphasising the Western type of modernisation with its institutions, values, and customs, such as rule of law or democratic norms, China, with its successful state capitalism, is creating its own modernisation path and model. Potentially, at least if we should rely on lessons from previous large-scale historical periods of change, China will eventually also seek to shape the world in its image, or at least it will challenge the current global order.[4]

In the era of globalisation the countries, to some extent, necessarily converge in terms of their economic and political systems; even so, a rather obscure and non-standardised type of 'new' authoritarian capitalism, or perhaps state capitalism, has arisen. This hybrid has formed an alternative to the Western model for a whole group of countries, especially in Asia and Africa (in spite of the Arab 'democratic' uprisings in 2011), in their efforts to deal with the challenges of modernisation and globalisation. The global financial and economic crisis of the latter part of the first decade of the new millennium, which revealed many structural weaknesses in the Western model, has enhanced the power and attractiveness of the state–capitalist model for the non-Western countries' *elites*, who are looking for their own route of modernisation which would enable them to stay in power. The illusion of supremacy of Western liberal–democratic capitalism, especially the once so celebrated neo-liberal version of it, has been rapidly broken down, or at least lost its attractiveness as a path to follow. After the end of ideological competition between capitalism and communism and the seeming victory of the Western model, this victory was never completely finalised and it seems possible that a new global ideological competition between liberal–democratic capitalism and a new kind of authoritarian state capitalism is taking shape.

In this book, we take a closer look at the experiences of two major post-communist countries, and great powers, who have chosen not to follow the Western liberal–democratic modernisation example, but who are taking their own authoritarian state–capitalist modernisation paths. Russia's and China's historical experiences are different, but are linked in more than one way. The Soviet Union did *not* originally choose the 'Chinese way' of Deng Xiaoping – though it perhaps was one of the options during the short-lived Yuri Andropov period in the early 1980s, when reforms were understood to be necessary, but were limited to those within the economic system only. China's later policies were in turn created by a determination to *not* follow the 'Soviet way' in terms of what happened under Mikhail Gorbachev and later with Boris Yeltsin. Instead of the double-reform of the political and economic systems in the Soviet Union, and later in Russia, which simultaneously broke down leading to downfall and chaos, China chose to maintain a focus on state-led market-economic reforms while keeping the political system virtually untouched. For an observer committed to Western liberal values, the obvious success of this path is still an anomaly. In order to deal with this perceived anomaly, the question put forward by some scholars has been framed as asking why the Chinese authoritarian one-party system is so 'resilient',[5] thus implying that this resilience nevertheless has its limits, and that sooner or later China has to democratise and adopt Western political values and forms of governance if it is to remain economically successful.

Russia would also be an anomaly for the same observer: why did it not democratise, and why is its 'new authoritarianism' so resilient?[6] The popular anti-regime protests which started in Russia at the end of 2011 are easily interpreted from this perspective so that this resilience has been pushed to its limits and Russia is on the brink of both socio-economic and political collapse. In any case, things in Russia did not evolve in the beginning as they 'should' have done from the 'Western' point of view. True, Russia made some progress in liberalising both its political and economic systems. In the mid-1990s it was not rare to hear both Russian and Western leaders to proclaim that Russia and the West share the same, 'universal values'. "From the perspective of universal values", President Boris Yeltsin declared in 1996, "our country has made a strategic choice in directing its development: civil society, rule of the law and the market economy. Civil society is the guarantee of freedom, democracy and justice."[7] However, during recent years it has been more or less acknowledged – both in policy analyses and by Western political leaders – that Russia has not followed a linear path from a totalitarian or authoritarian state and command economy towards a Western type of liberal democracy and market economy.

Russia came out of the post-*perestroika* anarchy with a new kind of leadership. Vladimir Putin[8] and his more liberal counterpart Dmitri Medvedev[9] were both hand-picked by their predecessors and did not have previous reputation as politicians. Both have openly relied on the idea that Russia is *not* mirroring or copying the Western model but, rather, that the country should leap over this model to somewhere new. While there might have been some differences in the fine-tuning of the political system within this four-year tandem-regime, there has been (at least publicly) a clear elite agreement on the building blocks of the new and lasting order. This would be a combination of economic–technological modernisation: building a high-tech, great power Russia relying on lessons and technology borrowed from the West, and political modernisation based on Russia's own national political culture, which most notably expresses itself in the striving towards 'political wholeness' through centralisation of power functions and the personification of political institutions.[10] Accordingly, Prime Minister Putin announced that he will choose to retake his position as the next elected President of Russia in March 2012, whereas Medvedev would in turn be formally downgraded to prime minister. This scenario – which at the time of writing, has a realistic chance of materialising – will again establish a clear-cut Putin-regime, potentially for the next twelve years according to the Constitution. While we may look for specific characteristics of this kind of post-communist, new- or post-modern authoritarian regime, one should not forget that this is the same formula that, in various forms, has been used in Russia at least since Peter the Great. The current application, even if called 'sovereign democracy' by Russian leaders themselves, effectively builds upon the legacy of Russian authoritarian and communitarian traditions.

In any case, the 'third wave of democratisation'[11] seems not to have fulfilled its promises to Russia, and even less so to China. True, Samuel Huntington, when introducing this concept in a rather optimistic spirit, never claimed – unlike Francis Fukuyama advocating 'the end of history' – that the third wave of democratisation would be the final storm leading to the ultimate democratisation of the whole world. The question, then, is whether a hybrid regime will prove to be a tangible alternative. Yet, there seems to be not one form of hybrid regime and not one path to those different hybrids. The current modernisation strategies of Russia and China, led by their elites who try to redefine their respective countries' role and future in a complex environment, were launched from very different starting points. Originally they chose different paths, and these countries' current solutions to their socioeconomic and political systems coincide only at a very general level.

Both of these post-communist countries have experienced extensive socioeconomic and political transformations, as well as foreign policy reorientations, during the past two or three decades. While it is often tempting to emphasise the historical legacies of the old cultural, political, and socioeconomic systems in non-Western countries, one cannot overlook the tremendous changes caused by globalisation (particularly of capital and values) – changes that are still going on. This book will deal with the challenge of understanding what has happened and, in part, what is still happening in post-communist Russia and China in the context of global post-modern capitalism, and why. To be sure, individually the changes in Russia and China have been a rather popular subject for academic study; they have been popularised in applied research and, naturally, they are regular elements in policy debates and news reports. However, very few scholars have taken advantage of the opportunity to study the developments in Russia and China in a comparative perspective.[12] This lack of Russia–China comparisons is probably due to the fact that while the Soviet Union as a political system and geopolitical entity collapsed almost overnight, the major changes that China has undergone have been almost silent in comparison, appearing to be evolutionary in form and only revolutionary when seen over time. One can still argue about when China actually ceased to be a socialist or communist state. Some – perhaps even many – political scientists, completely ignoring earlier definitions of this particular political and economic system, continue to claim that China remains a communist country, simply because its ruling party calls itself a communist party. In any case, during the whole of the 1990s most analysts implicitly held that the two countries had increasingly fewer common features.

In a way, this threw them into different analytical categories and made them a rather 'odd couple' when used for comparative purposes.

In early 2010s the situation seems to be different, even if we do not have a clear picture about where developments in Russia and China are ultimately headed. But in order to tackle the issue of why such developments have taken place in Russia and China respectively, and what might be their societal and wider global consequences, a comparative approach has several clear advantages. It may lead to a better understanding of both country-specific and residual peculiarities, as well as providing a clearer picture of more general tendencies in political and socioeconomic transformations of this type of country. Additionally, it will perhaps lead also to some more generalised comparative politics arguments, applicable to any country. We should start by asking why Russia and China chose, or perhaps were thrown onto, such different initial paths through their post-communist transitions. At what junctures were the crucial choices made? How do their strategies differ today? How are they interrelated and where are they now? On the basis of this analysis, we will come to questions such as: what are the strategic choices yet to be made by Russia and China? What are the available alternatives, how are they constructed, and what are the internal and external settings that facilitate and constrain the choices between different future policy lines?

The bias of comparison

Broadly speaking, comparative politics aims to provide answers to questions such as why societies are run so differently, why their socioeconomic and political systems are designed in such various ways, and what are the societal consequences of the different constellations. Most comparative politics is done by political scientists and, even more importantly, it is applied to the study of democracies or democratisation. Mainstream comparative politics often discusses some rather technical binary patterns of democratic governance, such as majoritarian versus consensus governments, two-party versus multiparty systems, executive versus legislative, centralised versus decentralised models, and so forth. In this genre, the aim is to identify the pros and cons of differently governed *democratic* political system.[13] If the emphasis is more on long-term historical perspectives, questions such as how do democracies initially appear, why and how do they consolidate, why do they sometimes become unstable, and how could they collapse into dictatorships, are the central issues.[14] From a wider perspective, one should also include Marxist and post-Marxist analyses into the scope of comparative politics, as these analyses are mostly truly comparative by definition, though ideologically more explicitly deterministic. In this case, the focus is not so much on Western liberal democracies but on world politics in general, on the interrelationship of the world economy and domestic politics, issues of hegemony, and emancipation. The overall spirit of analysis would, from a Marxist point of view, be much less 'technical' and more 'ideological' than in mainstream comparative political science.[15]

But in any case, and as is widely accepted, all possible theoretical solutions carry some ideological and teleological predetermined elements into empirical analysis, indeed much more than in non-comparative politics. For instance, in their comparative analysis of modernisation paths, Kopstein and Lichbad consciously try to use a more 'neutral' concept: 'development paths'. But they then divide the countries studied into four categories: early, middle, late, and experimental developers. Both Russia and China would be late developers in this typology. Characteristic of these countries, economic development occurred so late compared to the early developers that the state was forced to play a very strong role, society remained weak, and the middle classes remained small and powerless. The societal response in these largely peasant countries, as an alternative to a liberal development path, was a communist revolution led by the intellectual middle-class elite.[16] In a way, this approach allowed the countries to leap over many phases of Western capitalist development, or at least their leaders thought so.

When putting countries not only into comparative perspective, but also into implicit or explicit preference-ordering – early versus late, developed versus underdeveloped, consolidated versus unconsolidated, modernised versus pre-modernised, and so forth – bias is not easy, and may even be impossible, to avoid. By definition any comparison, implicitly or explicitly, has to deal with ideal types; it has to choose some criteria and comparative elements that are not and cannot be value-free. It is extremely difficult to use even 'neutral' language and concepts when discussing countries in comparative perspective. This is primarily the case with that part of comparative politics literature which is closely connected to post-communist developments, precisely because the tradition of comparative politics calls us to focus on democratisation, or at least on modernisation with democracy as a teleological goal. Indeed, even a short look at the mainstream comparative politics literature is enough to convince one that the vast majority of it has Western democracies and the West-dominated realist–liberal world order as explicit or implicit ideal reference points. Mainstream comparative politics has implicitly adopted the idea that the history (of modernisation) really has a predetermined direction; Marxist historical and dialectical materialism does the same, but in more explicit terms. The end point is assumed; some countries go more straightforwardly towards it, whereas the modernisation paths of others are characterised by harmful zigzags or slowness.

Even if we would *consciously* try to find a less teleological comparative theory or yardstick for comparison, all theories related to the comparative study of post-communist politics, and their respective methodologies, tend to predetermine the outcome of empirical observations, or at least tell us what to look at. If our liberal theory states, for instance, that the existence of a developed network of independent non-governmental organisations is an important feature in a democratic political system and that this, in turn, is the best frame to facilitate long-term development and modernisation, we are likely to pay attention to that particular empirical fact and make our conclusions accordingly. If we, in the spirit of post-Marxist or post-structuralist approaches, would look for emancipation instead, we are likely to find the proof for our deductive theoretical arguments in the empirical evidence. Even more important is the understanding that even such supposedly neutral concepts as 'transition', 'modernisation', 'development', or even 'transformation' bring with them some teleological goals.[17]

Thus, we *cannot* avoid the bias of explicit or implicit ideal types in comparing Russia and China. In order to avoid over-simplified theorising, the most important theoretical choice in this book is therefore that our overarching social science theory element is not one school of thought, not one single theory or single-level analytic factor, but rather a debate between several schools and theories. Our reference point is the large body of literature, including a number of theories and related methodologies and concepts, that deal with issues such as social change, social transformation, transition, modernisation, regime change, and so forth, even if these ideas are labelled differently depending on the particular school or theory. In so doing we refuse to accept the idea of explaining the social, economic, and political changes of Russia and China by any one single-factor or single-level model.

This brings us, however, to the issue of dealing with several levels and units of analysis simultaneously, as the theories and related explanations move on and are rooted in these different levels. There is no unambiguous way to deal with this challenge. Our solution, in general terms, is to lean towards the constructivist side of metatheoretical social science debates. This emphasises the importance of the *interplay* between different theoretical levels of reality and analysis: macro and micro, structures and agents, processes and individuals, culture and institutions, identities and interests, and so forth. We rely upon and elaborate upon this interplay in order to describe, interpret and, perhaps, understand or explain what has been and what is currently happening in Russia and China. How the structure–agency or macro–micro interplay is manifested in different issues is, in our analysis, not a theoretical issue but, rather, a largely empirical one.

Structural preconditions

Let us start with 'structures'. The literature that focuses on structural elements, and which can be applied to comparative studies of post-communist societies, has in some typologies been summarised into two broad schools of thought. The *modernisation school* would be understood as one which, generally speaking, focuses on the observed positive empirical correlation between socioeconomic development and levels of democracy, emphasising, however, the problem of causality (or direction of the 'causal arrow') in this context. What has been labelled as an independent *structural approach* in this context, and being more closely connected to traditional Marxist analysis, looks at the historical processes from the perspective of power structures, and focuses mainly on social class structures, class relations, and their consequences.[18] However, to our mind, these two schools overlap considerably and their concepts and hypotheses have often been applied interchangeably. Therefore we choose to treat these two structural schools as one source of theoretical and conceptual inspiration, not so much emphasising their differences, but rather their combined generalised argument; namely that structural factors should receive due attention as causal factors in analysing large-scale social changes.

Let us first take a short look at what these 'structural' factors might be. As a school, modernisation theory has been, and remains, rather heterogeneous and open to interpretation.[19] Usually such 'material' structural processes as urbanisation, industrialisation, demographic development, improvement in living standards, development of welfare systems, and similar socioeconomic processes are included in the toolkit of modernisation theory. Sometimes, the development of democratic institutions is included as a similar structural modernisation process, as it is held ideologically that a society cannot be truly 'modern' without some level of democracy. This in turn has brought attention to 'non-material' structural factors such as civic virtues and value systems – of the elite or of society at large – and the argument goes that these values play a crucial role in the emergence and flourishing of working democratic institutions.[20]

On the other hand, and in much more neutral and general terms, modernisation can be seen as an increase in the capacity for social transformation that does not presuppose any one model of linear development. "If the starting point and the end state each comprise a variety of social structural types, and if we allow for the notion of a variety of developmental paths, even for similar societies, we are committed to evolutionism only in the loosest sense."[21]

True, modernisation theory often provides tools for rather deterministic interpretations. When the Soviet Union and other East European communist systems collapsed, modernisation theory was adopted by many to explain post facto that the collapse was inevitable due to the fact that communist systems could not facilitate further modernisation processes even if they did have resources – basically in the same way as was discussed above and as will be elaborated in more detail in the next, historical chapter. The simplified argument of this faction is that top-down systems could not deal with the bottom-up driving forces of post-industrial society; furthermore, it was concluded that the resulting collapse was the triumph of modern liberal capitalism. However, this argument was rapidly criticised for providing too teleological a model for approaching such complex developments as post-communist Russia.[22]

In turn, the Marxist and post-Marxist structural schools emphasise class structures when dealing with societal changes from a structural point of view.[23] One should start by noting that class analysis does not only consist of drawing maps of the class structure, slotting people into those different classes, and counting the proportions they represent. This is merely the first step, and is certainly inadequate for establishing whether those classes exist only in the researcher's typology or whether they actually exist in social reality.[24] Yet this first typological step is necessary in order to make sense of the situation, and the identification of classes has to be based upon some clearly operationalised principles.

However, if class analysis was merely this kind of statistical exercise it would not have any relevance. A class analysis, as we see it, is necessarily rooted in the philosophy of structure–agency (see below in this chapter), even when it leans towards discussing the structural side of the issue. A class may be without any collective identity or agency, or it may develop its own identity and act as a collective agent. For an individual, belonging to a class, that class is a structural factor. An individual can, certainly at least in one's personal life, choose whether or not to identify with one's own 'objective' class. Yet the class structure is, according to this school, a major structural factor explaining the outcome of social change.

Class analysis, however, is a highly complex process which involves many conceptual levels and research strategies. A very basic distinction which needs to be made is that between class position and class situation.[25] Class position has to do with ownership and domination within production. The concept of class situation, then, refers to more concrete phenomena: the reproduction situation such as income, education, labour market position, and working conditions. Studies of class organisation and class consciousness cannot base their explanations on class structure without an analysis of class situation. Class interests cannot be identified without taking into account class situation. For example, in order to analyse the potential interests of the Russian or Chinese middle classes today, we have to start from the historical and concrete living conditions instead of, as many orthodox Marxists would do, looking at the 'objective historical mission' of a class. Class interests, we argue very clearly, are not objectively given within the structure of capitalist or socialist societies. It is precisely the historicity and contextuality of interests that constitute the biggest challenges to class analysis today.

It must also be noted that social classes are not only socioeconomic realities, but are also cultural constructions. This means, among other things, an openness to rival explanations, even if our focus would be on class. It is thus important to recognize that class analysis is not about reducing everything to class. Indeed, we have not seen this kind of essentialism or class reductionism in the last thirty years or so. There are other identities which may, and often do, leave class overshadowed. Other collective communities, or even 'imagined communities',[26] such as nations or religious identities are particularly important in a situation where both class and civil society are poorly developed – which, of course, is particularly applicable to present-day Russia as well as China.

So what about the causality of these structures? While many deterministic studies have been written in the name of the modernisation and structural schools, Barrington Moore's seminal 1966 *Social Origins of Dictatorship and Democracy*,[27] a philosophical and illustrative study, rather than a true sociological or empirical analysis, is helpful in illustrating how we understand the logic of causality in this school. Moore tried to list the structural preconditions, mainly focusing on social classes, for the different paths that modernisation has taken in the twentieth century: bourgeois, fascist, and communist. At first glance, one can interpret Moore so that these preconditions could not only explain the emergence of a certain political system or, in general, the modernisation path, but that they more or less determine the outcome. However he also argues that in principle the modernisation paths are open-ended, and in passing he implies that governments, or possibly other actors, if they are informed about the necessary preconditions, may adopt the appropriate strategy to reach 'modern democracy' if they so choose.[28]

Thus, while the focus on 'objective' structural conditions in modernisation literature often speaks in the language of determinism, these preconditions, we argue, are better understood as structural factors which delimit or enable the possibilities inherent in a given historical situation.[29] These preconditions, it must be clearly stated, can naturally also be shaped by the actions of social agents, and not only the other way round as in orthodox Marxism. We must also emphasise the interplay of exogenous and endogenous structural factors in conditioning social change. With some danger of simplification, one can state that mainstream comparative politics focuses more on endogenous factors, whereas traditionally the exogenous sources have been emphasised in the variety of dependency and neo-Marxist theorising on underdevelopment. While we discuss many country-specific endogenous issues in terms of explanatory causal factors, we cannot overlook the notion of the importance of external context. This especially includes the previous spread of industrial capitalism and post-modern capitalist globalisation as an all-encompassing phenomenon – profoundly affecting and conditioning even large countries such as Russia and China.

Short-term processes and agents

While we stress the importance of 'structures', it must be clear by now that we do not claim that they – or perhaps more clearly structural *preconditions* – determine the outcome. Agency must be brought into the picture as well. For our theme, the most relevant theoretical school that focuses on agency is the so-called transition school. Here, to choose between the structure and agency, it is not only a question of the length of the time period being analysed. While structures or preconditions are usually understood as long-term phenomena by definition, when applied to countries such as Russia or China in the light of their recent history it seems obvious that even within a relatively short term (of twenty years or so) socioeconomic preconditions, along with many other structural preconditions and even social class structures, have changed considerably. To become convinced by argument it is enough to study some of the figures and tables in Chapter 3 of this book, which show the socioeconomic and class structure changes in Russia and China.

Nevertheless, the transition school's zoom is much more limited. It prioritises short-term political agency-determined processes over structural changes in order to explain outcomes and longer-term developments, rarely paying any attention to economic or socioeconomic variables. A good way to present the transition approach very briefly and in its 'pure form' is to look at it from the point of view of its critics, and then to look at how it has defended itself. In 2002 Thomas Carothers published his essay *The End of the Transition Paradigm*,[30] which argues that, after about a decade of post-communist reforms, it is time to recognize that the school had outlived its usefulness and one should look for a better lens. His criticism culminated in the argument that the reality was no longer conforming to the model. This model, according to Carothers, is built upon five core assumptions. First, any country moving away from dictatorial rule can be considered to be a country in transition towards democracy. Second, this democratisation is supposed to follow a set sequence of stages, more or less. This starts with an opening period, such as the political liberalisation of the dictatorial regime. It is followed by a breakthrough, such as the collapse of the old regime and the rapid emergence of a new democratic system and related institutions, and it ends with a slower process of democratic consolidation. Third, the paradigm is rooted in a belief in the determining importance of elections not just as a foundation stone, but as a key generator, over time, of further democratic reforms. Fourth, underlying conditions such as socioeconomic level, political history, institutional legacies, sociocultural traditions, and so on, are not major factors in starting the transition process or in its outcomes. Finally, the paradigm assumes the existence of a largely coherent and functioning state, where the democratic transition will include some redesign of existing state institutions.

Carothers' article created a lively debate, which inspired a special issue of the *Journal of Democracy*, wherein many of the representatives of the transition school defended themselves quite successfully. One of the contributors was Guillermo O'Donnell,[31] who replied that under the heading of the 'transition paradigm', Carothers had lumped together a large and uneven body of work and then proceeded to concentrate his criticisms on some of the weakest parts of it. He agreed with Carothers on many points, but noted that Carothers did not draw a true picture of the transition literature. In particular, O'Donnell emphasised that the work which he had co-edited, the 1986 four-volume *Transitions from Authoritarian Rule*,[32] which Carothers had claimed to be the seminal and pioneering work defining the content of the transition paradigm, was *not* entitled *Transitions to Democracy*. There was, O'Donnell remarked, nothing predestined about these transitions; their course and outcome were open-ended and uncertain.

In general, however, it seems to be true that within the democratic transition literature, structural factors – such as levels of socioeconomic development, literacy rates, urbanisation, and so on – have been challenged, and have to some extent even fallen out of favour, as explanatory causal variables. This is largely an intellectual rejection of the modernisation theory and its functionalist approach to understanding political change. Instead of emphasising preconditions as causal factors, since the 1970s scholars have focused on the *process* of transition in order to gain insights into how authoritarian regimes exit from power and new democracies emerge. In particular, political bargaining, strategic interaction between the ruling elites and the opposition, uncertainty, and contingency have been viewed as more important in influencing the choices made by authoritarian ruling elites and the outcome of the transition process.[33]

Some applications of the transition school on post-communist developments go so far as to state that "structural factors do not determine outcomes; individuals do".[34] We do not share that view either, as it leans too much on the power of the process and overlooks the structural preconditions for action. The old Marxist wisdom that although man makes his own history, he does not make it out of conditions chosen by himself but, rather, out of such things he finds to hand, is still valid. Agency-based and process-based theories have limited explanatory utility mainly because such theories offer only a few parameters for analysing probable transition outcomes. As reductionist theories, they *alone* do little more than emphasise the high degree of uncertainty and the difficulty in using a given set of variables to predict the outcomes of the transition process.[35]

In this book, we nevertheless argue for the usefulness of the transition paradigm, not as a dogmatic teleological road map or a collection of reductionist single-factor process-based and agency-based explanatory variables, but rather as a toolbox of rather well-defined concepts and empirically tested hypotheses, which under some conditions have proved to be crucial and causally measurable factors, and in others, have not. Indeed, even the firm transition theorists often need to refer to structures. For instance, a classic text on democracy by Robert Dahl (perhaps a kind of a father of the transition school) emphasises the impact of structural preconditions – ranging from the level of socioeconomic equality, sub-national cultural diversity, the concentration of economic resources, and elite attitudes towards democracy – on the emergence and consolidation of democratic regimes.[36] More recently, especially with regard to the question of whether or not a move from authoritarian rule leads to democratic consolidation, structural preconditions have been accepted by some transition theorists as a *part of the explanation* even if the researcher's emphasis is on processes.[37] Thus, we argue that in its more sophisticated versions the transition school does not claim to explain everything, but focuses on those issues that are difficult to understand and explain on the basis of structural changes alone.

Structure–agency interplay

In many empirical comparative politics studies it is claimed that situations such as, for example, why democratisation leads to consolidation in one case but not in another, cannot be explained by a single factor. Nor can any one theoretical approach alone account for the variety of experiences of different countries.[38] Indeed, while in individual chapters we sometimes emphasise structures over agency or vice versa, put together and understood in a flexible way the structural and process-related approaches seem to catch the main features which are relevant to studies of the modernisation of Russia and China. But is it possible to use structural and process-level approaches in combination? We believe so, on the basis of the non-deterministic interpretation of these approaches presented above.

A 'positivist' way to put these factors, elements, or variables – which obviously operate on different levels of analysis – together would be to treat the structural factors as independent factors, the process-related factors as intervening factors, and the outcome of the change as the dependent factor. This, however, would limit our analysis as we believe that the structural factors, especially in our cases, have been and continue to be in constant flux and cannot easily be 'frozen', even for analytical purposes. We therefore adopt a more flexible structure–agency approach. We argue that there is nothing to hinder us from understanding social realities as a continuous interplay of material and non-material structural preconditions on the one hand, and conscious or unconscious action that may in turn either reinforce these structures or introduce some changes into them, on the other. Basically this type of structure–agency reasoning does not differ greatly from a detailed and well-structured historical interpretation, and in a way it justifies the old-fashioned multilevel historical analysis in the context of contemporary social science debates. Thus, when the different variables, moving at seemingly different levels of analysis, are consciously put into the context of structure–agency relations, we believe that we can produce plausible interpretations and even explanations, at least in some cases.

This choice brings the issue of causality and 'rationality' into the picture. Causality is a complex mix of different variables at a variety of analytic levels and time periods, but one can safely state that structures, material or non-material, always predetermine, or are embedded in, the context where the agency-driven processes take place. In contrast to those who understand agency–structure analysis, including value- or discourse-based choices, as opposite to rational decision making, we instead claim that rationality is not in any way merely a theoretical possibility in these processes. Rather, states, people, and other actors tend to behave largely in rational ways, in that they prefer an option that they perceive as the better one over a worse option. Yet even when we put the structural preconditions and agency together, this mix does not predetermine the outcome, and at best we can forecast only some loose development alternatives or highly conditioned probabilities. Structural preconditions can always be interpreted by the agent in different ways. Moreover, while the agents' preference-ordering of the perceived options is, in most 'normal' cases, based on clearly identified interests rooted in more obscure identities and values, the process of concrete decision making is often constrained by residual factors resulting from complexity, limited information on the consequences of one's choices, and so on. This makes individual decisions and policy-making more broadly not rational, in any ideal sense of the word. This irrationality of rationality is particularly true in such complex issues as the choice of a country's modernisation strategy, with the many actors, decision-making situations, and unintended outcomes. Therefore, we emphasise the open-endedness of the historical processes, but at the same time expect that the choices of Russia and China were not randomly or 'irrationally' chosen.

The dimensions of change

Each of the following chapters discusses a particular comparative dimension of social change. These dimensions are naturally interrelated and overlapping; not separate 'dimensions' of social reality, but rather analytic categories. While many other dimensions could be added we consider that the dimensions chosen here together catch the essence of the post-communist modernisation processes in Russia and China in the context of comparative politics.

The current introductory chapter has outlined the motivation of and some very general *theoretical* underpinnings of the book. Chapter 2 can be seen as a *historical* introduction to the subsequent chapters as it discusses the pre-communist and communist modernisation strategies of Russia and China respectively. In this kind of a book, we felt that we could not do without a short review of the history which has shaped the material and mental structures still involved in current developments. The chapter argues, in the spirit of comparative politics rather than area studies, that the modernisation of Russia and China cannot be discussed without understanding the global competitive position within which it has taken place over a number of centuries and, more importantly, that this competitive environment has so far been framed by the success of the Western-born liberal–capitalist model. This is particularly necessary for understanding countries such as Russia and China. Thus, the chapter's main message is that, for centuries, both countries have shared the same challenges: pressure from the economic, technological, political, and military aspects of Western modernisation. The chapter outlines the minimum of necessary historical conditions for understanding the respective 'catching up' modernisation strategies of Russia/Soviet Union and China, and their similarities and differences in historical development from this angle.

Chapter 3 deals with *socioeconomic development*, the main issue for both Russia and China being to choose, or rather find a balance, between the free-market based privatised social security model and a state-dominated welfare state model. The chapter analyses these issues on the basis of a detailed review of the emerging class structures, looking at the position and situation of the different classes and the respective interests and power positions in both countries. This analysis is naturally closely connected to the results of the privatisation processes in both countries, and in China to the changes in rural–urban relations in particular. The analysis provided in this chapter puts forward an evidence-based argument (an argument that has not been sufficiently elaborated in earlier literature) that while Russia and China clearly originally chose the rather liberal or 'US' – as compared to social–democratic and 'European' – model of welfare state development, China is reconsidering its original liberal approach and consciously redirecting towards a more balanced and state-regulated, or perhaps a 'European', social welfare regime. It remains to be seen whether Russia will ultimately make the same turn in its policy.

Chapter 4 focuses on *political change*; the main axis of choice being between authoritarianism and democracy. The book argues that in both Russia and China the political systems have, in a way, reached a balance between multiple elite interests and that no conscious or well-organised efforts towards further democratisation can be identified. Both countries seem to challenge the Western liberal democracy model as a culture-centric rather than a universal system, and they seek a model of governance better suited to their respective traditions. A question then arises about the long-term stability of this equilibrium. Both countries have weak state–society relations, which in certain conditions may undermine the stability of these rather top-down systems. For China in particular – the more authoritarian of these two countries, at least in formal terms – the regime earns its legitimacy from its performance and there is no institutionalised bottom-up mechanism of replacing the current political elite if it fails. In Russia, a 'dominant party system' seems to have been formed, at least for the time being, that in practice provides no way for the opposition to gain power through elections. However, the conditions in both countries hint that potential change may be initiated from above, or from within the ruling elite itself, rather than from below, contrary to developments in the Arabic autocracies with their bottom-up revolts in 2010–2011. Potential change is very much dependent not only on the domestic performance of the regime, but also on the comparative reference performance of Western capitalism. The question, then, is which model is seen in China and Russia to be the most promising in creating best-case conditions for the elite survival in the respective countries and also for the welfare of post-modern Chinese and Russian societies and peoples in general?

Chapter 5 discusses *international relations and foreign policies*. In this dimension, Russia's international position can be characterised as that of a declining great power, whereas China's relative great power ranking is rapidly rising. This state of affairs leads them to search for their place and role in the evolving structures of international politics. We emphasise the binary concepts of sovereignty and interdependency, between which both countries have to find a balance. This book demonstrates how both Russia and China are still searching for their new roles, but how Russia's 'nostalgic revisionism' fails to provide foreign policy successes, whereas China has adapted much more successfully to new conditions and effectively uses new soft power instruments to promote its interests. Furthermore, while Russia may often turn to protectionism and economic isolationism, China has concluded that its own modernisation depends on the continuation of a liberal international economic order, thus currently only demanding smooth and gradual changes within the established international order.

It must be emphasised that the binary concepts, used in the titles for Chapters 3, 4 and 5 – namely 'free-market state or welfare state', 'authoritarianism or democracy', and 'sovereignty or interdependency' – are not to be understood as strict predefined dichotomies between which the two countries have to choose. Rather, they are used in this book as zero variables to facilitate structured identification of the different development alternatives in a comparative perspective. In a way – before any other unexpected dichotomies, dimensions, or mutations, emerge – they represent the three interrelated two-dimensional continuums of possible change where the current choices are located in order to find their balance. Also, these are not the only dimensions of change discussed in the respective chapters; taken together, however, these three different main dimensions of social change generate several interesting questions. How are the socioeconomic and political systems interlinked, what are the most plausible combinations, how do they construct and condition each other? How are the political systems and the countries' international roles interrelated? These cross-sectoral questions, amongst others, are elaborated within the individual chapters, and also in the concluding chapter, which summarises the comparison of the post-communist modernisation paths of Russia and China.

Notes

1. Wilhelm Fucks, *Formeln zur Macht*, Stuttgart: Deutsche Verlags-Anstalt 1965.
2. Francis Fukuyama, 'The End of History?', *The National Interest*, Summer 1989, pp. 3–18, here p. 4.
3. Robert Kagan, *The Return of History and the End of Dreams*, New York: Vintage 2009.
4. This view is expressed, among others, in: Martin Jacques, *When China Rules the World. The End of the Western World and the Birth of a New Global Order*, New York: The Penguin Press 2009; Stefan Halper, *The Beijing Consensus: How China's Authoritarian Model will Dominate the Twenty-first Century*, New York: Basic Books 2010; Ian Bremmer, *The End of the Free Market: Who Wins the War between States and Corporations?*, New York: The Penguin Press 2010; C. Fred Bergsten, Charles Freeman, Nicholas R. Lardy and Derek J.

Mitchell, *China's Rise: Challenges and Opportunities*, Washington DC: Center for Strategic and International Studies 2009. For an opposite view, arguing that China instead has chosen to play according to the rules of "the Western game", at least in terms of integrating into the Western economic order, see: Edward S. Steinfeld, *Playing Our Game: Why China's Rise doesn't Threaten the West*, Oxford: Oxford University Press 2010.

5. Yumin Scheng, 'Authoritarian Co-optation, the Territorial Dimension: Provincial Political Representation in Post-Mao China,' *Studies in Comparative International Development*, 44, no. 1 2009, pp. 71–93; Richard Baum, *The Limits of Authoritarian Resilience*, CERI – Debate, January 17, 2007, available at http://www.ceri-sciencespo.com/archive/jan07/art_rb.pdf; Andrew J. Nathan, 'Authoritarian Resilience', *Journal of Democracy*, Volume 14, Number 1, January 2003, pp. 6–17; Bruce Gilley, 'The Limits of Authoritarian Resilience', *Journal of Democracy*, Volume 14, Number 1, January 2003, pp. 18–26.
6. Ivan Krastev, 'Paradoxes of the New Authoritarianism,' *Journal of Democracy*, Volume 22, Number 2 April 2011, pp. 5–16.
7. Boris Yeltsin, 'O Natsionalnoy Bezopasnosti. Poslanie Prezidenta Rossiyskoy Federatsii Federal'nomu Sobranomu', *Nezavisimaya Gazeta* 14 June 1996, p. 7.
8. See Putin's last master plan on Russia's modernisation during his second Presidency: Vladimir Putin, *Speech at Expanded Meeting of the State Council on Russia's Development Strategy through to 2020*, 8 February 2008, available in English at http://archive.kremlin.ru/eng/speeches/2008/02/08/1137_type82912type82913_159643.shtml.
9. See Medvedev's master plan on Russia's modernisation: Dmitry Medvedev, *Go Russia!*, 10 September 2009, available in English from the official Kremlin site at http://eng.kremlin.ru/news/298.
10. As put by the 'chief regime ideologist' and First Deputy Chief of Staff of the Presidential Executive Office Vladislav Surkov, 'Russian Political Culture: The View from Utopia', *Russian Social Science Review*, Volume 49, Number 6, November–December 2008, pp. 81–97.
11. Samuel P. Huntington, *The Third Wave: Democratisation in the Late Twentieth Century*, Norman: University of Oklahoma Press 1991.
12. As checked in September 2011, there seems to be no up-to-date English-language books on the market which compare Russia and China in the same holistic spirit as this current volume does. The book by Minxin Pei, one of the authors of this book, should be mentioned though: *From Reform to Revolution: The Demise of Communism in China and the Soviet Union*, Harvard University Press 1994. However, due to the time in which it was written, that study focuses more on the collapse of the old systems than on the building of new ones.
13. A good example of this genre is Arend Lijphart, *Patterns of Democracy: Government Forms and Performance in Thirty-Six Countries*, New Haven and London: Yale University Press 1999.
14. This approach is well represented in Jeffrey Kopstein and Mark Lichbad, *Comparative Politics: Interests, Identities, and Institutions in a Changing Global Order*, Cambridge: Cambridge University Press, 2nd edition, 2005.

15. A case in point is Etienne Balibar and Immanuel Wallerstein, *Race, Nation, Class: Ambiguous Identitites*, London and New York: Verso 2002.
16. Kopstein and Lichbad, *Comparative Politics*.
17. Ibid. See also Robert A. Dahl, *On Democracy*, New Haven: Yale University Press 1998.
18. David Potter, David Goldblatt, Margareth Kiloh, and Paul Lewis (eds), *Democratisation*, Cambridge: The Open University and Polity Press 1997.
19. Ian Roxborough, 'Modernization Theory Revisited. A Review Article', *Comparative Studies in Society and History*, Volume 30, 1988, pp. 753–761.
20. Ronald Inglehart and Christian Welzel, *Modernization, Cultural Change, and Democracy: The Human Development Sequence*, Cambridge: Cambridge University Press 2005.
21. Roxborough 1988, 'Modernization Theory Revisited', p. 756.
22. Michael Burawoy, 'The End of Sovietology and the Renaissance of Modernization Theory', *Contemporary Sociology*, Volume 21, Number 6, November.1992, pp. 774–785; cf. Rudolf Andorka, 'The socialist system and its collapse in Hungary: an interpretation in terms of modernisation theory', *International Sociology*, September 1993, Volume 8, pp. 317–337.
23. The section on class structures is largely based on a draft by Markku Kivinen which was originally part of Chapter 3.
24. See John Goldthorpe, *The Constant Flux: A Study of Class Mobility in Industrial Societies*, Oxford: Clarendon Press 1992; Erik Olin Wright, *Class Counts: Comparative Studies in Class Analysis*, New York: Cambridge University Press 1997; Markku Kivinen, *Progress and Chaos: Russia as a Challenge for Sociological Imagination*, Helsinki: Kikimora Publications 2002; Markku Kivinen, 'Classes in the Making. Russian Class Structure in Transition,' in Göran Therborn (ed.), *Inequalities of the World*, Verso 2007, pp. 247–294. For readers who are not familiar with class theory, a detailed operationalisation may seem quite cumbersome. There are, however, three fundamental reasons for this. First of all, the operationalisation of class theories is a difficult and demanding task because there is such a huge number of occupations and professions in modern society. John Goldthorpe and his colleagues took several years to establish which occupations can genuinely be operationalised as occupying middle class positions on the criterion that the real labour process involves decision-making authority and autonomy. Secondly, although there may be differences in how individual occupations are classified, there is in fact a rather broad consensus of opinion on the basic structure, whether we start out from Goldthorpe's, Olin Wright's or Kivinen's class theory. In particular, there is broad agreement on the position of professional and managerial groups. Not even the critics of class analysis deny the role of professionalisation or 'credentialism'. Thirdly, although different kinds of operationalisation lead to somewhat different conclusions about the sizes of class groups, the picture that emerges when we proceed to analyse the structuration of class situation and consciousness is, in the end, rather similar. The only theories that differ from the mainstream (and which in empirical terms appear more or less untenable; see Kivinen 1989, pp. 164–197) are those that deny the significance of professional and managerial positions and that define the middle class as consisting of such groups

as state workers; see *Projekt Klassenanalyse: Materialien zur Klassenstruktur der BRD I-II*, Berlin/West 1973; cf. Markku Kivinen, *The New Middle Classes and the Labour Process – Class Criteria Revisited*, Helsinki: University of Helsinki: Department of Sociology 1989.

25. Kivinen, *The New Middle Classes and the Labour Process*; Raimo Blom, Markku Kivinen, Harri Melin and Liisa Rantalaiho, *The Scope Logic Approach to Class Analysis*, Aldershot: Avebury 1992; cf., Erik Olin Wright, 'The New Middle Classes and the Labour Process: Class Criteria Revisited by Markku Kivinen Huomautuksia Kivisen luokkateoriaan,' *Tiede ja edistys*, Vol. 15, 1990/2, pp. 142–146.
26. Benedict Anderson, *Imagined Communities*, London and New York: Verso 1983.
27. Barrington Moore, Jr, *Social Origins of Dictatorship and Democracy: Lord and Peasant in the Making of the Modern World*, Boston: Bacon Press 1993.
28. See his discussion on India, for instance: Moore, *Social Origins of Dictatorship and Democracy*, pp. 407–410, 430–432.
29. See the discussion by Adam Przeworski, 'Some Problems in the Study of the Transition to Democracy', in Guillermo O'Donnell, Philippe C. Schmitter and Laurence Whitehead, *Transitions from Authoritarian Rule, Comparative Perspective*, Baltimore and London: The Johns Hopkins University Press 1991, pp. 47–63, here pp. 47, 48.
30. Thomas Carothers, 'The End of the Transition Paradigm', *Journal of Democracy*, Volume 13, Number 1, January 2002.
31. Guillermo O'Donnell, 'In Partial Defense of an Evanescent "Paradigm"', *Journal of Democracy*, Volume 13, Number 3, July 2002.
32. Guillermo O'Donnell, Philippe Schmitter and Laurence Whitehead (eds), *Transitions from Authoritarian Rule*, 4 vols, Baltimore: Johns Hopkins University Press 1986.
33. Dankwart A. Rustow, 'Transitions to Democracy: Toward a Dynamic Model', Comparative Politics, April 1970, 2, pp. 337–63; Guillermo A. O'Donnell and Philippe C. Schmitter, *Transitions from Authoritarian Rule: Tentative Conclusions about Uncertain Democracies*, Baltimore: Johns Hopkins University Press, 1986.
34. Michael McFaul, *Russia's Unfinished Revolution: Political Change from Gorbachev to Putin*, Ithaca and London: Cornell University Press 2001, p. 341.
35. For criticisms of process-based theories of transition, see Terry Lynn Karl, 'Dilemmas of Democratisation in Latin America', *Comparative Politics* October 1990, 23, pp. 1–21, and Stephan Haggard and Robert Kaufman, 'The Political Economy of Democratic Transitions', *Comparative Politics* April 1997, 29, pp. 263–283. Juan Linz and Alfred Stepan emphasised the nature of the old regime as a key variable: see Linz and Stepan, *Problems of Democratic Transition and Consolidation*, Baltimore and London: Johns Hopkins University Press 1996.
36. Robert Dahl, *Polyarchy*, New Haven: Yale University Press 1971.
37. See, for instance, Mark J. Gasiorowski and Timothy J. Power, 'The Structural Determinants of Democratic Consolidation: Evidence from the Third World', *Comparative Political Studies*, Volume 31, Number 6, 1998 pp. 740–771, and

Robert A. Dahl, 'Development and Democratic Culture', in Larry Diamond, Marc F. Plattner, Yun-han Chu, and Hung-mao Tien (eds), *Consolidating the Third Wave Democracies: Themes and Perspectives*, Baltimore and London: The Johns Hopkins University Press 1998, pp. 34–39.

38. James Putzel, 'Why has democratisation been a weaker impulse in Indonesia and Malaysia than in the Philippines?', in Potter et al., *Democratisation*, pp. 240–263.

2
A Short History of Catching Up

Christer Pursiainen

In the context of Western political science, the developments in Russia and China over the last twenty years are very hard to understand and may be regarded as 'anomalies', if one does not provide a proper historical background to today's situation. While there are naturally several interpretations, it is argued here that historically these countries' domestic modernisation strategies are, to a considerable degree, shaped by pressure created by the developments in Western capitalism and the connected great power politics. Russia and China were forced to adopt modernisation strategies in order to adapt to – or even survive the pressure of – the ever-enlarging, Western-dominated global capitalism. Even the communist periods of these countries can be seen as a defensive reaction to this global pressure. At the same time, the current developments in Russia and China can be understood as efforts to adapt to the developments of Western global capitalism and to change the direction of global development into one that would better match the perceived Russian and Chinese national interests and identities.

The Russian Westernisers and slavophiles

The ideological roots of Russia's present modernisation debates derive historically from the contentious term, the 'Russian idea'. This term defines the relationship between Russia and the West – or rather, Russia's difference from the West – beginning with Russia's so-called Byzantine heritage. After the collapse of Constantinople in the middle of the fifteenth century, Russia, under the leadership of Ivan III, adopted the role of the 'Third Rome', as well as developing a suspicion of the Catholic (and later the Protestant) West. A new phase of modernisation began with Peter the Great, which was defensive in motivation.

When the Russians made this attempt to master Western manners and technology – as they have done many times since – they did so in order to save themselves from being forcibly Westernised, though paradoxically in the process they had to partially Westernise themselves.[1] As a result of pressure from the West, two significant and rival trends in Russian political thought developed: *zapadnichestvo* or Westernism, and *slavianofil'stvo* or Slavophilism, with the former advocating Western-type modernisation and the latter opposing it.

The concept of *zapadnichestvo* derives from the Russian word for the West, 'zapad'. This 'Westernism' does not suggest an automatic emulation of Western political institutions or a Western-minded foreign policy. Rather, it considers Russia in the spirit of Enlightenment, developing toward a conclusive universal end of West European or Western modernisation. According to the spiritual father of *zapadnichestvo* in the early nineteenth century, Pyotr Chaadaev, Russia had in no way participated in the development of humankind, and it had merely distorted everything that had been left over from the progress achieved elsewhere. In his much debated *Philosophical Letters*, Chaadaev urged Russia to adopt Western thought and development, and to abandon its old culture and traditions.[2]

Chaadaev's letters were a reaction to the political doctrine of nationalism. Articulated by Sergey Uvarov in 1832 and confirmed by Nikolai I, nationalism remained the official ideology until 1917. This ideology emphasised three elements: the orthodox religion, autocracy, and nationalism. Its essence was to keep Russia apart from Western European liberal and socialist thought and to isolate Russia ideologically, though not economically or technologically.[3] In his later (unfinished) essay *An Apology from a Madman*, Chaadaev advanced a more positive outlook for Russia's backwardness. Only after adopting all the knowledge and education of the West could Russia fulfil her mission in the world, he argued. By learning faster than others and avoiding their mistakes, Russia's delay could be turned to her advantage. Then the day would come when Russia would stand at the heart of Europe. Like many of today's *zapadniks*, Chaadaev believed that the logical result of Russia's long isolation would be its rise to the vanguard of countries destined to answer the most important questions facing humankind.[4]

Slavianofil'stvo, or Slavophilism, instead emphasised the uniqueness of Russia and Russian-ness, striving for social development within Russia's own cultural traditions. In the same spirit as those ideologies which in today's Russia oppose the argument that Russia should 'join the West', early Slavophilism opposed the *zapadnik* linear historical philosophy of a single worldwide civilisation, instead proposing cultures as the basic units of world history. Like Chaadaev, Aleksey Khomyakov, the most famous of the early nineteenth-century slavophiles, emphasised Russia's difference from the West, but not in terms of backwardness or underdevelopment. For Khomyakov, the spiritual and social uniqueness of the Russian people lay in their orthodox faith in God, their community, and conciliation within the Church.[5] Most early slavophiles were educated landowners, humanists, and lovers of freedom, with spiritual roots deep in the Russian soil. As would later happen in China under Mao Zedong's influence, these early Russian slovophiles considered the peasantry to be the eternal foundation of Russia, the guarantee of the country's distinct identity.

The peasant spirit of community contrasted strongly with Western individualism. Western economic modernisation, starting with the spread of capitalism, was delayed in Russia until after the reforms of the 1860s. Russian modernisation, unlike that of the West, was authoritarian and imperial, creating and preserving the military and bureaucratic complexes. The motivation for this model was geopolitical. Governance of the huge empire was thought to require authoritarian control. In this model of modernisation enforced from above, innovators were distanced from the people and entrepreneurs were not encouraged. Russia's raw materials were exchanged for Western technological inventions that mainly benefited the bureaucratic and military sectors. Thus, although Russian capitalism basically developed independently on a national basis, its main features became dependence on the export of raw material, foreign capital and foreign debt, and foreign technology. It was reliant upon state orders and infrastructure projects, and heavy industry was started with foreign capital. Domestic markets remained underdeveloped. While within these limits Russia was rapidly 'catching up' with the major Western powers in terms of economic development,[6] as a whole this top-down effort failed to produce a balanced modernisation strategy. When economic modernisation finally began, the lack of commensurate political modernisation distorted development. Western-style social and political modernisation, which arose from civil society as a kind of 'natural process', was lacking in Russia. The political elite tried to compensate for this by guiding the modernisation process.[7]

It is often argued that it was exactly the failure of European-style modernisation in imperial Russia that led to Russian communism, or bolshevism. In a sense it was a social reaction against an uncontrolled and too rapid economic modernisation that happened without commensurate changes to the political system. Totalitarianism in the Soviet Union, as most mainstream post-Soviet Russian analysis argues, was a "socio-political mutant" born of the inability of Russian leaders "to face the challenges of modern times, to find the way of co-operation with huge masses that had lost their fixed social position".[8] Top-down efforts to isolate Russia ideologically had failed. While the conservative strand of *zapadnik* thought approximated official Russian ideology, late nineteenth-century liberal *zapadnik* ideas provided the roots for revolutionary movements in Russia. This leftist movement drew explicitly upon West European political radicalism: first on French socialist ideas and later, Marxism. Originally, the leftist *narodniks*, like the earlier slavophiles, believed in 'the Russian people'. To the disappointment of the *narodniks* the Russian peasantry did not live up to expectations, having no interest in revolution. So the revolutionary intelligentsia turned to itself, placing the destiny of Russia on its own heroic shoulders. But the revolt petered out, limited to acts of terrorism by small outlaw groups. Marxism offered a way out of this intellectual and spiritual deadlock because it abandoned an agrarian worldview, instead adopting the idea of a developing proletariat as the social basis and power of the revolution.

But Russian socialists faced a moral dilemma: how to welcome capitalism, and the emergence of the proletarian class in capitalist industrialisation, while opposing the evil it represented? This was the dilemma that bolshevism solved. First Leon Trotsky, and then Vladimir Lenin, emphasised the feasibility of socialist revolution in Russia before society as a whole had reached the capitalist phase of development. Instead of a real proletariat class as a social basis for revolution they created the idea – the illusion – of a revolutionary class.[9] Trotsky in particular was to put forward the (then) novel idea that an underdeveloped country such as Russia could leap over others to join the vanguard of worldwide modernisation by staging the world's first socialist revolution. However, unlike Josef Stalin later, Trotsky was careful to note that this political revolution would not lead very far without world revolution. In particular, the developed capitalist West should produce its socialist revolutions, too, which would enable 'state help' from these more developed countries to assist Russia to modernise in cultural, socioeconomic and technological terms.[10]

The Middle Kingdom's early modernisation attempts

A parallel historical situation to that of nineteenth-century Russia can be found in China. Like the Russian slavophiles, the Chinese imperial court "did not seem to think that Western industrialisation mattered much" until the second half of the nineteenth century.[11] Industrial power would be no match against the superior Chinese civilisation. Nevertheless, in the 1860s, the pressure to modernise and, to a certain extent, to 'westernise' began to surface in the Middle Kingdom under the Qing Dynasty in response to the country's experiences of debilitating internal crises in the form of peasant rebellions coupled with external crises of Western aggression.[12] The so-called Foreign Affairs Movement (*yangwu yundong*), also known as the Self-Strengthening Movement, was China's first modernisation attempt and lasted for over 30 years. It was led by members of the Qing Dynasty ruling class and was intended to emulate the Western development of science and industrialisation.[13]

Like its Russian counterpart, the Qing court adopted a model of modernisation that emphasised keeping Western technologies apart from Western values.[14] Thus the reformers of the late Qing Dynasty were intent on modernising China while still preserving Chinese civilisation. This is emulated by Chinese leaders today. As Lucian Pye points out, Chinese are "supposed to only be learning practical matters from alien cultures".[15] An underlying current still reflected today in the way many Chinese express their views of China's place in the world is the 'Middle Kingdom Complex',[16] a curious mix of superiority and inferiority: superiority because of their great civilisation and where they feel their rightful place is in the world, but inferiority because they were helpless against superior Western technology and military power. It is easy to trace the same spirit in current Chinese and Russian debates about the West.

Events during the late Qing Dynasty were not only humiliating for China because of the superior scientific and technological developments of the West; it was also the first time a Western power was able to present a threat to Chinese civilisation.[17] The inability of China's military to deter foreign aggressions created a deep sense of political insecurity and hopelessness among China's intellectuals and the ruling elites of the Qing court. When the Foreign Affairs Movement began in the early 1860s, China had already lost the two Opium Wars against Britain and been forced into submission by numerous unequal treaties and territory secession by outside powers.[18] Consequently, many educated Chinese began to seek solutions in the technologically superior West.[19]

China's scientific and technological modernisation efforts continued to expand throughout the late 1800s, especially after China's defeat in the Sino–Japanese War of 1894–95 and, again, as the Qing Dynasty limped towards its final downfall in 1911.[20] An important contrast between the modernisation attempts of the late Qing and post-imperial China was the motivation behind them. Under the Qing, modernisation had the dual purpose of strengthening the country as well as resuscitating the power of the Manchu imperial court, whereas after 1911 modernisation efforts were inspired by nationalism: a common sentiment shared among the population at large was that China was in danger of ceasing to exist in the face of unrelenting foreign aggression.[21] A sense that the nation was embroiled in a struggle for survival culminated in the May Fourth Movement of 1919, with 'Science and Democracy' as its rallying cry. The movement was spurred by large student demonstrations in Beijing after the Chinese delegation failed to secure China's interests in the negotiations leading to the Versailles peace treaty.[22]

Five years later, Sun Yat-sen, known as the father of modern China, produced a blueprint for a modern democratic state, a modern society, and a modern economy (*sanmin zhuyi*). Sun had advocated political revolution in order to overthrow the Manchu emperor. He wanted to temporarily establish a new government by military law, and then adopt a government structure based on a constitution. Many disagreed with Sun's vision, arguing that the Chinese people were not ready for modernity, and that an 'enlightened autocracy' was required for an undefined period of tutelage.[23] Others argued that "the requirements of modernisation ran counter to the priorities of Confucian social and political order."[24] As in Russia, authoritarian control was regarded as the only way to govern the huge Chinese empire. Sun, for his part, was concerned that nation-building efforts were hindered by traditional family and lineage loyalty, the defining traits of Chinese society throughout the ages. [25] For almost two thousand years, the network of centralised political authority in China ended at the seat of the county government. Families, lineages, professional groups and villages were, to a great extent, only obliged to cooperate with the central imperial authorities in matters of large-scale public works, local security, and external defence. As a result, throughout China's history, sub-county level entities were relatively free to govern according to local conditions and rarely confronted the central imperial authorities.[26] Interestingly, in the late 1970s, when Deng Xiaoping loosened central government authority in the economic domain and allowed local authorities to implement reforms suitable for the development of their locality, he was reinserting elements of traditional society.

The economic independence of local authorities has been key to the success of the reform policy.

The 1911 revolution overthrew the Qing emperor, but failed to provide a viable or lasting political alternative. After decades of warfare – internal rebellion, civil war and the prolonged war against Japan – the communists rose to power under Mao Zedong's leadership in 1949 with the support of the rural population.

The forced Soviet modernisation

Both the People's Republic of China and the Soviet Union were huge and rabid modernisation – or perhaps postmodernist – projects. Often, almost overnight, they created illusions to legitimise utopian policies. They manufactured these illusions – extreme versions of a belief in progress – based on the Marxist idea of an inevitable, objective and inescapable modernisation process. For many Russian and Chinese citizens looking to the West as a point of comparison, these illusions filled the vacuum of pessimism. The Marxist version of modernisation which was based on a succession of different socioeconomic phases – feudalism, capitalism, socialism, and communism – seemed to lead inevitably towards the final end.

As mentioned, although the Bolshevik wing of the Russian Marxists believed that a socialist revolution might begin in Russia, not even Lenin thought that Russia could build socialism by itself. Socialism was seen as the proletarian-led effective modernisation model which preceded the classless society of communism. This, in turn, would ultimately be the most rational and effective way to organise economic development and, through that, create a win-win situation for the society at large. But Russia had scarcely achieved the capitalist phase of development, and therefore it was thought that world revolution, or revolutions in at least some of the more developed countries, would be necessary to help build socialism in Russia. Stalin, once in power, turned the idea the other way around; it was the Soviet Union who became the basis of world revolution. In domestic politics, his socialism-in-a-single-country theory was first posited, almost by accident, in 1924 in the process of a power struggle against Trotsky. Stalin emphasised the possibility of building the ideal society without waiting years or decades for world revolution.[27]

Critics of Stalin's opportunistic concept – again, most notably Trotsky – claimed that socialism would conquer capitalism only if productivity, and hence living standards, became higher under socialism. Since the

Soviet Union was not capable of building socialism without outside 'state help', the revolution would fail and capitalism would return to Russia if the world revolution (or, at least, the German revolution) did not come to assist Russia in its modernisation.[28] But Stalin, after opposing the Trotskyist domestic rapid modernisation model in the early 1920s in order to make the leap into an industrial society, adopted Trotsky's forced modernisation project in 1928, with the difference that he claimed that industrialisation led by the proletarian government, utilising Russia's huge territory and natural resources, would make it possible to organise a socialist economic system in a single country. Stalin prevailed. In 1930, firmly in power, he declared that the Soviet Union had achieved the socialist phase of development.

Although the goal of catching up with the West characterised the Soviet Union's modernisation, its relations with the West passed through different stages. Each of these stages implied a different role for the West to play in the Soviet Union's modernisation. Before the Second World War, Stalin strove to establish trade relations with the West. In the early Cold War era, Stalin's policy became more isolationist, minimising not only the ideological, but also the economic, influences of the outside world. Nikita Khrushchev's 'peaceful coexistence' was instead based on the over-optimistic idea that the power of the Soviet Union was inevitably increasing: it had already surpassed Western Europe by the early 1960s and would soon overtake the United States. In this self-confident, if illusory, spirit, Soviet leaders believed that Soviet world influence would flourish in a context of interdependency and cooperation rather than in the context of revolutionary war – an approach that was closely linked to the fear of mutual destruction in the era of nuclear weapons. Under conditions of 'peaceful coexistence' – or rather competition – the Soviet Union could show everyone the superiority of its system.

However, Khrushchev, along with his advisors, realised that the Soviet system needed changes in order to keep its promises. He tried to accelerate the modernisation process by reorganising agriculture, increasing the emphasis on consumer goods and social benefits, improving housing, and putting science and technology in service to economic development as well as in non-military spheres of production. He tried to reorganise the bureaucracy and the *Gosplan* (state plan) system that he saw hindering the economy.[29] But Khrushchev failed both internationally and domestically. The currency deficit severely limited the Soviet Union's economic cooperation with the Western countries, and politically Khrushchev's strategy of peaceful coexistence was met with suspicion in the West, as a covert propaganda tool for ultimate world domination. At home, the nomenklatura and bureaucracy resisted Khrushchev's reforms and finally replaced him. His administrative reforms were largely repealed, although his foreign policy reforms were not.

Only gradually and reluctantly, during the Leonid Brezhnev and Aleksei Kosygin years, did the Soviet Union reassess its own economic and technological modernisation process. Soviet leaders realised the country required closer cooperation with the West for its own survival. Oil and gas exports to Western Europe partially resolved the currency problem, and with that currency the Soviet Union bought available technology from the West. In the eighth five-year plan of the Soviet Union (1966–70), Western technology already played an important role. In the next five-year plan, the role of Western technology was enlarged further. Besides importing machinery and even whole factories from the West, the Soviets made efforts to conclude scientific–educational cooperative agreements with Western countries.[30]

However, in a political and economic system that did not facilitate spontaneous innovation, the Soviet Union's scientific and technological development suffered under the pressure of falling further behind. In the late 1960s, Kosygin tried to modernise the Russian economic system by giving more freedom to enterprises and experimenting with a new price reward system. The aim was to utilise selected market economy instruments within a command economy system; an incommensurable combination, and the reforms were bound to fail without free markets. Enterprises which took this greater freedom seriously were consequently punished the following year with higher production quotas required by the *Gosplan*. From the early 1970s until 1982, when Yuri Andropov tried to start some technocratic and economic reforms, no efforts were made to break the deadlock of systemic inertia. Yet in the early 1970s the Soviet economy was still growing in volume with the power of its forced modernisation efforts. It did not stagnate until 1975.

In terms of Soviet social (though not really 'political') modernisation, the Khrushchev period – the 'thaw' – was naturally more free compared to the repressive totalitarian Stalinist political system. But this 'liberalisation' did not increase the general level of political activity; it merely intensified the internal struggle of Russian nomenklatura and strengthened certain local interest groups within the party elite. This state of affairs continued during the Brezhnev era, until the beginning of Mikhail Gorbachev's reforms in the mid-1980s. Yet, while surely an era of political and economic stagnation, the "1970s were a period of major social and socio-psychological shifts" with far-reaching consequences in terms of modernisation. The essence of these changes was that "an industrial society was definitely formed" in the country, "the process of urbanisation was completed and a new generation grew up, shaped by the conditions of Europeanized city life."[31]

As a whole, however, Soviet development proved to be unbalanced, in many ways merely continuing the imperial model. The Soviet Union's dependence on the export of raw materials and the import of Western technology, as well as the need to preserve the military balance of power, led to a structural crisis in the economy. "The military-industrial sector operated as a black hole in the Soviet economy, absorbing most of the creative energy of society and making it disappear in an abyss of invisible inertia."[32]

A commonly held psycho-sociological interpretation is that the roots of this structural crisis lay deep within the souls of individuals suppressed by totalitarianism, in the absence of impulses from below, in a society governed from above.[33] Forced modernisation might be appropriate for the great leap of industrialisation if we omit the human sacrifices, but not for the challenges of late modernity. The incapacity to develop science and technology at the level of practical applications that would benefit the society at large showed that the forced modernisation model was bankrupt. Mere large investments, had such been available, were not enough. New technology and modes of production presupposed a less bureaucratic, more democratic political system or, at least, a less bureaucratic, less centralised and more democratic production system.

After the death of Brezhnev in 1982, Andropov's unfinished reforms, as well as Gorbachev's reforms from 1985 onwards, were the first conscious efforts to deal with the country's systemic crisis since the half-hearted and unrealistic Kosygin reforms, which had petered out by the beginning of the 1970s. Andropov wanted to modernise and intensify the economic system while leaving the political system untouched, an approach some Russian politicians and scholars refer to as the 'missed possibility of the Chinese way'. Gorbachev's approach was more ambitious, but was badly organised, based on ad hoc improvisation. However, as is usual during revolutionary times in Russia, Gorbachev's era was the heyday of new political phraseology that imitated a more concerted approach. The discursive components of this reform were *perestroika*, the general reconstruction of the system; *glasnost*, an instrument of constructive criticism of the system; *uskorenie*, a technocratic acceleration of the economy; *novoye politicheskoye myshleniye*, a more cooperative foreign policy line; and *sotsialisticheskaya demokratiya*, that is, humanising the communist political system under the slogan of 'not less but more socialism'.

But this project's goals did not conform to the rules of the system within which the goals were to be achieved. *Perestroika* was intended to liberalise the political system while preserving the hegemony of the Soviet Communist Party, and to modernise the economy while preserving the command system. Within these strictures, the nomenklatura had no cohesive strategy for national development. The political elite soon began to divide into several groupings. One might classify them, for instance, into four main factions: orthodox (neo-Stalinist) Marxists; Gorbachevian 'social–democrat' centrists; more liberal radical 'democrats'; and right-wing Slavophilism or Eurasianism-inspired nationalists – each with a different view of how to proceed. In the end, after a failed coup d'état in August 1991 by the conservatives, the 'democrats' won the battle, establishing a new Russian Federation after the collapse of the Soviet Union as a geopolitical entity.

Mao and utopian optimism

In China, Mao Zedong set out to completely break with the past. Contrary to the imperial court's hesitation to set China on a path toward comprehensive modernisation, Mao wanted literally to create a 'New China' by, among others, doing away with the 'four olds': old ideas, old culture, old customs, and old habits. Yet, there was also a new element for comparison besides the Western model. In China, during the first decade of the People's Republic, the Soviet experience influenced policy-making. The existence of not only the goals, but the means as well – the Soviet model – was crucial to the initial success of the communist initiatives in China.[34] Even today, elderly Chinese remember the call in the early 1950s to be 'Modern and Soviet'. Subsequently, the Chinese Communist Party shifted its focus from the countryside to the cities. China's industrialisation at this stage was heavily dependent on Soviet aid, advice and technology. The approximately 150 large capital-intensive industrial projects of the first five-year plan (1953–1957), which were built with Soviet assistance, accounted for nearly half of all industrial investment.

Mao Zedong set about building a new government according to the ideas expressed in *New Democracy*, his major theoretical work from 1940, in which he adapted Marxism–Leninism to the Chinese situation during the transition directly from semi-colonialism and semi-feudalism to socialism. The classic pattern, from Karl Marx and Friedrich Engels, of societal development from feudalism to capitalism to socialism did not apply in China, for the stage of capitalism did not properly exist there – as it did not for the most part in pre-revolutionary Russia.[35] However, the difference was the unexpected long-term survival of the Soviet Union, and the idea that feudal countries could leap over the capitalist phase of development with the assistance of existing socialism was how Mongolia and less-developed areas of the Soviet Union were supposed to have reached socialism. In the 1960s this approach was applied to Third World countries, and labelled a 'non-capitalist way of development' and later 'the path of socialist orientation'. Mao adapted this concept to Chinese conditions.

In China too, as in the Soviet Union, an almost utopian optimism marked the Communist Party's frenzied attempts to speed up the pace of industrialisation in the late 1950s. The rural population were included in Mao's definition of the 'revolutionary masses', but it was the industrial workers who made substantial gains in lifetime security, generous welfare benefits, and a rise in social status. However, Mao's novelty was his decision to discard Soviet-style policies as the modernisation strategy model, which was in part grounded in the realisation that conditions in China were not comparable with those in the Soviet Union. China's vast impoverished peasantry could not shoulder the burden of financing investment for heavy industry. In early 1958, he launched the Great Leap Forward – a programme based on mass mobilisation that forced nearly every citizen to participate in industrial production. Within six months, hundreds of thousands of furnaces had sprung up all over the country. Mao talked about catching up with, or even surpassing, British industrial capacity within fifteen years. Some Chinese parents named their children 'Surpass Britain'. In reality, the Great Leap Forward produced an economic disaster, resulting in the deaths of almost 36 million Chinese people from starvation.[36]

The Great Leap Forward turned out to be just one of the first steps – albeit a catastrophic one – in Mao's creation of a grand illusion of successful modernisation. In pushing through collectivisation and the establishment of People's Communes, Mao is said to have been influenced by the late Qing reformer Kang You-wei, who argued for the creation of a utopia with no private property, private ownership, sale of land, or private industry, but with public hospitals, public education, public welfare, and public homes for the aged. The fundamental features of this utopia would be the destruction of the family and the emancipation of women. Mao called for the birth of a new Socialist Man, who would have no regard for face and put the state before family – paradoxically, an approach that can be found in some of Trotsky's writings. Mao's division of the population into mass organisations, and his continuous mass campaigns marked by intense indoctrination sessions, aimed to transform the Chinese people, once described as a loose pile of sand, into a population more tightly-organised than any other in the world.[37]

The Great Proletarian Cultural Revolution (1966–1976) was Mao's desperate attempt to cling to his position as supreme leader and eliminate colleagues who favoured a more realistic economic reform program. It was also a sign of Mao's "restless quest for revolutionary purity in a post-revolutionary age".[38] It was, yet again, a way to divert the Chinese people's attention by mass mobilisation from the reality of Western supremacy in living standards and technological development, and from acknowledging the failure of previous policies to narrow the gap in the promised timeframe.

The Cultural Revolution precipitated a decade of frenzied political activism, political indoctrination, class struggle, and the militarisation of Chinese politics. The danger of a Sino–Soviet war, following the Sino–Soviet split that started to show itself from 1960 onwards, and of which the population was reminded at regular intervals, provided useful fodder for Maoist efforts to justify China's isolation. China was brought to the brink of civil war, and virtually shut off from the rest of the world.

The Maoist illusion disintegrated long before Mao himself passed away in 1976; with his death it was buried irreversibly. Deng Xiaoping's ascension to power in the latter part of the 1970s dramatically changed China's course. Ideology was replaced with pragmatism, ideological purity with ability and know-how. Not overnight, exactly, but within a few short years innovation and entrepreneurship became acceptable, sought-after qualities. Yet again, the populace was admonished to rally around the goal of making China strong and powerful, to make it the equal of the Western countries. But this time the citizenry was spurred by rising living standards and personal gain.

After the establishment of diplomatic ties with Washington in 1979, Deng actively proceeded to integrate China into the world economy. Foreign investment was sought and foreign experts welcomed. In the 1980s tens of thousands of Chinese students were permitted to travel to the West to pursue degrees. At the Twelfth Communist Party Congress in September 1982, less than three years after the pivotal Party Plenum decision to pursue opening and reform (*gaige kaifang*), Deng Xiaoping declared that the Party's main task for the remainder of the decade was to intensify the socialist modernisation drive with "economic reconstruction at the core."[39]

Deng did not only fling open the country's doors to the West. He appealed to all Chinese compatriots to put aside ideological differences and participate in his modernisation programme for the motherland. Up to 75 per cent of all 'foreign' investments in China between 1979 and 1994 had 'Chinese roots'. While Gorbachev, several years later, may be compared to Deng as a leader who, by way of his personal power and courage, managed to reorient his country, the conditions for reform were at variance. Investment by overseas Chinese, and the know-how of Hongkongese, Taiwanese and ethnically Chinese Thai, Indonesian, Malaysian, American, Canadian, and Australian businessmen, constituted a crucial difference between Gorbachev's and Deng's reform movements. When Gorbachev launched *perestroika,* he could not turn to tens of millions of overseas Russians, as Deng turned to the massive Chinese diaspora. More than 26 million overseas Chinese live in Asia alone. Overseas Chinese felt no calling whatsoever to communism.[40] In fact, many of them had fled mainland China when the communists won the civil war. But devotion to one's roots, the birthplace of one's ancestors (*laojia*), is quintessentially ingrained in Chinese culture. Besides providing a new range of hitherto unexplored business opportunities, Deng's opening and reform policy made it possible for millions of overseas Chinese to fulfil their dream of visiting and paying tribute to their ancestral homes. It is impossible to estimate the monetary value of the donations made by overseas Chinese during the past two decades. The Chinese landscape is dotted with hospitals, schools, libraries, and research centres built with overseas Chinese money.[41]

As the reform period progressed, citizens of the People's Republic of China were not motivated by any deep conviction in communism either. Rising standards of living spurred Chinese to work hard for the betterment of their own lives and the strengthening of China (as opposed to a communist ideal). In the China of the late 1980s, the demonstrating students in Tiananmen Square and their intellectual supporters, as well as reform-minded groups within the bureaucracy, advocated political reform, but also believed that change from *within* the Communist Party was the right recipe for restructuring the Chinese political system. The vast majority of Chinese felt that China was on the right track. Economic modernisation was progressing rapidly. In addition, the havoc of the Cultural Revolution was still vivid in everyone's memory. Neither the reformist bureaucrats nor the majority of the intellectual community wanted to risk *luan* – chaos. Analysts often cite this fear of chaos as an essential component of the traditional Chinese worldview. China's history abounds with periods of rebellion, civil war, and instability. Those in power are naturally inclined to reinforce the view that strong government and stability go hand in hand. They point to examples from history: when the empire has been united and stable, Chinese civilisation has flourished; when China has disintegrated into several parts, chaos and stagnation has prevailed.[42]

Two roads towards market economies

The so-called IMF orthodoxy, formulated in the late 1980s for the transition of all post-communist states from state-centred to market economies, suggested four basic policies: monetary stabilisation in terms of controlling money supply and thus inflation (instead of, for example, creating jobs or maintaining production); liberalisation of prices, entrepreneurship and foreign trade; privatisation of state-owned companies; and structural changes to enable efficiency and competitiveness.[43] While most Eastern European countries applied this rather technocratic model, which did not pay much attention to culture and traditions, more or less successfully, the former Soviet Union (excluding the three Baltic States) appears, in many perspectives, to have failed during the first two decades of its post-communist reform. It is regarded as an unfinished case in terms of a successful modernisation process. China followed its own unique path which is regarded, at least economically, as a very successful modernisation model.

While these developments will be discussed in some detail in the chapters which follow, it is enough to emphasise here the fundamentally different roads the Soviet Union and China adopted early on their respective modernisation journeys. In the steps towards a market economy during Gorbachev's *perestroika* in the Soviet Union, privatising the state sector was not a top priority. Rather, *perestroika's* goal was to improve the performance of the stagnant state sector. Encouraging private entrepreneurship was a second-hand by-product of the reforms. And when a limited privatisation programme was accepted, the Soviet model turned out to be a top-down privatisation based on – as it has been called – a 'formal–legal' approach, the opposite of the Chinese 'pragmatic–entrepreneurial' approach, which allowed a considerable amount of grass roots developments to take place in the private sector. Moreover, privatisation in China has, to a large extent, been implemented ahead of official legislative acts, whereas in the Soviet Union, laws typically preceded their corresponding privatisations.[44]

The comparative sizes of the socialist welfare states provides the most plausible structural explanation as to why no widespread grass roots movement for privatisation and market reforms existed in the Soviet Union, as it did in China. Soviet citizens simply had too much to lose by risking their socialist welfare security, even if it was modest when compared to most developed Western capitalist countries. In China the benefits of the existing system for the majority of the people (that is, for the rural population) were minor compared to the potential benefits of reform. In 1979 less than one-fifth of the population of China was classified as urban. Only one-quarter of the labour force worked in the non-agricultural sector. In Russia, two-thirds of the population in 1986 were urban residents, with around 80 per cent of the population employed in the non-agricultural sector.

The structural preconditions for privatisation and market reforms which China consciously created during the reform period – most notably, fiscal decentralisation, lifting restrictions on foreign investments and foreign trade in the domestic private sector, and partial price reform – were absent in Gorbachev's Soviet Union. Instead of the major reforms that were implemented relatively quietly in China, in the Soviet Union market reforms and privatisation were the subject of heated public debate and political struggle among proponents, opponents, and those who tried to balance the new and the old systems. Indeed, Soviet privatisation began in 1986 with a modest effort to legalise part of the shadow economy, particularly the service sector, and was limited to those persons outside the productive state sector, such as pensioners and students. In a later phase of *perestroika,* the focus shifted to the small cooperatives, something that in the current Western terminology could be called the seeds of small- and medium-size enterprises (SMEs).

In spite of bureaucratic restrictions connected to their legal functioning, cooperatives in the Soviet Union grew rapidly. By early 1990 they produced almost 6 per cent of the GNP and employed more than five million people. Another measure was to legalise semi-private firms through the leasing of state companies. In 1990 a proposal which anticipated full-scale privatisation was opposed by the conservatives with a plan, which limited the reforms in the service sector. On the eve of the attempted coup in August 1991, Gorbachev made an alliance with the liberals, or 'democrats' – who had already adopted laws on privatisation in the republic-level parliaments – to put forward a Soviet-level law on the basic principles of large-scale privatisation. For the first time, privatisation was made a main element of reforms. These efforts remained unfinished, however, when the Soviet Union collapsed in December 1991.

There did seem to be considerable variation between the Soviet republics, hinting that some cultural or mental preconditions played a role. Indeed, the private sector developed most rapidly in the non-Russian regions and republics of the Soviet Union. By 1991 more than 75 per cent of joint stock companies and 80 per cent of private farms were in the Baltic republics. Local government officials were most negative towards the development of the private sector in the Russian Federation and in Central Asia. Furthermore, organised crime and negative public attitudes threatened the development of the private sector. It should also be mentioned that genuinely private firms constituted only a minor part of the sector that was considered private during *perestroika*. Most were connected to state enterprises, one way or another. Rural privatisation never got started in the Soviet Union, unlike in China. The land-leasing programme introduced by Gorbachev was heavily resisted by lower-level bureaucrats as well as by the collective farm workers at the grass roots level.[45]

In China, a 'societal revolution', as it has also been called, took hold in the 1980s. It relied, not on the state, but on bottom-up societal forces through the market, and resulted in important institutional–structural changes. Parts of China's economy were transformed from state-dominated to increasingly market-oriented. China doubled its GNP, internationalised its economy, and experienced rapid industrialisation. After just one decade of reform, China had undone many of the legacies of the state–socialist development of the previous twenty years.[46]

Deng's revolution took place in the countryside, as had Mao's. Mao's revolution has been described as having two "marching legs": agrarian reform and nationalism.[47] The same can be said of Deng's revolution. In both cases it is fair to say that the peasantry had little or nothing to lose and were willing to take risks for a fresh start. Politically, the rural population had become alienated from China's Communist Party, which had long since risen to power thanks to their support, but had now transformed into an urban political establishment, or nomenklatura. During the 1980s, when the so-called Chinese economic miracle took off, the Chinese socialist welfare state covered only about one-fifth of the total labour force. Though official statistics reported the income of the urban population as being, on average, twice the annual income of country residents, in reality, the gap was much wider due to numerous welfare benefits.[48] The legacy of this structural income distribution is still visible today: for instance, in 2010 urban residents earned four times as much as rural residents, according to official statistics.[49]

The first historical clue to explain this would be to note that, even before the reform politics, the Maoist welfare state had not spread its tentacles to the countryside. Peasants were excluded from welfare programmes, which consisted of food subsidies, free health care, guaranteed employment, and income security. While industrial workers were, and in certain industrial sectors still are, dependent on the state, the rural population retained a high degree of independence from the state. The growth of market forces led to an informal coalition of rural residents, private entrepreneurs, local rural elites, and foreign investors (especially overseas Chinese), which in turn spurred the development of the private sector. By the early 1990s, China's private and quasi-private sectors had become overwhelmingly larger than the state-controlled sector.

By the time of the collapse of the Soviet Union in 1991, China had surpassed its 'Soviet big brother' in terms of economic reforms. Opening the discussion on democratic reforms that would threaten and most likely replace the majority of the (then) current political elite in the Soviet Union was paralysing the country's economic reform policy and led to half-hearted zigzags. By contrast, in China economic self-interest was the driving force. The private sector made no open demands on the regime.

Conclusions

Though they began from different points and have adopted different means, Russia and China share the same impetus to modernise: 'catching up with the West' is the ultimate goal and, indeed, a historical mission. The elites' power position has been – and remains – connected to fulfilling that mission. In Russia the historical roots of this goal go back at least three hundred years; in China, more than one hundred. For both countries the original urge to modernise was a reaction to the challenge of the modern capitalist West, and for China a response to the challenge of Japan as well. Both countries were forced to break from their traditional social models.

The original success of the communist revolutions in Russia and China can only be understood in this competitive context. Both revolutions were reactions to a failure to meet the challenge of Western modernisation. But, despite rapid industrialisation in both countries, communist modernisation projects proved ineffective compared to Western achievements. The Soviet Union created fantastic utopias about how the world's first socialist state would lead universal progress, but totalitarian state–society relations stifled the innovations necessary for post-industrial developments. At first, the Chinese attempted to follow the Soviet model, but they could not adapt it to Chinese conditions. Seeking rapid solutions, Mao Zedong created his own version of the socialist illusion, plunging the country into one disastrous experiment after another.

It is argued above that it was China, not the Soviet Union, whose leaders first realised that abandoning the communist modernisation strategy offered the best chance of survival, not least for the ruling political elite itself. If communist modernisation is characterised by the pursuit of equality on ideological grounds, a command economy, rural collectivisation, and industrialisation reliant to a great extent on state-run enterprises, China took the first step toward post-communist modernisation in the late 1970s, when the opening and reform policy was officially endorsed. China continued forcefully in that direction, dismantling the communes and rapidly expanding the private sector during the 1980s.

In 1992, when Deng Xiaoping acknowledged economic prosperity to be the foundation on which the legitimacy of the Communist Party rests, China's modernisation drive had already pushed the *economy*, though not the formal political system, into the post-communist phase. During the 1980s Deng had already declared that some people, and implicitly some regions, must be permitted to get rich first. The landmark decision to make mention of the private sector in the Constitution in 1998 was merely a belated legal acknowledgement of a *fait accompli*.

Thus the Soviet Union began the slide towards post-communism later than China. Although *perestroika* created many slogans, in real terms it was only in the late 1980s that concrete changes to the system took place, and they were often implemented half-heartedly. While the Soviet Union's emphasis was on ad hoc political reforms leading to both economic and political chaos and turmoil, China concentrated on economic modernisation, maintaining its political system under one-party rule and leadership of the Communist Party. Chinese leaders managed to avoid opening the Pandora's box of democracy, despite the 1989 Tiananmen Square democracy movement, whereas the whole Soviet Union as a geopolitical entity and its economic–political system collapsed almost overnight at the end of 1991.

Notes

The author is grateful to Linda Jakobson for her comments and suggestions on the parts about China, as well as her cooperation on a 2001 conference paper about the modernisation paths of Russia and China, which served as an inspiration for this book project.

1. See Toynbee's 'Russia's Byzantine Heritage' in his *Civilisation on Trial*, London, New York, Toronto: Oxford University Press 1949, third edition, pp. 164–183, here especially p. 167. See also Dmitri Obolensky, 'Russia's Byzantine Heritage', in Michael Cherniavsky (ed.), *The Structure of Russian History: Interpretive Essays*, New York, Random House 1970, pp. 3–28. See also Dimitri Strémooukhoff, 'Moscow the Third Rome: Sources of the Doctrine', in Cherniavsky, *The Structure of Russian History*, pp. 108–125.
2. P. Ya. Chaadaev, 'Filosoficheskie pis'ma', in A.F. Zamaleev (ed.), *Rossiya glazami russkogo. Chaadaev, Leontev, Solovev*, Sankt-Peterburg, Nauka 1991, pp. 19–138. See especially the first of the 'Philosophical Letters', published for the first time in Russian in 1836.
3. S.V. Utechin, *Russian Political Thought: A Concise History*, New York, London: Fredrik A. Praeger Publisher 1963.
4. P.Ya. Chaadaev, 'Apologiya sumashedshego', reprinted in Boris Trasov, *Chaadaev*, Moskva: Molodaia gvardiia, pp. 558–573.
5. See A.S. Khomyakov, *Izbrannye sochineniia*, New York: Izdatel'stvo imeni Chekhova 1955, especially pp. 79–101.
6. V.A. Krasiltshchikov, V.P. Gutnik, V.I. Kuznetsov, A.R. Belousov, and A.N. Klepatsh, *Modernizatsiya: zarubezhny opyt i Rossiya*, Moscow: Rossiyski nezavisimy institut sotsialnykh i natsionalnykh problem 1994, here especially Ch. IV.
7. V.A. Krasiltshchikov et al., *Modernizatsiya*, Ch. IV.
8. G.A. Belov, *Politologiya. Kurs lektsiy*, Moscow, Chero 1996 p. 153.
9. Nicolas Berdiaev, *The Origins of Russian Communism*, Ann Arbor: The University of Michigan Press 1972, originally printed in Russian in 1937. See also Nikolai Berdiaev, *The Russian Idea*, Hudson, NY: Lindisfarne Press 1992; Tim McDaniel, *The Agony of the Russian Idea*, Princeton, New Jersey: Princeton University Press 1996.
10. Trotsky had elaborated this approach already in 1906 in his *Results and Prospects*, whereas Lenin adopted the same position considerably later, around 1917: Leon Trotsky, *The Permanent Revolution and Results and Prospects: Revolutionary Strategy in Underdeveloped Countries. With Introductions by Michael Löwy*, London: Socialist Resistance 2007.
11. Suzanne Ogden, *China's Unresolved Issues: Politics, Development, and Culture*, Englewood Cliffs, NJ: Prentice Hall 1989, p. 21.
12. J. Chen, 'Recent Chinese Historiography on the Western Affairs Movement: Yangwu Yundong, Ca. 1860–1895', *Late Imperial China*, 7, no. 1, 2011 pp. 112, 115.
13. A literal translation of the Chinese term *yangwu yundong* is 'foreign affairs movement'. *Yangwu* could mean literally anything about contact with foreign countries. The movement is also referred to as the 'self-strengthening movement'. Ibid., p. 113.
14. Immanuel C.Y. Hsü, *The Rise of Modern China*, Oxford University Press, 1995, pp. 169–219.
15. Lucian W. Pye, 'China: Erratic State, Frustrated Society', *Foreign Affairs*, 69, no. 4, 1990 p. 61.

16. Ibid., p. 62.
17. T. Wei-Ming, 'Cultural China: The Periphery as the Center', *Daedalus* 120, no. 2, 1991, p. 4.
18. Hsü, *The Rise of Modern China*, pp. 169–219.
19. Jonathan D. Spence, *The Search for Modern China,* New York: W.W. Norton & Co 1990, p. 271.
20. Chen, 'Recent Chinese Historiography on the Western Affairs Movement: Yangwu Yundong, Ca. 1860–1895', p. 118.
21. Spence, *The Search for Modern China*, pp. 200, 301–302.
22. Hsü, *The Rise of Modern China*, pp. 501–502; V. Schwarcz, *The Chinese Enlightenment: Intellectuals and the Legacy of the May Fourth Movement of 1919*, University of California Press 1986, p. 107.
23. Ramon H. Myers, 'The Chinese State During the Republican Era', in David L. Shambaugh (ed.), *The Modern Chinese State*, New York: Cambridge University Press 2000, p. 45.
24. H. Lyman Miller, 'The Late Imperial Chinese State', in David L. Shambaugh (ed.), *The Modern Chinese State*, New York: Cambridge University Press, 2000, p. 39.
25. See, for example, David Strand, 'Community, Society, and History in Sun Yat-sen's *Sanmin Zhuyi*', in Theodore Huters, R. Bin Wong and Pauline Yu (eds), *Culture and State in Chinese History*, Stanford: Stanford University Press 1997, pp. 326–338.
26. Marie-Luise Näth, 'From Doctrine to Ethics', in *Russia and China: On the Eve of a New Millennium*, Jan S. Prybyla and Carl A. Linden (eds), New Brunswick: Transaction Publishers 1997, p. 151.
27. E.H. Carr, *Socialism in One Country 1924–1926. Volume III*, London: MacMillan & Co Ltd 1964.
28. See Trotsky, *The Permanent Revolution and Results and Prospects.*
29. Manuel Castells, *End of Millennium*, Manuel Castells (ed.), *The Information Age: Economy, Society and Culture*, Malden, vol. 3, Mass: Blackwell Publishers 1998, Chapter 1.
30. John P. Hardt and Ronda A. Bresnick, 'Brezhnev's European Economic Policy', in G. Ginsburg & A. Z. Rubinstein (eds), *Soviet Foreign Policy Toward Western Europe*, New York: Praeger 1978, pp. 200–232.
31. Boris Kagarlitsky, *The Dialectics of Change*, London and New York: Verso 1990, p. 284.
32. Castells 1998, *The Information Age.*, p. 22.
33. Krasiltshchikov et al., *Modernizatsiya*, is a sophisticated version of this argument.
34. Another important factor was the unity of the leadership. In contrast to the purges in the Soviet Union, Chinese Communists remained united until the mid-1960s.
35. Hsü, *The Rise of Modern China*, p. 651.
36. Jisheng Yang, *Tombstone: A Record of the Great Chinese Famine of the 1960s*, vol. 2, Hong Kong: Cosmos Books 2008, p. 464. Original Chinese title 楊繼繩, *墓碑: 中國六十年代大饑荒紀實. 各地情況展現*, 下篇 (天地圖書有限公司, 2008).
37. Hsü, *The Rise of Modern China*, pp. 657–58.

38. Harry Harding, 'The Chinese State in Crisis, 1966–9', in R. MacFarquhar (ed.), *The Politics of China: The Eras of Mao and Deng*, Cambridge University Press 1997, p. 148.
39. Deng Xiaoping's Opening Address to the Twelfth Congress of the Chinese Communist Party on 2nd September 1982. Available at http://cpc.people.com.cn/GB/64162/64168/64565/65448/4429495.html, original Chinese title: 邓小平在中国共产党第十二次全国代表大会上的开幕词.
40. Min Zhou, 'The Chinese Diaspora and International Migration,' in Y. Bian, K.B. Chan, and T. Cheung (eds), *Social Transformations in Chinese Societies: The Official Annual of the Hong Kong Sociological Association, Volume I*, Leiden, Boston: Brill 2005, pp. 161–190.
41. Linda Jakobson, *A Million Truths: A Decade in China*, New York: M. Evans & Co 2000, pp. 238–239.
42. This often-cited view is not founded in fact. For example, the Song (960–1279) was a weak dynasty, in terms of political control, but it "was the highpoint of intellectual and economic achievement, the pinnacle of China's artistic history". See D. Lary, 'Regions and Nation: The Present Situation in China in Historical Context', *Pacific Affairs*, 1997, p. 181.
43. Pekka Sutela, *The Road to the Russian Market Economy: Selected Essays, 1993–1998*, Helsinki: Aleksanteri Institute 1998, pp. 23–39.
44. Minxin Pei, *From Reform to Revolution: The Demise of Communism in China and the Soviet Union*, Harvard University Press 1998, pp. 118–149.
45. Pei 1998, *From Reform to Revolution*, pp. 118–149.
46. Ibid., pp. 43–44, 71.
47. Castells, *The Information Age*, p. 303.
48. Qingfang Zhu, 'The Urban-Rural Gap and Social Problems in the Countryside', *Chinese Law & Government* 28, no. 1, 1995.
49. National Bureau of Statistics of China, '2010 Statistical Report on National Economic and Social Developments in the People's Republic of China,' National Bureau of Statistics of China, available at http://www.stats.gov.cn/tjgb/ndtjgb/qgndtjgb/t20110228_402705692.htm, original Chinese title: 中华人民共和国2010年国民经济和社会发展统计公报.

3

The Free-Market State or the Welfare State?

Markku Kivinen and Li Chunling

When Russia and China started their socioeconomic reforms, their starting points were institutionally rather similar. Both were one-party states. They had eliminated the private ownership of the means of production and classes based upon that. Their social policy was also built on the labour collective and state-provided welfare benefits for special groups. However, as far as their level of modernisation was concerned they were quite different. Russia was an industrialised and urbanised society, and China was still a predominantly agrarian society. These differences exist even today, as can be read, for instance, from the UNDP's Human Development Report 2010 (Table 3.1), although the results of the comparison are no longer so unambiguous.

In any case, both Russia and China faced the challenge of developing a new socioeconomic model and a new social contract between the state and society in the context of the reality of a market economy. So, the question arises whether the new model would be based on the idea of the power of the market place, namely a liberal welfare system model, with a strong private service sector and perhaps a third sector taking care of many of the previous responsibilities of the state, or whether a new state-based welfare system will be developed on the ruins of the old socialist welfare state. We connect these questions to the analysis of class structures.[1] Given the large-scale privatisation of the Russian and Chinese economies, how has this changed the structure of classes in these countries? Who are the representatives of the owning classes today? What are the situations, internal divisions, and organisation of the working classes and the middle classes in the two countries? What are their roles, relative resources, and perceived interests concerning the preferred welfare model? What kind of socioeconomic systems

Table 3.1 Selected indicators from UNDP's 2010 Human Development Report

			USA	Sweden	Russia	China
Satisfaction with freedom of choice	*Total*	*2009*	83	90	50	70
(% satisfied)	*Female*	*2009*	85	81	51	68
Democracy	*Score (0–2)a*	*2008*	2	2	1	0
Human rights violations	*Score (1–5)b*	*2008*	3	1	4	4
Press freedom	*(index)c*	*2009*	4	0	60.9	84.5
Journalists imprisoned	*(number)d*	*2009*	0	0	1	24
Corruption victims	*(% of people who faced a bribe situation in the last year)*	*2008*	9	6	21	–
Democratic decentralisation	*Score (0–2)e*	*2008*	2	2	–	2
Political engagement	*(% of people who voiced opinion to public officials)*	*2008*	32	29	13	–
Employment to population ratio	*(% of population ages 15–64)*	*1991*	59.4	62	56.8	75.1
		2008	59.2	57.6	56.7	71
Human Development Index (HDI) value		*2010*	*0.902*	*0.885*	0.719	0.663
Life expectancy at birth	*years*	*2010*	*79.6*	*81.3*	67.2	73.5
Mean years of schooling	*years*	*2010*	12.4	11.6	8.8	7.5
Expected years of schooling	*years*	*2010*	15.7	15.6	14.1	11.4
Public expenditure						
Education	*% of GDP*	2000–2007	5.5	6.7	3.9	1.9
Health	*% of GDP*	2000–2007	7.1	7.4	3.5	1.9
Research and development	*% of GDP*	2000–2007	2.7	3.7	1.1	1.5
Military	*% of GDP*	2008	4.3	1.3	3.5	2
Tax revenue	*% of GDP*	2008	10.3	–	15.7	9.4
Urban population	*of total*	1990	75.3	83.1	73.4	26.4
		2010	82.3	84.7	73.2	47

Source: UNDP Human Development Report 2010.

are taking shape based upon these structural changes and deliberate choices by elites in Russia and China?

Russia

It is clear that the official version of working-class power in the Soviet Union was at variance with the real dominant position of the nomenklatura; political processes developed and unfolded out of this tension. In fact, the relationship between the working class and nomenklatura represented one fundamental aspect in a more general strict duality of the Bolshevik culture. If it was the opposition between the bourgeoisie and the working class that gave the impetus to the revolutionary action of workers, the nomenklatura appears to have been an unintended result of the project. As Michael Burawoy has pointed out, it is far more difficult to legitimise privileges in a system that does not accept inequality.[2] This makes the nomenklatura an absolute taboo in the public sphere. At the everyday level the nomenklatura proper, for the absolute majority of people, was only a distant reality: 'they' were out there somewhere.

New elements began to appear in the class structure from the 1930s onwards. When Stalin criticised excessive equality, he was in effect appealing to the new social forces, the middle class, which Stalinist politics itself had paradoxically produced, in this case professional–managerial groups. These were major groups born out of industrialisation, education, and bureaucratic expansion: 'our own intelligentsia', as opposed to the 'old bourgeois intelligentsia' with whom all accounts had been settled in the early 1930s. During the Soviet era a constant tension prevailed between the 'holy proletariat' and the real-life working class. Whereas the former was assumed to be disciplined, organised and hard-working, the latter turned out to be rural, carnivalistic, restless and heavy-drinking. A similar situation is unfolding today with the idealised middle class. All Russian political forces are hankering after the middle class. In spite of these semiotic structures of the hegemonic project, class analysis cannot be reduced to the cultural level: such a move would deprive us of the possibility of secularising and deconstructing such sacred codes.

The phase of insider privatisation

Compared to Eastern Europe, Russian privatisation could be called a 'nomenklatura privatisation' and in this sense it can be seen as a failure.[3] However, private ownership of the means of production emerged and the process was irreversible. As was briefly discussed in the previous chapter, privatisation in Russia got uneasily under way during Gorbachev's reign. The purpose of privatisation was to replace the means of 'administrative' regulation with 'economic' regulation, that is, to create a new kind of control system, rather than release companies from the shackles of government control. Valentin Pavlov's government passed the first all-union privatisation law, which made it possible for companies to be collectively or cooperatively owned. Joint-stock companies and even direct private ownership were now possible. Although the law did not set out any specific procedures for privatisation, most of the first projects were based on cooperative or rental arrangements. Shares were sold to workers at reduced prices, with the company offering loans. As far the workers were concerned, all of this seemed to promise a secure job and an opportunity to break free from centralised wage control. For managers, it meant the company became legally independent of state control. At the same time it effectively legalised various financial arrangements for full-scale privatisation.

In the new Russian Federation, Yegor Gaidar's government initially aimed at a form of state privatisation that was oriented against the industrial nomenklatura. Gaidar was opposed to releasing any property for free and did not want to relinquish control to the former company managers in the name of the 'labour collective'.[4] Privatisation was to create a new 'propertied class' and at the same time generate income to stabilise the national economy. However, the industrial nomenklatura mobilised strong pressure both in parliament and through the old trade unions for privatisation based on labour collectives.[5] Many neo-liberal economists in Russia were persuaded to support this model, because there was very little popular resistance and because, for them, the chief concern was not ownership but getting the markets up and running. The privatisation programme adopted in the first year of the new Russia marked an almost complete surrender to the demands of the industrial nomenklatura.[6] Companies were offered several options for privatisation. The decision was to be made by a meeting of the labour collective. According to the first model, workers were entitled to 25 per cent of the company's shares without a vote; in addition they would have the option of buying 10 per cent of the shares at a reduced price. Top management would be allowed to buy a further 5 per cent of the share stock. The rest would remain in the hands of state or local privatisation committees to be sold at a later date by auction. This was the model that privatisation committees tended to favour, but it was also preferred by those liberal democrats and worker activists who were still hoping to break the power of the industrial nomenklatura. However, the results of the Russian privatisation process were exactly the opposite: the new bourgeoisie was growing out of the old industrial nomenklatura.

Thus, in the new Russia, state property passed first into the hands of those already in power, following an approach that is called nomenklatura privatisation or spontaneous privatisation. To some extent, this phenomenon was already present in the Soviet Union, especially from late 1980 onwards: "Managerial elites of SOEs [state-owned enterprises] were the driving force behind this movement, and they persuaded employees to go along by promising various benefits. Some SOEs were converted into joint-stock companies, with employees receiving a minority stake in the form of shares, and the management usually controlling a majority stake."[7] The new Russia only continued this trend of privatisation. Those in high positions, the 'red barons' of enterprises or administration, transferred "the property of state companies to themselves or their own firms".[8] The early phase of Russian privatisation therefore resulted in a much larger scale of insider control than in most other transition countries. While some economists saw this development as natural, and even as beneficial for the Russian economy, most have agreed that it reinforced "state intervention, corporatism, favouritism, corruption, paternalism and protectionism".[9] An ownership structure that is by nature antagonistic to structural changes and further market reform does not welcome domestic or foreign investments in the existing enterprises.

This was the opinion of the neo-liberal market-reformers – who rose to power together with President Yeltsin – about the rather unintended ownership structure. Most notable amongst them was Anatoly Chubais, in Gaidar's government. Following the initial 'democratic' approach, they modestly started to reform the ownership structure by introducing the mass privatisation approach, that is, vouchers or privatisation checks that were distributed to the whole population. Reaching a compromise with the conservative Supreme Soviet, where the allies of the 'red barons' were against further privatisation, the law on privatisation was adopted in June 1992, still giving the insiders (that is, the managers and workers of enterprises) the right to keep 51 per cent of each enterprise whereas the rest would be sold or kept by the state. However, the original idea was never to follow the Yeltsin slogan 'we need millions of owners, not hundreds of millionaires', but to use the vouchers as a way to enable the 'outsiders', a new capitalist class, to enter the enterprises by collecting these vouchers into larger funds.

From oligarchic capitalism to bureaucratic capitalism

Allowing this kind of a new class to be formed in Russian society[10] meant that Russia's economic reforms had been undemocratic and unequal in spirit; however, they were to become much worse with the wild capitalism that followed. Most of the future so-called oligarchs were *not* part of the former nomenklatura. They had made use of market opportunities since the late 1980s by starting cooperatives and trading whatever was possible. These new 'NEPmen' were originally speculators and swindlers, who utilised the absence of general rule and law in the late-Soviet and early new Russia era, especially the lack of legislation regulating financial and economic activities. If one was endowed with entrepreneurial spirit and had enough luck and energy, small fortunes could easily be made in several ways in the late-Soviet and early new-Russian times. These included, for instance, collecting huge profits by currency speculation in an era of hyperinflation; releasing worthless 'shares' in investment funds which the public ran to invest in; working as a middleman for managers of state property, especially buying state-owned raw materials at artificially low domestic prices and selling them illicitly on foreign markets at export prices, sometimes with profits of several hundred per cent. The money made was then used to generate even greater riches: buying or collecting (with false promises) large numbers of privatisation vouchers from the population to make voucher funds and thus becoming shareholders in, or completely taking over, formerly state-owned companies. The shares of these companies were sold by the State Property Committee at ridiculously low prices, enabling the future oligarchs to virtually 'steal' the property of the state.

As a consequence, a kind of a quiet revolution in ownership structures took place around the mid-1990s. The new owners started to replace the old managerial elites, the rent-seeking 'red barons' who had based their success on state subsidies for non-competitive production rather than on market-oriented entrepreneurship. Early on, these future oligarchs had entered the banking and stock market sector in order to administer their operations, with licenses received from state authorities on the basis of personal connections. If they were lucky in making contacts with corrupt politicians and bureaucrats, their banks became 'authorised', meaning state bureaucracies financed regional or other state economic and social programmes through them, including the salaries of public workers and civil servants. The backstage idea for this arrangement was that instead of paying funds immediately to where they were owed, the unregulated system enabled the banks to use these huge amounts of cash to carry out short-term currency and other speculations and collect huge profits.

By the mid-1990s, the oligarchs had found firm allies in the market-reformers around President Boris Yeltsin, who held power in important government positions relevant to economic policy. After several failures to get rid of the old conservative managerial elites, and dissatisfied with the rather small-scale achievements of voucher privatisation, the market-reformers were now interested in privatising state property as fast as possible and at any price. The ideological purpose was to finally get rid of the threat of the return of communism, without paying any attention to what this would mean for the population at large or the democratic values at stake. The final innovation that materialised in this ideology was the so-called loans-for-shares approach, that is, auctions that were organised to sell off the most lucrative natural resources and main state companies to a hand-picked group of oligarchs. Formally, the banks received shares in state companies for safekeeping, in exchange for a loan to the government. As the bankrupt government, according to the plan, did not pay back the loans, the banks had the right to sell the shares, which they did. However, they sold the shares cheaply to themselves via backstage operations. In this way a handful of oligarchs took over the largest and most lucrative state-owned enterprises and resources, including those dealing with oil, metallurgy, pulp industry, and so on.

A third change in the ownership structure started with President Vladimir Putin in the early 2000s. He first made a deal with most of the oligarchs that they would not interfere excessively in politics; those who were too ambitious were either put in prison or driven abroad. This development, which was understood by many Western analysts and scholars as an authoritarian move as it touched on the property rights of the new capitalist class, was generally welcomed by the Russian people. At the same time, the new ruling elite under Putin emphasised the necessity of re-establishing the great power role of Russia, which led to the conclusion of the need to tighten control over what were seen as strategic or sensitive sectors, such as raw materials and energy. The new approach that was introduced has been called 'renationalisation' or 'state capitalism'; the state enterprises started to buy attractive private companies either at a high price, or the sale was forced and therefore the price was low. While many oligarchs have, at least so far, remained in these companies, others have been forced out, especially in the energy sector. The *siloviki* (the people from security structures), as well as other people close to the Putin administration, were installed to lead many of the main Russian enterprises.[11] Thus, what was originally labelled as oligarchic capitalism became what is currently labelled as bureaucratic capitalism. Yet the private sector remains dominant, and even critics of the current renationalisation claim that Russia "became a market economy after a couple of years of transition, with no significant reversal", and that its "economic freedom holds firm".[12]

Russian peculiar class structure

In their book *Making Capitalism Without Capitalists,* Gil Eyal, Ivan Szelenyi and Eleanor Townsley analyse the class formation and elite struggles in post-communist Central Europe. They make a basic distinction between Central Europe and Russia. In the former case the revolution by the nomenklatura was blocked by an independent intelligentsia. In those countries privatisation proceeded more cautiously than in post-Soviet Russia, and typically produced diffuse ownership rights.[13] The result was a 'capitalism without capitalists': relatively developed capital and labour markets, functioning mechanisms of stock exchange and budding capitalist forms of corporate governance, all administered by the intelligentsia in its role as 'cultural bourgeoisie', but without a propertied class. In Russia the nomenklatura managed to convert itself into a propertied class via spontaneous privatisation,[14] then via oligarchic privatisation, and later with Putin bringing back the bureaucrats to the sources of economic power. The result is a powerful propertied class thriving in the context of weak, rudimentary, or even absent, capitalist market institutions – 'capitalists without capitalism'. Ivan Szelenyi had suggested that China followed a different trajectory, which he has labelled 'capitalism from below' or 'entrepreneurial capitalism'. In a more recent article, however, Szelenyi argues that these differences seem to be vanishing.[15]

The Russian transition has intensified sociological studies on class structure; in particular, the formation of a middle class has been the focus of many Russian sociologists.[16] This approach has been significantly inspired by a rather essentialist approach to class identity, consciousness, and habitus of classes.[17] The middle class is suggested as being in its essence legalistic, disciplined, and full of entrepreneurial spirit. Theoretical discussions in Western sociology on the special and non-benign interests of the middle class have not been broadly discussed in Russia. In empirical analysis, Russian class research tends to be oriented towards constructing multidimensional stratification models[18] and opinion scales. Except on some totalising new openings,[19] in most cases the class analysis is restricted to defining the limits of the class, at best adding hypothetical constructions on class interests. This limited scope can be challenged, and analysis can instead focus on the structuration process of classes in concrete terms, taking into account the concrete levels of class situation and forms of organisation. It is especially important to understand the neglected connection between class structuration and the formation of the welfare regime.

In the Soviet Union, as in the West, the question of the alienation and autonomy of labour was a crucial distinguishing dimension between the middle class and the working class.[20] On the other hand, the middle class in the Soviet Union had far fewer resources available to protect their own positions than is the case in advanced capitalist countries. How is it possible to operationalise classes such as the new middle class? For us, the core of the new middle classes consists of all types of professional, scientific technical, managerial or administrative-bureaucratic autonomy, regardless of managerial status. In addition, people in leading positions of office work are included. By contrast, care workers, skilled workers and autonomous employees of small enterprises, as well as those in performance-level autonomous office jobs, constitute a contradictory class location in the middle ground between the core of the new middle classes and the working class. In this operationalisation, autonomy serves as a class criterion in two different ways. Firstly, occupations are classified as autonomy types on the grounds described above. Secondly, membership of the core of the new middle classes has required at least unambiguous medium autonomy on the following scale: 1. High, unambiguous; 2. High, probable; 3. Medium, unambiguous; 4. Medium, probable; 5. Low; 6. None. Autonomy can be measured with three different questions concerning product design, performance design, and genuine problem-solving in the work process. These dimensions can be combined into a measure of autonomy by weighting the product design and problem-solving components on the basis of rules of deduction borrowed from Wright's original theory of autonomy. The professional and managerial groups included in the core of the middle class are therefore groups who possess this kind of real autonomy.[21] However, on account of their lack of power resources, Russian professionals have had less autonomy than professionals in capitalist countries. To highlight this phenomenon we have formed one new class group, which is called marginal group 2 in Table 3.2. This group comprises those wage earners whose occupation would imply a position in the core, but who do not really possess autonomy. Examples include doctors, teachers, lawyers, and engineers with no autonomy. Additionally, we have operationalised

Table 3.2 Class structure by autonomy criterion, autonomy index = 2

		Frequency	Per cent
Core of m/c	*1998*	197	14.8
	2007	172	14.3
Marginal group 1	*1998*	94	7.1
	2007	101	8.4
Marginal group 2	*1998*	210	15.8
	2007	155	12.9
Marginal group 3	*1998*	120	9
	2007	145	12
Working class	*1998*	672	50.5
	2007	558	46.3
Entrepreneurs	*1998*	37	2.8
	2007	73	6.1
Total	*1998*	1330	100
	2007	1204	100

Source: The class structure rests on the premises presented in Markku Kivinen, 'Classes in the Making? The Russian Social Structure in Transition', in Therborn Göran (ed.), *Inequalities of the World: New Theoretical Frameworks, Multiple Empirical Approaches*, London, New York: Verso 2006, pp. 263–264.

a third marginal group, which comprises those wage earners who have at least some supervisory tasks.[22]

An unintended result of the Bolshevik's modernisation project was, eventually, a broad potential middle class; there were more teachers, engineers and medical doctors than in many developed Western countries. [23] However, the middle class was not allowed to organise or articulate its own interests. This constellation can still be observed as the most significant difference between Russia and the developed Western societies as far as the internal differentiation of wage working groups are concerned.

We have studied Russian class structure in the years 1991, 1998 and 2007 using survey methods and a representative sample of the population. Table 3.2 shows that because of the weak power resources during the Soviet years, the actual middle class in Russia is still rather small compared with the core of the middle classes in the West. In all developed Western societies this class comprises more than 20 per cent of the population.[24] However the marginal group 2, which is almost non-existent in the West, [25] in Russia is almost as large as the core of the middle class. The table also shows the considerable growth of the entrepreneurial middle class during the transition to a market economy. The size of this class group has grown rapidly but is still lagging behind the respective figure for the most developed market economies as well as that for China.

Comparative class analysis indicates that differences between developed market societies are minor at the level of class structure.[26] If we make the conceptual distinction between class position and class situation we notice that the latter is the level of structuration where the differences emerge, although at this level the relative differences (e.g. in mobility or permeability) are also, to a large extent, unchangeable.[27] However, the differences in construction of the class agency are vast between different societies. This agency creates conditions for different models of welfare. To a large extent, these can be explained by the concrete differences in class situation.

During the first years of transition Russia was in deep economic crisis. Between 1991 and 1998 the GDP fell 40 per cent; more than during the 1930s in Western societies. At the same time the traditional safety nets of Soviet society were eroded, and poverty increased dramatically due to the fall in GDP and growing inequality. However, since the economic collapse of 1998, the Russian economy has been growing by about 5–7 per cent a year. Real incomes have been growing rapidly, as can been seen in Figure 3.1. Table 3.3 in turn shows, however, that the relative income differentiation (measured by the index in which the average income is 100) between class groups has remained exactly the same.

As far as measuring inequality is concerned, it seems to be the case that when social classes organise themselves outside of the real interest

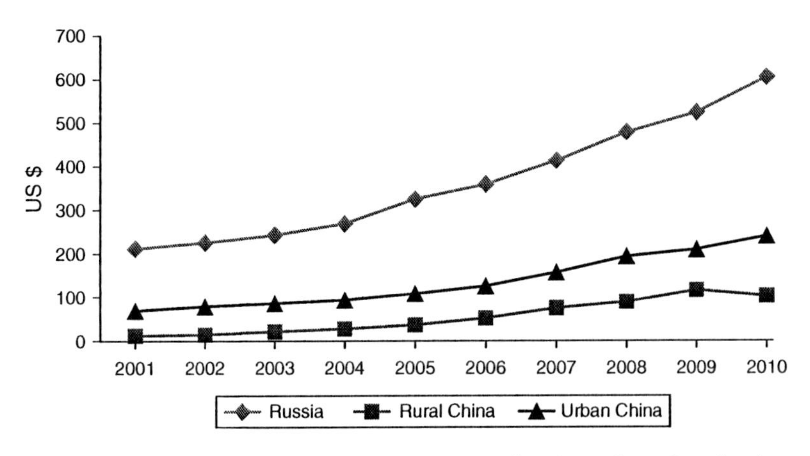

Figure 3.1 The development of real incomes in Russia and rural and urban China (in USD)

Source: Institute for Economies in Transition (Bofit) Bank of Finland.

Table 3.3 Income in roubles by class (average for the year = 100)

1998	Year	Absolute Income	Index	N
Core of m/c	*1998*	1184	133	189
	2007	12007	133	158
Marginal group 1	*1998*	1158	130	23
	2007	6615	73	27
Marginal group 2	*1998*	961	108	200
	2007	10305	114	149
Marginal group 3	*1998*	1062	119	120
	2007	9398	104	141
Working class	*1998*	725	82	705
	2007	7512	83	610
Entrepreneurs	*1998*	1455	164	33
	2007	13031	145	65
Total	*1998*	889	100	1270
	2007	9013	100	1150

Source: Institute for Economies in Transition, Bank of Finland (Bofit). Income in roubles. Survey was performed late October – early December 1998. During this time one dollar was worth approximately 16,41 roubles in October, 17,21 in November, 20,83 in December, and approximately 25,58 roubles in 2007.

politics, a society is being created where social inequality is very insignificant. Should we consider the Nordic countries in Northern Europe, for instance, they are placed at the top of the list of most developed countries when measured with the Sen-index. This is calculated by taking into account GNP per capita as well as the Gini-index[28] measuring inequality. Measured with this instrument, the United States, where the working class has weak power resources, is placed among the least developed countries among the Western market economies. The development of the Chinese and Russian Gini-index are shown in Figure 3.2. Since in Russia interest policy and representation is weak, the Gini-index has increased significantly during the transition period. However, this development of inequality should not be seen in too straightforward a way; the polarisation of society because of the formation of the middle class is a real process.

When we take into account the growth of inequality (Figure 3.2) measured by the Gini-index, and also the regional differences in Table 3.4, we can suggest the following conclusions concerning the relevance of income differences in contemporary Russia. First, the growing differences in Gini-index should not be interpreted as a polarisation of society, nor does this indicate growing relative differences between classes. The growing inequality during the Putin and Medvedev regimes

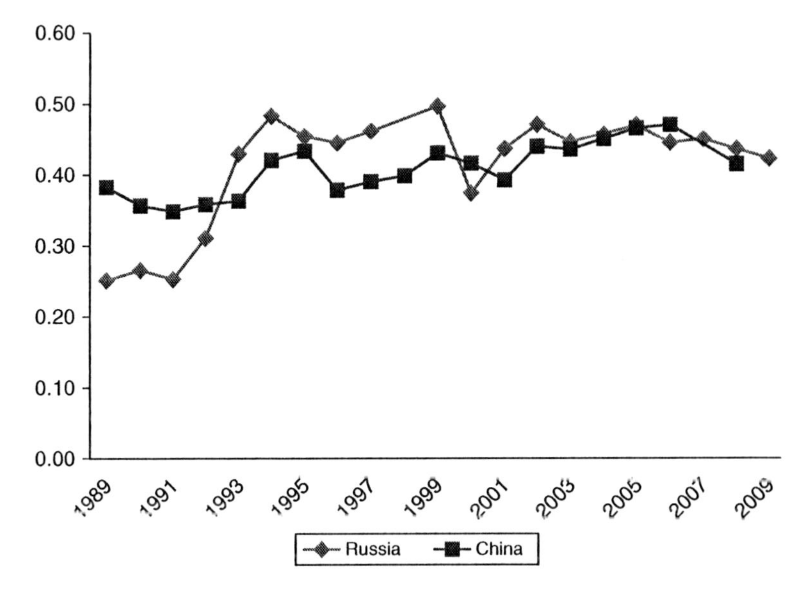

Figure 3.2 The development of Gini-index in Russia and China, 1989–2009

Source: World Bank Development indicators; UNU-WIDER World Income Inequality Database, Version 2.0c, May 2008.

seems to be due to *regional differentiation* instead. Second, the relative differences between the middle class and working class seem to have stabilised. They have a strong structuring effect on life perspectives in conditions that are characterised by paid and chargeable welfare services and a lack of progressive taxes. Third, for the working class experience in Russia, the relative differences between classes may be less significant than the growth of real incomes and consumption possibilities. To some extent, the transition situation is in a phase similar to that of the decades after World War II in Western Europe.[29]

Anyhow, the structuration of class situation also has other dimensions, which we are able to analyse using our survey data. Table 3.5 is shown here as an example of the indicators concerning working conditions. It clearly shows that the 'potential middle class' significantly improved its position after Putin took over the Russian presidency in 2000. Consequently, this group seems to be in the process of receiving a real middle class position. But the table also shows (and all the other indicators show the same thing) that improving corporate governance is a real phenomenon in contemporary Russia, touching all wage labourers in everyday life. This underlines the thesis above, namely that

Table 3.4 Income in roubles by class and area (average of the year = 100)

Class	Area	Year	Absolute Income	Index	N
Core of m/c	*Moscow & St. Pet*	1998	1927	217	32
		2007	23143	257	28
	Cities > 500 000	1998	2336	263	14
		2007	10417	116	18
	Other Cities	1998	990	111	106
		2007	10437	116	74
	Villages	1998	662	74	37
		2007	7611	84	38
	Total	1998	1184	133	189
		2007	12007	133	158
Marginal group 1	*Moscow & St. Pet*	1998	0		
		2007	13500	150	4
	Cities > 500 000	1998	5450	613	2
		2007	8833	98	3
	Other cities	1998	853	96	16
		2007	5346	59	13
	Villages	1998	608	68	51
		2007	5825	65	78
	Total	1998	961	108	200
		2007	10305	114	149
Marginal group 2	*Moscow & St. Pet*	1998	1665	187	34
		2007	16150	179	30
	Cities > 500 000	1998	1152	130	26
		2007	15658	174	19
	Other cities	1998	838	94	89
		2007	8199	91	72
	Villages	1998	608	68	51
		2007	5825	64	28
	Total	1998	961	108	200
		2007	10305	114	149
Marginal group 3	*Moscow & St. Pet*	1998	1807	203	17
		2007	17125	190	16
	Cities > 500 000	1998	1442	162	6
		2007	8750	97	30
	Other cities	1998	987	111	75
		2007	8782	97	74
	Villages	1998	638	72	22
		2007	6795	75	21
	Total	1998	1062	119	120
		2007	6398	104	141

Continued

Table 3.4 Continued

Class	Area	Year	Absolute Income	Index	N
Working class	*Moscow & St. Pet*	1998	1293	145	76
		2007	13269	147	65
	Cities > 500 000	1998	949	107	94
		2007	9414	104	100
	Other cities	1998	694	78	343
		2007	6794	75	298
	Villages	1998	446	50	192
		2007	5126	57	147
	Total	1998	725	82	705
		2007	7515	83	610
Entrepreneurs	*Moscow & St. Pet*	1998	500	56	1
		2007	22567	250	6
	Cities > 500 000	1998	1650	186	4
		2007	14923	166	13
	Other cities	1998	1496	168	27
		2007	11303	125	35
	Villages	1998	500	56	1
		2007	13031	145	65
	Total	1998	1455	164	33
		2007	13031	145	65
Total	*Moscow & St. Pet*	1998	1549	174	160
		2007	16499	183	149
	Cities > 500 000	1998	1219	137	146
		2007	10434	116	183
	Other cities	1998	832	94	656
		2007	7948	88	566
	Villages	1998	512	58	308
		2007	5949	66	252
	Total	1998	889	100	1270
		2007	9013	100	1150

Source: Institute for Economies in Transition, Bank of Finland (Bofit). Income in roubles. Survey was performed in late October – early December 1998. During this time one dollar was worth approximately 16,41 roubles in October, 17,21 in November, 20,83 in December, and approximately 25,58 roubles in 2007.

the absolute improvement may be more significant than relative differences in contemporary Russia.

Weak class organisations

If we want to understand the specificity of class organisations in Russia today we have to start with the position of the trade unions under Soviet

Table 3.5 Job changes in five years: the opportunity to use skills (%)

		Got worse		No change		Got better		Total	
		%	N	%	N	%	N	%	N
Core of m/c	*1998*	19.8	34	45.9	79	34.3	59	100	172
	2007	4.0	4	35.0	35	61.0	61	100	100
Marginal group 1	*1998*	11.1	2	38.9	4	50.0	9	100	18
	2007	4.2	1	50.0	12	45.8	11	100	24
Marginal group 2	*1998*	24.6	43	53.7	94	21.7	38	100	175
	2007	7.8	7	34.4	31	57.8	52	100	90
Marginal group 3	*1998*	21.4	21	56.1	55	22.4	22	100	98
	2007	4.1	3	40.5	30	55.4	41	100	74
Working class	*1998*	26.3	142	62.0	335	11.7	63	100	540
	2007	5.3	17	64.6	208	30.1	97	100	322
Entrepreneurs	*1998*	24.0	6	36.0	9	40.0	10	100	25
	2007	2.70	1	62.20	23	35.10	13	100	37
Total	*1998*	24.10	248	56.30	579	19.60	201	100	1028
	2007	5.10	33	52.40	339	42.50	275	100	647

rule. In both China and the Soviet Union a trade union organisation used to be unequivocally a branch of enterprise management. They used most of their resources to administer the enterprise level social and welfare system which played a central role in the reproduction of the labour collective (or *Danwei* in China). The trade union did not represent the workers in relation to management; they could act as mediators between workers and management in disputes but they were not seen as representatives of separate interests. The trade union president and the enterprise director were both seen as representing the labour collective, although with different functional responsibilities. At the national level, trade unions were deeply embedded in the structures of the party-state. As such they had a limited role as junior partners in lobbying for resources, and there were no collective agreements. Collective agreements had existed in the years immediately following the revolution, but they were abolished in the Soviet Union in 1934 and in China in 1958. By this the trade unions were subordinated to the party-state apparatus.[30]

It was not in the interests of Soviet managers to control production; all that mattered was how much the workers produced. The main obstacle to reaching production targets was not the resistance of workers, but a shortage of parts and materials. It follows that the key concern of enterprise administration was to secure the supply side of the production chain. It was much easier for the administration to fight for less restrictive plans from the Ministry, to fiddle the figures, or to force the workers to intensify their labour than to take direct control of the production process. Workers had considerable control over how they produced, but limited power in terms of collective resistance or in terms of influencing how much they had to work or how they were paid. They had various individual strategies to cope with the oppression: they stayed away from work, changed jobs, or turned to drink. People frequently talked about the lack of discipline and motivation problems. On the other hand, the concept of production management did not exist.

The federation of independent trade unions in Russia was established in September 1989, on the basis of organisational and economic assets of the official trade union organisation of the Soviet Union. It is still the largest class organisation in contemporary Russia: about 22 per cent of wage workers belong to this union. According to sociological surveys, most of them expect the unions to protect their interests, but most of them also feel that this does not occur.[31] Russian trade unions, like their Chinese counterparts, face a dilemma: whether to reconstitute their traditional role through collaboration with management and the state apparatus, or whether to develop their ability to defend the rights and interests of workers.[32] Post-socialist trade unions have to construct their own practices on the basis of inherited structures and within a societal framework which is not of their own making.

Perestroika was essentially an effort to make a transition to a 'socialist market economy'. This involved replacing the administrative-command system with market relations. The idea was that private entrepreneurship and foreign investment would be allowed, but medium and large enterprises would remain under state ownership. At the same time, the authority of the party in the workplace should be reduced. Employment relations should be regulated on the basis of the law and collective bargaining. This implied a new role for the trade unions alongside the institutions of democratic participation. During the 1989 strike wave, Gorbachev made an effort to generate *perestroika* from below by the reform of the trade unions.

When the transition to a socialist market economy eventually developed into a transition to a capitalist market economy, the erosion of the institutions of workplace democracy implied an increasing role for the trade unions. In this context they should have represented the employees' interests in negotiation with enterprise management. During the 1990s the miners' trade unions played a significant political role in promoting the market economy as allies of the 'democrats'.[33] They viewed the market economy as promising because of the export prospects for coal in the new political situation. However, the rapid pauperisation of miners in 1992–1993 broke this alliance, and in 1997 the miners trade unions demanded the renationalisation of the coal industry, which had been privatised in just three weeks a couple of years previously; by then, however, they lacked political power. Still, in the 1990s the rights of the unions were respected. Since 2000 these collective rights have gradually been eroded and the harassment and persecution of independent activists has become common.[34]

The problem in Russia was that the change in the political role of the trade union had done nothing to change its institutional form within enterprises. The old trade unions were still drawing on enterprise resources and performing managerial functions. To a large extent, they maintained considerable resources of property and legal privileges dependent on the state authorities. On the other hand, capitalist development implied an increase in the potential for industrial conflict. New trade unions emerged after the collapse of the Soviet Union; however, they had a weak institutional basis and this led them to turn to political patronage and participation in institutions of social partnership as the means of their institutional reproduction.[35] The 1990s saw a remarkable convergence between the traditional and new trade unions in their structures and forms of activity.[36] The legitimacy of the enterprise trade unions has been further undermined by the fact that their role as the beneficent provider of social benefits has been eroded. When grievances develop into overt industrial conflict, the trade union typically tries to dissuade workers from taking any kind of collective action and will, at best, appeal to the courts or political bodies to redress their individual grievances.

The erosion of the power resources, as well as the structural contradictions of trade unions, contribute fundamentally to the demobilisation of the rank and file. According to official statistics, strikes had almost withered away during the latter half of the first decade of the millennium (Figure 3.3). This is partly due to new labour legislation which makes official strikes very complicated,[37] but even illegal strikes are rare – only 35 in 2007, for instance[38] – because of the weak micro-level structural conditions of the trade unions.

As far as civil society in general is concerned, the boom in the late 1980s was followed by a slump in the first decade of post-communist politics. In particular, activism in associations was in dramatic decline. Nevertheless, one should not exaggerate the weakness of Russian civil society; even if it is difficult to get a picture of the exact number of NGOs based on official statistics (which give a variety of figures and definitions, as will be discussed in the next chapter), or of the extent

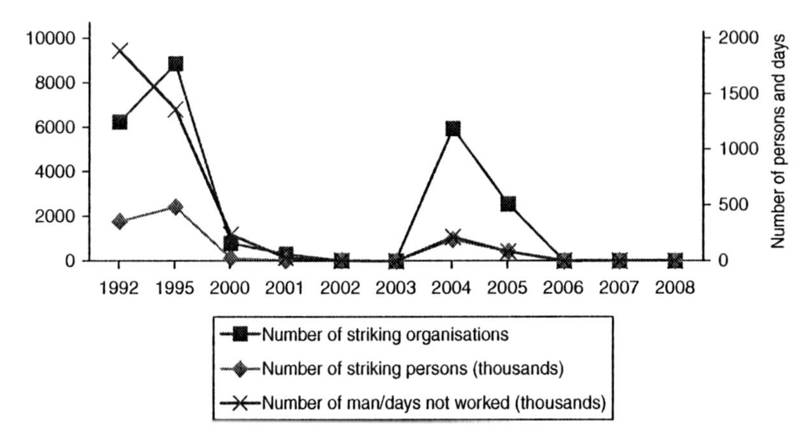

Figure 3.3 Strikes in Russia
Source: *Federal State Statistics Service*, Russia in figures.

of their real activities, there are hundreds of thousands of civil or public organisations in Russia.[39] Russia is rather different from Western societies in the role that organisations play in civil society. During the Putin regime (2000–2008) and the Putin-Medvedev first tandem regime (2008–2012), although the leaders paid lip service to the terms of civil society, a growing number of groups that are informally called GONGOS (government organised non-governmental organisations) has appeared.[40] In most cases, professional organisations for the middle class have followed this path as well. They seem to work in a 'constructive spirit' with the government, as well as with regional and local authorities. As to the political organisation, our survey shows a low level of party membership in general. However, the analysis hints that members of the middle class are more and more willing to promote their careers by joining the ruling *United Russia* party.

In formal terms Russia is a democracy. However, since societal interests are very weakly organised in Russia, we would use the concept of mass democracy to characterise the contemporary Russian political system.[41] This concept refers to a system where all of the social classes are weakly organised and represented in the political system. The real power struggle is going on within the elite, and the media is a major player in linking the elite and the unorganised masses. Particular to Russia as a mass democracy is the post-Soviet political culture. We would characterise this culture using the concept of palimpsest: representing a vision of history according to which the past can be suppressed but not erased, the palimpsest is a metaphor for preserving cultural memory that lies submerged below the surface.[42] We can hear the echo of this in questions of the following kind: does Putin know? What is the power vertical? What is the role of the *siloviki* in Russian elite? Was the case of Mikhail Khodorkovsky a show trial? These questions all reflect the heavy burden of authoritarian culture in Russian politics. This is the dark background to contemporary Russia, where hankering for order serves as a strong civil religion.[43] As far as classes are concerned, a real representation of interests is still missing.

Creating a post-communist welfare regime

One of the core challenges for Russian society – as well as for Chinese society – is the creation of a new welfare regime. This is also one of the key issues in the mobilisation of class interests. In advanced capitalist countries many of the security needs of classes and individuals have come to be provided by 'welfare states', embracing a combination of pensions and social protection benefits, social services, and labour market regulation. Under these conditions social policies not only reflect, but also reproduce stratification outcomes in terms of power, as well as class and other forms of inequality. As Wood and Gough put it: "In this way, social policies shape political divisions and alliances, and usually reproduce them through time in a path-dependent way."[44]

The welfare systems of Russia and China should be analysed in comparative terms based on the method of ideal-typical models. In comparative social policy the first three ideal-typical models were introduced by Esping-Andersen in 1990.[45] He, as well as many of his followers, adhered to the political school of welfare studies, highlighting the crucial impact of politics on social welfare policy. In the beginning, the comparative analysis of welfare focused on European and Anglo-Saxon countries. Esping-Andersen distinguished three welfare state regimes in the OECD world. He labelled them liberal, conservative, and social democratic. The liberal model is found in Anglo-Saxon countries. This regime concentrates on poverty reduction and sees the individual and the market as relevant stake-holders. In continental Europe it was primarily Christian Democratic parties that created a conservative model which emphasised social insurance rights and saw both state and family as responsible agencies. In Scandinavia the ruling Social Democratic parties created a welfare model which focused on universal social citizenship rights with strong redistribution policies.

The East Asian model is closely connected with the fact that, with the exception of China, since 1945 conservative political parties have ruled in East Asia.[46] However, in the East Asian model the state is very active not only in the markets, but also in social investment and social development. At the same time the right to social security is moderate and much responsibility is put on the family and the market. Wood and Gough have used the concept of 'productionist welfare regimes' to characterise the East Asian model.[47] They also introduce the concept of informal security regimes to describe institutional arrangements where people rely heavily on community and family relationships to meet their social security needs. Insecurity regimes describe institutional arrangements which generate gross insecurity and block the emergence of stable informal welfare mechanisms. Many sub-Saharan states, more or less failed states, and criminal states fall into this category.

Both the Soviet Union and China had a distinct welfare regime during the post-war years, which were mainly based on the enterprise level. The Soviet welfare policy was built on two pillars. On the one hand, the state provided non-monetary social benefits for particular social groups. On the other hand, the firms in the planned economy were not enterprises as is understood in a market economy. Both of these old pillars are disappearing in the contemporary market system. The ideological representation characterised a Soviet enterprise as a 'labour collective': the labour collective comprised all those with a right to work in the enterprise, including, for example, women on extended maternity leave or young people in military service, as well as the pensioners of the enterprise. It is the labour collective that produces and reproduces itself through its activity in the enterprise (and it is the labour collective that was supposed to be the principal claimant to ownership rights in the process of privatisation). This meant that the achievements of an enterprise were not measured in money, nor simply in tons produced, but in the size, education and skills composition of the labour force, the number of houses built, kindergartens supported, and so forth, which dominate the iconography of the Soviet enterprise and of the achievements of socialism.[48] The idea of the enterprise as a labour collective was a fiction, but it is precisely in the name of the labour collective that management ruled the enterprise, and in the name of the labour collective that it pressed its interests vis-à-vis higher authorities and required that workers be subjected to managerial authority.

While China will be discussed in more detail below, it should be mentioned that before the communist revolution the traditional Chinese welfare model centred on the family and kinship.[49] The role of the state was limited to paternalistic concern in the case of natural disasters. In this sense the pre-revolution Chinese welfare state was close to the contemporary East Asian informal welfare regime. After the inception of the People's Republic of China the cherished egalitarian and collective values created a basic welfare system described as the 'iron rice bowl'. Also, the Chinese labour collectives provided their employees with considerable welfare benefits. As far as pensions were concerned, the replacement rate for those who retired with at least 20 years of service was set at 80–100 per cent of their final wage. In the case of health care, it was common practice that at least half of the medical expenses of employees were reimbursed by the employer.[50]

It should be kept in mind that this kind of right to social benefits was not a citizenship-based right that was enjoyed equally by the entire population in these countries.[51] The provision made by workplaces was dependent upon the nature (state-owned versus collective), size (big versus small), and the administrative level (central, provincial or county authorities) of the firms. When each firm had different kinds of benefits, the system of labour collective welfare had only a weak distributive effect.[52] During the transition period both Russia and China had to experience fundamental changes in their welfare systems. It may be too early to draw conclusions on this, and in contemporary studies neither the Russian nor the Chinese welfare system is or can be characterised as a clearly conceptualised type.

From benefits to cash

Let us take one step forward in this comparative conceptualisation of the welfare regime in the case of Russia. When the social system was changing, many of the social structures of the Soviet times began to erode. Enterprises were no longer responsible for social services. The more an enterprise has adopted the market principles, the more the labour collective has disintegrated. The moderate but real standard of living in Soviet society was based, to a large extent, on workplaces and the services that they produced. There was no unemployment, because under the conditions of a planned economy it was profitable to have a large pool of reserve labour within the enterprise. In fact it was not the sales, but production and resources, that were maximised. The more resources that could be lobbied for during the planning, the more successful the Soviet factory director was in his own eyes. Social security was built not only on the workplaces, but also on those free-of-charge services that certain special groups were entitled to.

Both of the social security systems of Soviet life are rapidly disappearing. The creation of a new model of welfare state is one of the big – and thus far unresolved – strategic tasks of Russian society. As Alfio

Cerami puts it, Russia is called to face a double burden of responsibilities: it must ensure protection against old and new social risks for a larger proportion of its citizens than in Western societies while, simultaneously, dealing with the most serious social, political and economic challenges stemming from transition.[53] Linda J. Cook has made a systematic analysis of how the Russian welfare state has developed during the transition, which emphasises the importance of the political factors.[54] Table 3.6 shows the main development stages. The first stage (1991–1993) included rampant and unrestricted liberalisation of the welfare model. There were no political counter-forces. Those with power during this reform period were the key ministries in social policy in the radical (neo-)liberal government. Because the structures of the state machinery had collapsed, the other stake-holders were paralysed and could not decelerate the process to any significant extent. During the second stage (1994–1999), political counter-forces emerged; these were predominantly the communists in the parliament, who could thwart the progress of the liberal reforms. The aim of the communists was to re-strengthen the system of the communist period and, in that manner, secure the position of the old, poor and more state-dependent Russians. Even the *Women's Party* and the *Yabloko* party tried to make reforms more moderate and maintain the structures of the former social

Table 3.6 Three stages of welfare state structuring in the Russian Federation

Stage	Executive	Representation of welfare stake-holders	Policy process	Outcome
1. 1991–1993	**Strong** *liberalising executive*	*No effective representation of statist or societal welfare interests;*	*Non-negotiated liberalisation*	*Unconstrained policy change*
2. 1994–1999	**Moderate** *liberalising executive*	*Representation of statist and societal welfare interests; ministries and legislature play veto role*	*Contested liberalisation*	*Policy deadlock*
3. 2000–2004	**Strong** *liberalising executive*	*Representation of statist elite and bureaucratic interests; bargain for institutional interests*	*Liberalisation negotiated within elite*	*Policy change with elite compensation*

security. Despite all that: "In the same manner as the economy, the welfare state in most respects went through a process of informalisation, spontaneous privatisation and cracking of the control of means of social security and social benefits."[55]

This development was mainly an unintended result of uncontrolled development, not of a systematic reform process. During the first Putin period (which started in 2000), the State Duma executed a significant number of laws which contributed to a welfare state model which was based more on the market than state structures. Pension systems were reformed, the legislation concerning privatisation of housing was strengthened, and a part of the labour market became unregulated. Also, in the essential sectors of health and education, the adoption of market-based routines became more common. According to Cook, the elites within the social sector and other state-based agents participated in the process to a completely different extent than they had done during the first years of the 1990s. It was not so much about creating rules of the game for the welfare state or the role of the state in general, but about how resources within the social sector should be dealt with. This power game between the professions and the elites requires closer analysis.

The welfare strategies and social policy choices are naturally conditioned by available resources. Figure 3.4 shows how the fiscal situation of the Russian state became stronger, especially during Putin's second

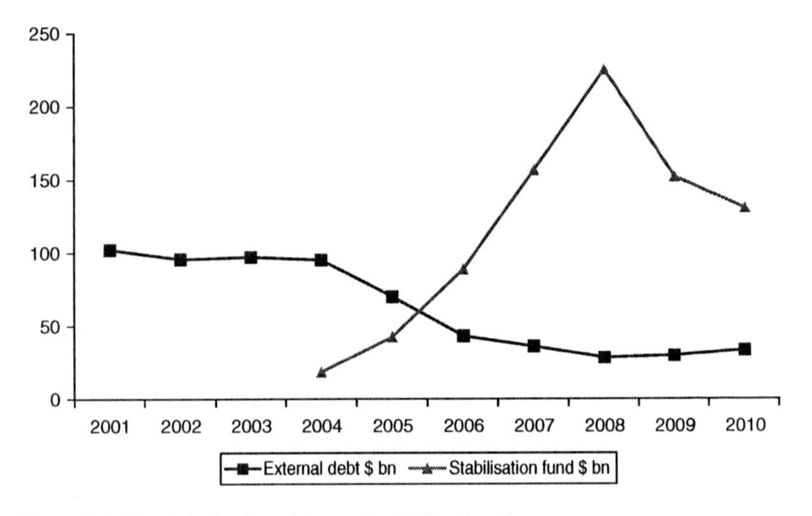

Figure 3.4 Russia's foreign debt and stability fund

Source: Institute for Economies in Transition, Bank of Finland (Bofit).

term from 2004 onwards. The entirety of foreign debt was paid in advance, while stabilisation funds and foreign currency reserves have grown rapidly. As the figure indicates, the crisis in 2008 hit Russia hard, but by the end of 2010 it seemed to be recovering rapidly, and the fiscal situation is still among the best in the world. While the fiscal situation was recovering there were two rather contradictory approaches to social policy. On the one hand, the government reformed and downsized the old social policy in a radical manner. On the other hand, presidential programmes were launched to support education, health, and social services.

From the beginning of Putin's second term it seemed like the old system and structures were being consigned to history. From 1 January 2005 the so-called benefit reform was enforced in Russia, which led to many reforms across the whole social security system. It was a question of a comprehensive package of laws, which was one of the most important decisions made during Putin's presidency at that time. The intention was to replace social benefits – which dated from Soviet times – with a simpler system allowing the possibility of a modern social policy, as recommended by Western experts. The target group was not small; the change directly concerned 34 million beneficiaries and, over a longer perspective, the change to social security would concern the whole population.

Typically for the Russian way of governing, public discussion about the total reform of social security only began after Putin had won the presidential election and *United Russia* had indisputably become the largest party. In parliament, the reform was passed by the *United Russia* party while the entire opposition was against it. The former system dated from the time of the Soviet Union. In addition to pension benefits, the system included 15 benefits, which were mainly different kinds of rights to free services. Some of them were rather insignificant, such as the right to free telephone installation or reduced telephone payments, but some of them were truly important. For example, ten million disabled people had the right to free orthopaedic treatment and free prostheses, which is a significant benefit. Free medicine and care services for the poor and the chronically ill have often been almost the only way to obtain care. The target groups of the old system represented 14 main categories; veterans of war and family members of war invalids, for example, belong in these categories, but also groups which were typical in Soviet times, such as heroes of labour or people who received the highest medals of honour. A number of people in these categories are elderly, such as the war veterans and those who lived in besieged

Leningrad, but these groups also include victims of Chernobyl, and Afghan veterans and those disabled in that war. Some people had a right to all benefits. For example, all veterans of war and heroes of the Soviet Union had comprehensive rights. Some groups, such as teachers who work in the countryside and residents of refugee camps, only had the right to free public transport.

The criticised new system

In order to evaluate the system in the making, we might ask: how well did the old system function? Thanks to the previous system, the grave economic difficulties caused by the transition have without doubt been diminished for some – in part, rather large – groups. On the other hand, in recent years, insufficient resources were budgeted for different kinds of support, and the execution of support was associated with irregularities and a malfunctioning administration. Pharmacies, doctors, and functionaries in the social administration were careless: the service was inefficient or did not exist at all, but benefits were recorded as having been given, and part of the budgeted resources did not end up with eligible beneficiaries. Besides corruption, one of the big problems was, for example, that the old system did not allocate support for those new groups which emerged during the economic crisis, such as the unemployed or the poor. Western experts saw this particular fact alone as being the biggest impediment in the old system. Nobody, however, had a clear picture of what sort of a role the system played, since there were no reliable registers of the people who used these services. That means that there was no way of knowing what kinds of risks were involved in the reform.[56]

The basic idea of the new social legislation was to pay benefits in cash. In the reform, all benefits that all target groups were entitled to were given a monetary value. The idea was that the social office *sobez* would pay the benefit directly into the beneficiary's bank account, and the beneficiary would then obtain the necessary services. In total, 11 benefits were abolished completely and, for example, war invalids who had received these benefits got 2000 roubles as compensation. The victims of Chernobyl, who had received eight benefits, got 1700 roubles; the family members of deceased invalids of war got 600 roubles; people with a significant record of blood donations got 500 roubles, and so on. The monetary amount was not fixed for all groups by the federation, but the support – for example, to victims of political oppression – was defined by the regions that were obliged to pay the support. Taking into account the low level monetary compensation, it is easy to understand the rebellious mood of the population.[57] The change was cushioned with a social package that included the three most frequently used services from the old system: free prescriptions, the right to the free use of local transport, and the right to a free annual visit to a spa. In 2005 the social package applied to everybody, but after that it was possible to exchange it for cash, namely 450 roubles.

Were the changes really about reform, or about cutting social security? Most likely, it was a bit of both. If a person loses the right to free health care, it is certainly a critical loss which cannot be compensated for with a small amount of cash. Many people were therefore understandably anxious. In the state budget, social expenditures were rising and, together with the reforms, the irregularities and corruption began to diminish. This is what people hoped for. The reform of social security was where Russian politics was clearly divided in two. All opposition parties were formed of Western-style liberals until the communists resisted the reform. Right-wing forces did not oppose the system of monetary benefits, but rather the way in which the reform was realised. The darkest predictions saw the reform as a decisive step towards Russia falling back into the category of a developing country. In the most shocking predictions, rural areas would be depopulated, the chronically ill would die prematurely, and AIDS and new forms of tuberculosis would spread more easily. The criticism expressed over the welfare reforms was part of wider discontent over living conditions. It is strongly symbolic when the fatherland seems to offer war veterans and others, its most loyal defenders, less.

Putin's inner circle was affronted by foreign critics who accused the government of forgetting the poor. In some cases these were the same Western experts who had proposed such a reform in the first place. The policy choices made in this respect were, like fiscal conservatism in economic policy, not specifically Russian, but the question is: are the monetary benefits making the system better? In Russia, even good ideas are not always implemented in the way that was expected. Can the Ministry of Social Development and the Ministry of Health carry the reform through in a consistent and productive manner? The reform is only one step; as we can see from Figure 3.5, where social security is concerned, pensioners have coped better than the unemployed or families with children. All this suggests that the welfare state model that has been created for the conditions of a market economy does not yet exist in Russia.[58]

Some scholars have spoken about a so-called Moscow consensus, which should include an overturn of the economic policy instituted

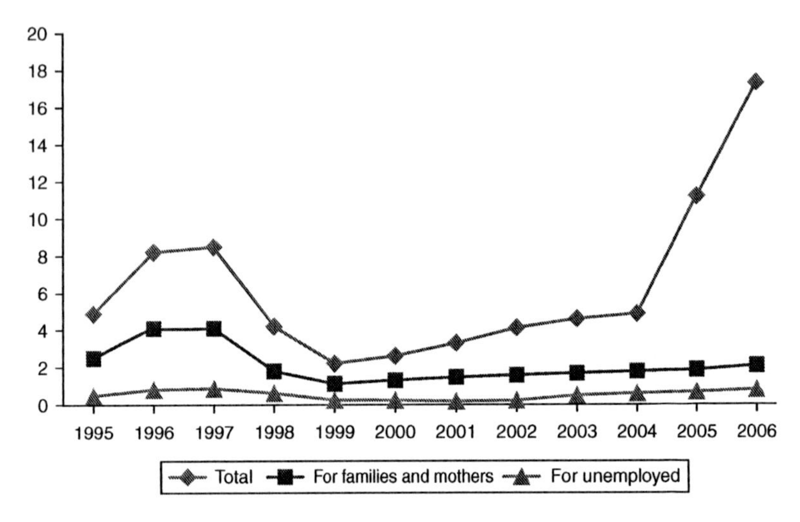

Figure 3.5 Government expenditure on social care, 1995–2006 (billion USD)

during the Putin period. According to Richard Sakwa, the starting points are, to a large extent, reminiscent of the original goals of the IMF, which are based on instructions from John Maynard Keynes, namely that the promotion and maintenance of high employment levels and the development of all productive resources of the members of society should be seen as the priority goal of the economic policy. If this is correct we may question to what extent this reliance on Keynes even suggested the strengthening of the universal welfare state in relation to the liberal model.

Our analysis of Russian class structure and the character of the political system as a mass democracy leads to a hypothesis that if no drastic reorientation takes place, eventually the outcome will be a liberal model of welfare state. Not even the strengthening of the middle class will present any counter-force to this model, because under current conditions Russia seems to try to secure its own interests by leaning on private services. In the West it has often been presumed that a stronger middle class would create the preconditions for a more democratic political alternative in Russia. However, empirical data suggests that it is much more likely that the middle class will organise itself into the party of power, *United Russia*. Studies at the local level, for example Meri Kulmala's studies on Karelia,[59] fortify this image of *United Russia* as a functionary party which serves the state, more than a forum for citizen activity.

What are the 'national programmes' brought in during the Putin presidency (2000–2008) which have important social and political dimensions?[60] Are they creating the preconditions for the re-establishment of universal social rights in Russia? Can these programmes be described as a return of some kind of authoritarian paternalistic model? Maybe it is too early to answer these questions. However, studies show that on a local level people know the contents of national programmes very well. At least on a local level it seems that some elements of a universal welfare state are being created. This is based particularly on women's civic activity, which partly seems to stem from social and political issues. Kulmala describes this in terms of a concept that Boltanski and Thévenot utilised in their 2006 study *On Justification: Economies of Worth*.[61] According to this study, regimes of action can be built on many kinds of rankings: creativity, respect/reputation, collective interest, price, and productivity/effectiveness. Russian activism at a local level seems to unite creativity, collective interests and respect/reputation. Women's networks unite enthusiasm, emotional commitment and emotional anchoring on a local level, especially through personal networks. In this manner, aspiration towards collective well-being is also created, partly built upon the networks of the Soviet era.[62] This situation is complicated by the fact that the state provides municipalities with additional responsibilities within the welfare policy, but they cannot manage them because well as there is no increase in tax revenue. This maintains continuity in the paternalistic forms of welfare services. This is particularly the case in numerous one-factory cities and villages.[63]

A poor man's version of the US model?

It is possible to identify many historically real power relations of classes. A social class may be regarded as strong when three conditions are fulfilled: the relations of ownership or power resources that lie at the heart of its position are firmly established, the basic dimensions of its class situation are well-established, and when it has strong organisations to fall back on. This, of course, is a simplification inasmuch as all these conditions do not necessarily apply at one and the same time. However, from this vantage-point we can compare Russia with other types of class relations and sketch possible courses of future development. Table 3.7 illustrates the different types of class relations on the basis of the strength or weakness of social classes. The classes included in this analysis are the bourgeoisie, the working class, and the new middle class. This, again, is something of a simplification in that

Table 3.7 Alternative models of class relations

Bourgeoisie	strong	strong	weak	weak
Middle Class	strong	weak	strong	weak
Strong	1	2	3	4
Working class				
Weak	5	6	7	8

Source: Markku Kivinen, *Progress and chaos: Russia as a Challenge for Sociological Imagination*, Helsinki: Kikimora Publications 2002.

peasants have played a crucial role in the class relations of many societies, and of course the urban petty bourgeoisie also has a relevance of its own.

In this analysis Western European countries (and Nordic countries in particular) are slotted into cell 1. In these countries relations of ownership are well-established and the core of the new middle classes, both managers and professionals, has certain undisputed privileges compared to the working class. On the other hand, the working class also has its own strong organisations, trade unions and parties through which it exercises an influence as part of civil society. Only a small portion of the societal residue goes directly into private consumption by the propertied class. That is why these societies cannot be regarded as exploitative societies proper.

Russia, then, seems to fall into cell number 8. Relations of ownership in Russia are still in the process of formation, and the middle-class power resources remain weak. Working class organisations are weak, and at the company level the power resources of workers are controlled by managers. No doubt the positions of the new bourgeoisie are already taking shape as the process of privatisation moves into its final stages. But, for the time being, the process of structural change in the economy is very much ongoing; it is still far too early to talk about profitable industries or about certain prospects. The organisations and interests of the middle class are beginning to take shape, although in many contradictory ways and under difficult circumstances. Indeed, the success of each class will largely depend on more general hegemonic projects in society and on their own successes, failures and struggles in formulating strategies.

It is unlikely that we will see Russia move straight from cell 8 into cell 1. But what other options are there? In this analysis the class structure of the Soviet Union immediately after the Civil War would come under cell 4, where both the bourgeoisie and the middle class are weak and the working class is strong. However, the organisations of independent working class power were overthrown during Lenin's rule, and destroyed forever under Stalin. The longer Stalin was in power, the weaker the working class independent organisations became, and the stronger the middle class grew – quite in contrast to the initial intentions of the Bolshevik project. In a sense, this brings us close to option 7, as is assumed in theories of a new dominant class. However, the force that really gains in strength is the nomenklatura; that is, not so much the middle class, but a new kind of ruling class.

In the privatisation process the nomenklatura has developed into a new bourgeoisie, but there are still various different ways in which the classes' power relations might take shape. Alternative 2 would resemble the situation in Germany during the Weimar Republic, where the middle classes were being crushed between a strong bourgeoisie and the working class.[64] In the 1990s there were some such elements to be detected in the position of the professional middle class in Russia.[65] However, our results for the era of the Putin regime do not support this kind of prospective development. Rather, the middle class situation has considerably improved and the potential middle class has become more a real one. At the same time the bourgeoisie has been growing stronger, whereas the previously numerically strong industrial working class has been inactive and marginalised because of a lack of independence of the trade unions.[66] It is not easy to classify the class basis for political forces that are at work in the Russian working class as either left-wing or right-wing;[67] even the Communist Party is now saying that an important task is to develop Russia's major power role on a national basis. In this sense, the model of authoritarian movements is not too remote a possibility. National self-assertion and a weak working class is historically a rather worrying combination.

The worst-case scenario for Russia today is the prospect of regression into being a developing country. If this were to happen, the class structure in Russia would begin to resemble the situation in countries where the bourgeoisie is so strong that most of the surplus production in society goes to the private consumption of the ruling class. There are plenty of examples of this in Latin America, Asia and Africa. These, quite literally, are societies of exploitation. The factor that is pushing things in this direction in Russia is the absence of the rationality of capitalism from a social equality point of view and strong dependency on the energy sector as a key to globalisation. But, after more than 12 years of economic growth, this does not seem to be a dominant trend in contemporary Russia.

Alternative 5 resembles the situation in the United States, where the middle class is so strong that even the working class has largely adopted middle class ways of thinking.[68] The working class is quite weak in terms of its organisation and there are no real left-wing projects. This is not any more an unlikely scenario in Russia, given the stronger and more stable position of the middle classes. In the United States this situation has been based on the country occupying a very special status at the hub of the world order and an exceptionally high level of affluence. Such middle class projects, which heavily stress the difference between performance and planning at the level of the labour process and that aim to create highly differentiated educational structures, are certainly not unknown in Russia. The more the market resources are decisive for access to education and health care, the further this kind of development is promoted. In this alternative the interests of the middle class and the working class seem to be rather antagonistic because the middle class has market capacities for welfare services, and the working class simply does not.

All in all, the fiscal conservatism of Russian economic policy,[69] a lack of strong political or trade union organisation amongst the working class, and the symbolic reference to middle class interests seem to be the characteristic features of the contemporary hegemonic project in Russia. On the other hand, raising living standards and creating order out of the chaos of the 1990s has helped to legitimise the contemporary political elites in Russia in the eyes of the ordinary working class. However, this American model will remain a poor man's version if the Russian economy fails to diversify and modernise its basic structures.

China

Since the beginning of the reforms and the opening-up in 1978, China's society, and its social structure in particular, has experienced dramatic changes. Rapid economic growth, speedy industrialisation, fast urbanisation, and successive marketisations have combined to bring about a series of changes in the composition, situation, organisation and interaction of the social classes. That accordingly impacts on the redistribution of resources, the re-establishment of a welfare system, the evolution of political institution, and the strategy of hegemonic projects. Although China has experienced the economic transition from planned economy to market economy, as Russia has, different choices of transition path and different historical experiences have created disparities in the changes in social structure between the two countries. One might, however, conclude that China's choices in this field were made more consciously than those of Russia.

From class struggle to economic development

In the winter of 1978, 18 peasants in a small village in Anhui province signed a land contract by fingerprint and embarked upon family-run agriculture. This event became symbolic of the beginning of China's rural economic reform. In the 1980s the reform extended to urban areas, and extensive privatisation and marketisation were carried out in the 1990s. Although the first actions of the economic reform were pushed from a grass roots level, the overall reform has been absolutely dominated by the government. An important change in the ideology of the state during the late 1970s and early 1980s became the juncture that led to later reform policies. The Communist Party stated it was transferring its priority from class struggle to economic development. In order to promote economic development, the Communist Party as government gradually tolerated the existence and development of a private economy, capitalist class and petty bourgeoisie, income gap, and class differentiation. These were considered as features of capitalism societies that were meant to be eliminated in socialist societies according to pre-1978 thinking. The change of communist ideology in China has been step by step, with intense debates making it very different from the dramatic, almost overnight, change in Russia. Even today, traditional communist ideology, with a stress upon egalitarianism, has a strong influence over the public, especially the working class and lower classes. This has long been a pressure on the policies of the government concerning welfare distribution and class interaction, and is one of the factors impacting upon the adjustment of class interests and the change of class structure. That is probably why dramatic institutional transition did *not* create a new poverty class and a group of economic oligarchies did not appear in China during the broad-scale privatisation.

Stable and fast economic growth and gradual institutional transition in recent decades has provided a basic background for the change in social structure. The annual growth of GDP in China was close to 10 per cent during the 1978–2009 period, as shown in Figure 3.6. Even with the worldwide economic recession in 2009, China still managed GDP growth of 8.7 per cent. The economic growth and incremental reform model has guaranteed a stable transition and avoided turbulence in reconstructing the class structure. A new ideology which focuses on economic growth has been widely accepted by the public and became a powerful means to strengthen social integration and ease interest conflict between classes.

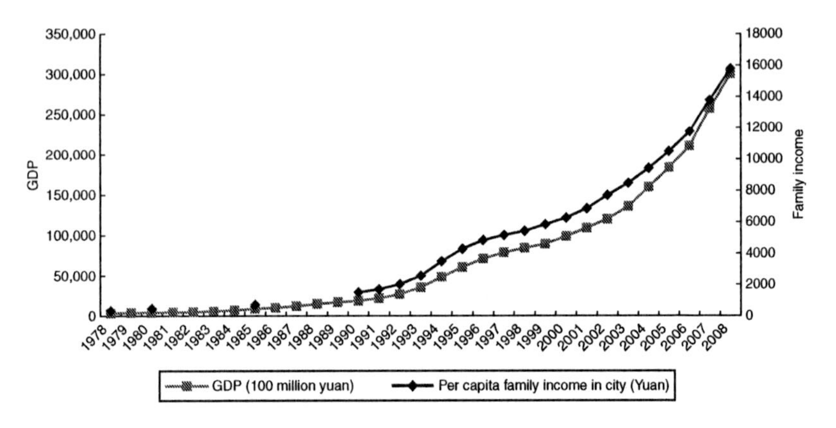

Figure 3.6 Growth of GDP and income, 1978–2006

Source: Statistics Bureau of China, *Zhongguo Tongji Nianjian* [China Statistical Yearbook], Beijing: China Statistics Press 2009, p. 53.

Most members of various classes display basic support for the reform policies of the central government, although some of them complain about certain behaviours of local governments.

Improvements with disparities

At the same time, marketisation, industrialisation and urbanisation have caused huge changes in the composition of the social classes. In 1978 almost 100 per cent of the labour force worked in the public sector and collective economy, which was strictly controlled by the government, but this was down to less than 25 per cent by 2005. Marketisation meant large numbers of people moving from the public sector to the private sector and new classes emerging in a domain which was out of the government's control. The proportion of the contribution of primary industry, secondary industry and tertiary industry to GDP were 31 per cent, 45 per cent and 24 per cent respectively in 1978, but this had changed to 11 per cent, 49 per cent and 40 per cent by 2008. Urban-dwelling Chinese made up just 20 per cent of the population in 1978, but this had risen to 46 per cent by 2009 (Figure 3.7). Industrialisation and urbanisation have resulted in a significant reduction of the peasant class, an increase in the working class in the 1990s, and the expansion of the middle class during this century. Opportunities for upward mobility in occupational and class positions have significantly increased during these processes. Most people have improved their socioeconomic condition even though disparities grew between classes.

Figure 3.7 The growth of the urban population

Source: Bureau of China, *Zhongguo Tongji Nianjian* [China Statistical Yearbook], Beijing. China Statistics Press 2009, p. 95.

China's education system has expanded rapidly since the 1990s. Educational opportunities have increased accordingly, and the average years of schooling for the population over the age of 15 grew from 4.3 years in 1982 to 8.4 years in 2007. Primary education was almost universal by the late 1980s and junior secondary education was universal by 2003. The enrolment rate for senior secondary education among graduates of junior secondary education was 79.3 per cent in 2007. China's government brought in a policy to increase the enrolment numbers in higher education during 1999–2003.[70] That resulted in a five-fold increase in the number of college students, and the opportunities for higher education doubled in these five years (Figure 3.8). In 2008, about 23 per cent of the college-age population received a college education. In turn, the expansion of higher education enrolment increased the proportion of the labour force with a higher education. At the same time, industrialisation has created ever more white-collared occupations. Consequently, the number of white-collared workers with a higher education has increased steadily (Figure 3.9). Consequently this has provided a basis for the emergence of a Chinese middle class.

Thus, education has played an increasing role in social stratification since the beginning of the economic reforms, and it has become a critical determinant of a person's socioeconomic status. The economic returns to education have increased very quickly. The rates of educational return in urban China are, respectively, 2.5 per cent in 1981, 2.7 per cent in 1987, 3.8 per cent in 1988, 5.9 per cent in 1995, 8.5 per cent in 2000, 10 per cent in 2002 and 11 per cent in 2006. The effect of education on occupational attainment has also strengthened.

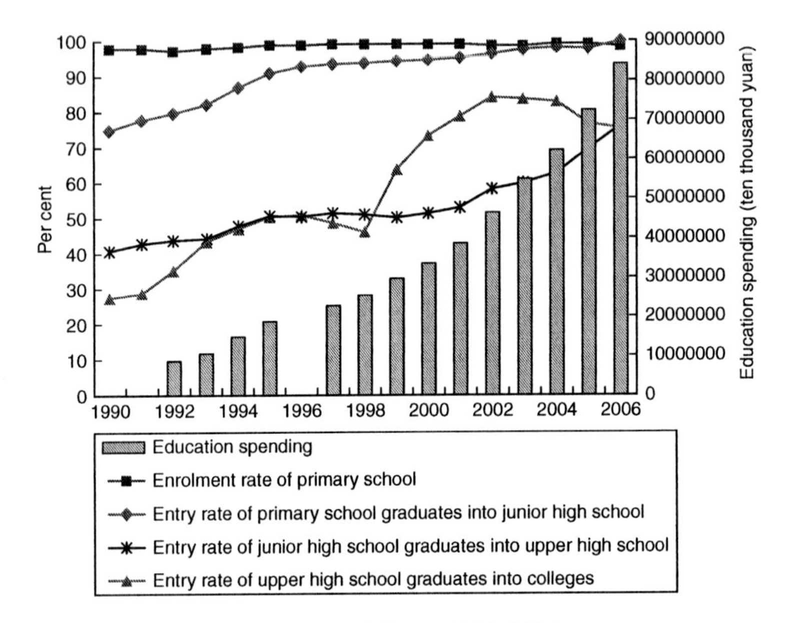

Figure 3.8 Educational expansion of China, 1990–2006

Source: National Bureau of Statistics of China, *Zhongguo Tongji Nianjian* [China Statistical Yearbook], Beijing: China Statistics Press 2009, p. 651.

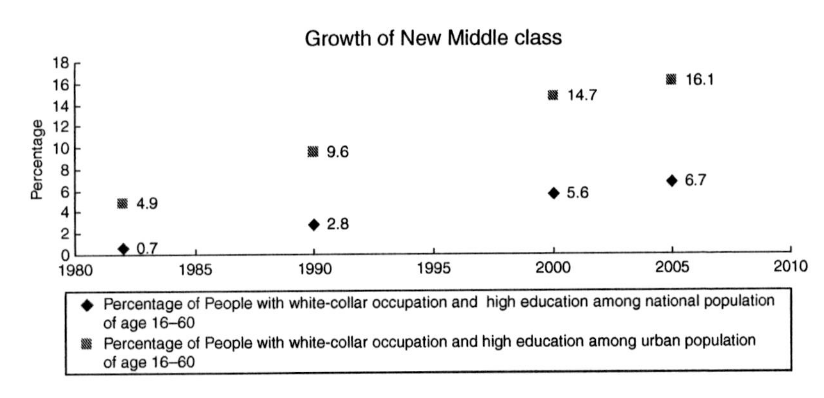

Figure 3.9 Growth in number of persons with white-collar occupation and higher education

Source: Calculation from Census Data of 1982, 1990, 2000 and 1% sample survey of national population of 2005.

Credentialism is the main mechanism of social stratification in China today. This has brought about fierce competition for access to higher education. The main directions of educational reform have been marketisation and elite selection, so that education costs are soaring and entrance examinations for all levels of education are increasingly strict. Children from the upper classes and privileged groups are the winners in this competition, while children from the lower class and rural areas lose out. The impact of family background on educational attainment, especially attainment in higher education, has increased significantly.[71] Inequalities in educational opportunity among classes and between urban and rural areas have been increasing in recent decades, even though educational expansion has provided more opportunities for education generally. In addition, the sharp expansion of higher education has brought about increasing unemployment amongst college graduates. Some parents from the peasantry and working class do not like to invest in their children's higher education because graduates from these families face serious difficulties in finding work. This enhances the intergenerational transmission of class inequality.

One of the salient consequences of the economic reforms is the rising income gap; this has been an issue which has perplexed the policy-makers in central government for a long time. The Gini coefficient, a major measurement of income inequality, was 0.27 during the early 1980s but it increased to 0.47 in 2009. This means Chinese society has changed from a society with low income inequality into a society with much higher income inequality during the past 30 years. Indeed, if China was one of the counties with the lowest income inequality in the world in the 1970s, it has now become one of the countries with the highest income inequality. Income inequality is especially reflected in regional differences, the urban-rural disparity, and in the gap between the rich and poor.[72] In 2009, the average income of urban residents was 3.4 times of the average income of rural residents; employees in Shanghai have 2.7 times the average income of employees in Jiangxi. To give some illustrative figures of households incomes in urban areas in 2007, the highest 10 per cent had an average per capita income 8.7 times greater than the lowest 10 per cent. In rural households, the highest 20 per cent had 7.3 times greater average per capita incomes than the lowest 20 per cent (see Figure 3.10).

Income inequality has become a main source of social discontent and public criticism against the government. In recent decades, widespread grievances against the rich and government officials have developed

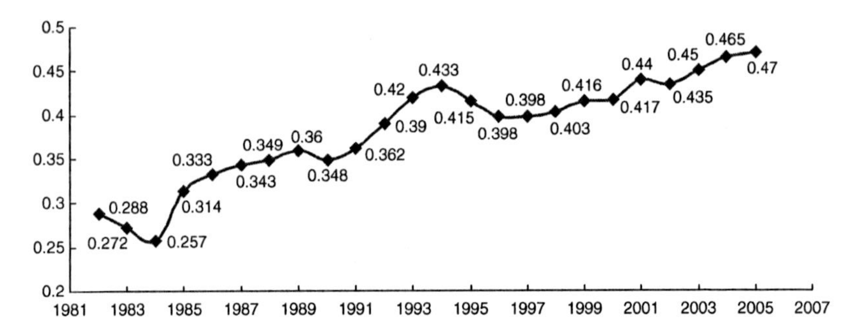

Figure 3.10 Gini coefficients of China, 1982–2006

Source: Figures of 1982–1999 are from Bi Xianping and Jian Xinhua, 'Relationship between change of economic structure and income gap,' *Review of Economics*, Number 8, 2002. Figures of 2000–2005 are from the publication of the National Bureau of Statistics of China. Figure of 2006 is from national survey data of CGSS.

among the citizens, facilitated by the internet. Many cases of large-scale protest and disturbances ignited by specific events in small cities or towns can be attributed to this feeling of dissatisfaction. Senior leaders in central government consider the rising income disparity to be a major threat to socio-political stability and have tried to control the income gap by such means as providing more economic assistance and social security to poor and vulnerable groups, as well as increasing taxation on higher income groups and disciplining corrupt officials. However, these measures have not restrained the continuous widening of the income gap.

From rural to urban areas, from the public to private sector

Before the economic reforms, the official definition was that in China there was 'a social structure of two-class and one-group'. While the workers and peasants were the two classes, the 'one-group' consisted actually of two groups, the cadres and the intellectuals. There was a pyramid-shaped structure to the population, stratified by the socioeconomic conditions of the different groups. Peasants made up the bottom 75 per cent, workers the middle 20 per cent, and about 5 per cent were the cadres and intellectuals situated at the top. Peasants suffered from lower incomes and less welfare than other classes and groups. The cadres, intellectuals and workers enjoyed similar income levels but they differed in terms of social welfare. However, there was a different stratification based on political criterion in which the cadres and the workers were at the top, peasants were in the middle, intellectuals were in the lower-middle and the approximately 1 per cent of the population who were political dissidents were at the very bottom.[73]

This original class structure has experienced differentiation since the beginning of the reforms. Almost half of peasants and their children moved from being in the peasant class to other classes. About 300 million peasants and their children have left agriculture and entered the manufacturing and service industries during the past 30 years. Most of them, named as 'peasant workers', joined the working class and have become its major constituent part; the traditional working class of employees in state-owned enterprises and collective enterprises has almost disappeared due to the privatisation of these enterprises. Consequently more than 60 per cent of members of the working class are currently peasant workers. The cadre group was separated into two major parts: party-government officials and managers of state-owned enterprises. In the process of differentiation, the socioeconomic status of the working class obviously declined and disparities between blue-collar and white-collar workers grew significantly. Among the white-collar workers, the socioeconomic status of party-government officials and managers of state-owned enterprises has improved continuously, increasing their distance from the socioeconomic positions of other regular white-collar workers.

The economic reforms have created a persistently expanding economic domain of private economy. In this new domain, new classes and groups have appeared and the numbers of these new classes and groups has increased in line with the development of the private economic sector. The most influential new class is the capitalist class or private entrepreneur class. The capitalist class had disappeared in the 1950s because of the elimination of the private economy. In the early 1980s, the government allowed a small number of people to engage in small business (the individual economy) but forbade the hiring of employees by business owners (the private economy). In 1987 the legitimacy of the private economy and private entrepreneurs was finally acknowledged by the government. Since then, the number of private entrepreneurs has increased steadily: in 2008, the number was 150.74 million. Another important new class is the petty bourgeoisie, that is, small business owners and self-employed people. These two new classes became the main part of the high income group.

At the same time, a new group of managers and professionals in multinational corporations and joint ventures has expanded quickly. This has resulted in a significant change in the composition of the professional class. Most members of the professional class formerly worked for party-government organisations and state-owned enterprises, but currently more and more are moving from the public sector to the private sector. These people have also become a part of the high income group, and their incomes are higher than those of their counterparts in the public sector. On the other hand, a lower-income group appeared in the private economy: the employees within the private economy. Some of them were laid-off workers from bankrupt state-owned enterprises, but most of them were peasant workers who migrated from rural areas into the cities. Their incomes are lower than the incomes of their counterparts in the public sector, they lack welfare services and security, and can suffer terrible working conditions.

A pyramid society or an olive society?

Thus a new class structure was formed in the late 1990s the following decade. There are different classifications for this new class structure, but none is operationalised identically with the one put forward in the Russian case and therefore they are not completely comparable. One of the most influential class categorisations has been proposed by a research team at the Chinese Academy of Social Sciences.[74] It differentiates between ten classes and ranks their hierarchical position in the class structure according their socioeconomic status. Put into the context of the social stratification of the adult population during the period of 1978–2006, Table 3.8 testifies to the tremendous changes that have taken place. Two new classes have emerged, namely the capitalist class and the petty bourgeoisie (small business owners and self-employed). White-collar classes, cadres, managers, professionals and clerks have all expanded. The peasant class shrank and the working class has kept its size but workers in manufacturing industries have decreased.

Recent survey data from 2008 shows the basic shape of China's social stratification as 22.5 per cent white-collar workers, 34.7 per cent blue-collar workers and 42.8 per cent peasants. When compared with Russia, China has much lower proportions of managerial and professional workers and the working class, but a much higher proportion of peasants in its class structure. Differences in the level of industrialisation results in the distinctive class structures of the two countries. Russia displays the typical class structure *of* an industrialised society, but China shows a dramatically changing class structure moving *towards* an industrialised society.

Currently a rather China-specific class structure element is the cadre, which refers to party and government officials, high-level managers of larger state-owned enterprises and the presidents or directors of institutions funded by the government (such as universities, schools, hospitals, industry or professional associations). Although this class is very small in number, it plays a decisive role in society. Some analysts consider it to be similar to what Milovan Djilas once labelled as the 'new class'

Table 3.8 The class structure of China

	Class structure of China				
10 social classes	**1978**	**1988**	**1999**	**2001**	**2006**
1. Cadres	0.98	1.70	2.1	2.1	2.3
2. Capitalists	0.00	0.02	0.6	1.0	1.3
3. Managers	0.23	0.54	1.5	1.6	2.6
4. Professionals	3.48	4.76	5.1	4.6	6.3
5. Clerks	1.29	1.65	4.8	7.2	7.0
6. Small business owners and self-employed	0.03	3.12	4.2	7.1	9.5
7. Workers in service industry	2.15	6.35	12.0	11.2	10.1
8. Workers in manufacturing industry	19.83	22.43	22.6	17.5	14.7
9. Peasants	67.41	55.84	44.0	42.9	40.4
10. Unemployed	4.60	3.60	3.1	4.8	5.9

Source: Figures for 1978, 1988 and 1999 for China are from Lu Xueyi (ed.), *A Research Report on Social Classes of the Contemporary China*, Beijing: Social Sciences Academic Press 2002. Figures for 2001 for China are from Li Chunling, *Cleavage or Fragment: An Empirical Analysis on the Social Stratification of the Contemporary China*, Beijing: Social Science Academic Press 2005. Figures for 2006 for China are from Lu Xueyi (ed.), *Social Structure of Contemporary China*, Beijing: Social Sciences Academic Press 2010.

in the Soviet Union. Since the state has maintained strict control over politics, society and the economy, the cadres, as operators of the state apparatus, have become the absolutely dominant class as it determines the distribution of resources. From a class stratification analysis point of view, this is indeed a distinctive feature of contemporary China's class structure which is different from today's Russia (at least, if the Russian state bureaucracy is not considered tantamount to the Chinese cadre) as well as most other contemporary societies.[75]

Because of the huge rural population in China, the peasant class is still the largest class in China even though it is rapidly shrinking. The working class has been growing since the manufacturing industry expanded and the service industry developed in the recent decades. Professional classes, including capitalists, the cadres, the managers and professionals, remain small in proportion, although members of these classes have increased. These conditions determine the pyramid-shaped structure of China's social stratification. Very few people (about 4 per cent: the cadres and capitalists) are members of the upper class, located at the top of this pyramid-shaped hierarchy. A few people (about 9 per cent: managers and professionals) are in the upper-middle whilst about 18 per cent of the population (the clerks, small business owners, and self-employed) are in the lower-middle of the hierarchy. However, most members of society (nearly 70 per cent: the working class, peasants and unemployed) remain at the bottom of the hierarchy. Such a structure leads large numbers of people in poverty and results in a serious income gap.

The middle class remains comparatively small in China, keeping the pyramid shape to the class structure. However, the rapid rise of the middle class in Chinese cities is a very obvious fact of recent decades. It means that the class structure in Chinese cities has been changing from the pyramid-shaped structure to an olive-shaped structure due to the growth of the middle class and the reduction of the lower class. The proportions of the classes in Table 3.9 illustrate the process of this transformation,

Table 3.9 Class structure and the middle class in urban areas, 1982–2006

Year	Capitalist Class	New Middle Class	Old Middle Class	Marginal Middle Class	Working Class
1982	0.0	13.9	0.1	19.7	66.3
1988	0.1	17.2	3.2	23.8	55.7
1990	0.5	19.6	2.2	19.9	57.8
1995	0.6	22.1	5.5	26.6	45.2
2001	1.5	16.6	10.3	33.2	38.4
2002	1.1	23.6	11.1	29.1	35.1
2005	1.6	21.0	9.7	31.4	36.3
2006	0.6	18.8	19.6	25.4	35.7

Source: Percentages for five classes for 1982, 1990, 2000 and 2005 are calculated from census data and 1% population surveys. Percentages for 1988, 1995 and 2002 are derived from household income surveys for Chinese cities. Percentages for 2001 and 2006 are from national surveys of social structure change and CGSS. 2001 and 2006 data includes cities and towns (with lower percentage for new middle class and higher percentage for old middle class), others are data for cities. Figures in Table 3.9 show that about 63% of the urban adult population are members of the middle class, which includes capitalist class, new middle class, old middle class and marginal middle class. Excluding about 3% of elite class from it, the percentage for middle class is about 60% in urban society. However, a lot of members of old middle class and marginal middle fail to reach socioeconomic conditions consistent with the status of the middle class. If we use the more strict definition of middle class with multi-dimensions of occupation, income and education, the percentages of middle class among the adult population are approximately 23% in cities and 12% in the whole country. Comparing this with the size of the middle class in Russia, China's middle class is very small. According to statistics from the Institute of Sociology of the Russian Academy, the proportion of middle class in the Russian adult population (20–60 years old) was 34% in 2008 and 36% in 2009.

listing percentages of working class (classes 7 and 8 in Table 3.8), capitalist class (classes 2 in Table 3.8), the so-called new middle class (classes 1, 3 and 4 in Table 3.8), the so-called old middle class (class 6 in Table 3.8), and the so-called marginal middle class (class 5 in Table 3.8) in urban populations aged 16–60 during the years 1982–2006. Even though different classifying variables in the various data sets cannot reach completely identical estimates,[76] the growth trend for the middle class is clearly reflected in this data. From 1982 to 2006, the new middle class increased by about 10 percentage points. The old middle class was almost non-existent in the early 1980s, while now it makes up more than 10 per cent.

Indeed, fast growth and a high percentage of the old middle class is a significant characteristic of the development of the Chinese middle class. In most Western countries, the expansion of the new middle class is usually followed by a diminution of the old middle class. However, in China, the old and new middle classes have expanded simultaneously. In fact, the size of the old middle class in many middle-sized and small-sized cities, and especially in towns, is larger than that of the new middle class. The marginal middle class had also developed quickly. The capitalist class has obviously also emerged, but its size is small compared to other classes. This emergence of the middle class has resulted in a significant decline of the working class.

The figures in Table 3.9 show that about 63 per cent of the urban adult population are members of the middle class, which includes capitalist class, new middle class, old middle class and marginal middle class. Excluding about 3 per cent of the elite class from it, the percentage of the middle class is about 60 per cent in urban society. However, many members of the old middle class and marginal middle fail to reach socioeconomic conditions consistent with the status of the middle class. If we use the more strict definition of middle class, with multi-dimension of occupation, income and education, the percentages of middle class among the adult population are approximately 23 per cent in cities and 12 per cent across the whole country. Compared with the size of the middle class in Russia, China's middle class is very small. According to statistics from the Institute of Sociology of the Russian Academy, the proportion of middle class in the Russian adult population (20–60 years old) was 34 per cent in 2008 and 36 per cent in 2009 (Polina Kozyreva 2010).

There is much controversy in China about the socio-political consequences of the emergence of the middle class. Is the middle class a stable force or an unstable force for the existing authority? Will the middle class promote a democratic transition or will it preserve the existing political order? Among Chinese analysts, one can easily find opposing answers. Some argue that the middle class is a social force which promotes a democratic transition, which will inevitably lead it to become a destabilising factor for the current government. Consequently, in order to preserve stability, the government should take measures to control this group. But others consider the middle class to be a social force which supports the existing political and social order. They say that the middle class functions as a socio-political stabiliser and is therefore a stabilising force for the authorities. They advise the government to follow a policy of enlarging the middle class. The most influential Chinese sociologists, who hold the latter view, think that the Chinese middle class is a socio-political stabiliser, because by definition it defends political conservatism.[77] Firstly, the Chinese middle class is the group which has benefited the most during the economic reforms and rapid economic growth. Secondly, the Chinese middle class is strongly dependent upon the state and has a propensity for state authoritarianism. Thirdly, the Chinese middle class, at least at present, is rather apolitical in attitude, preferring materialism.

The most prominent feature of the social stratification of contemporary China is a segregated structure between the urban and rural society; Chinese researchers refer to this as the 'dual social structure', and it results in the most serious inequality in China, namely the difference between urban and rural residents. Chinese society has long been segregated by institutional arrangement (the *Hukou* system) into two social systems. The *Hukou* system is a kind of household registration. Everybody in China has a *Hukou* status. People with different *Hukou* statuses hold different positions in the distribution of resources controlled by the government. Before 1978, urban residents with urban *Hukou* enjoyed a series of social welfare and security benefits provided by the state. These included employment security, stable income, free health care, almost free housing, and food allocation. Rural residents with rural *Hukou* were totally excluded from this welfare system. Since the beginning of the economic reforms, the government has invested a huge amount of funds in the cities to promote urbanisation, which has resulted in further enlargement of the gap between urban and rural areas in terms of welfare, income, education, health services and job opportunities. Figure 3.11 illustrates the increase in the income disparities between urban and rural households.

Large urban-rural disparities have led to a serious poverty problem in rural areas. According to the Chinese government, there were 15 million poor people in 2009, based upon the Chinese definition of poverty (namely, income per day of less than 0.31 US dollars).

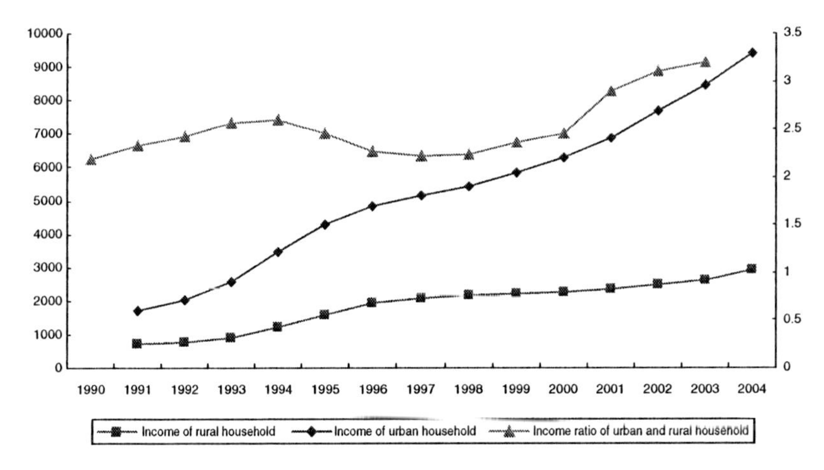

Figure 3.11 Income level and ratio of urban and rural households, 1990–2004
Source: National Bureau of Statistics of China, *Survey of Household Income and Consumption*.

However, if we adopt the poverty standard of the World Bank (income of less than 1.25 US dollars per day), there are 254 million people living in poverty. More than 90 per cent of these people live in rural areas. In order to escape poverty, a large number of rural workers migrate to the cities for employment or to seek new opportunities. However, because of their rural *Hukou* status, they continue to be labelled as peasant workers and suffer serious discrimination in the cities. In 2009, the total number of peasant workers was 149 million (Figure 3.12). Peasant workers constitute a lower-income group in cities and have become an essential part of urban class structure as an underclass.

Trading power for money

The powerful state is undoubtedly the most prominent feature of contemporary China. The Chinese state has a much bigger capacity to effectively control politics, economy and society than the state in most other countries. Through a system of bureaucratic organisations, the state plays a critical role in the distribution of resources among social classes. The closer to the core of the state organisation a class or group is, the more resources it will gain. Various classes and groups are trying to seek a favourable position in order to gain more resources from the state by influencing policy-making. On the other hand, there is one domain – the market – which is not entirely controlled by the state. Some people or groups may strive for a favourable position in

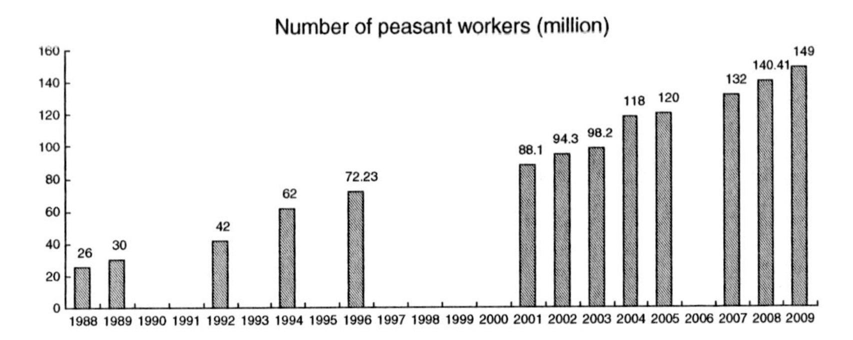

Figure 3.12 Number of peasant workers in cities, 1988–2009

Source: Figures of 1988-2007 are from Cui, Chanyi, 'Adaptation of peasant workers and adjustment of urban-rural relationship,' in Li Peilin ed. *Peasant Worker: Socioeconomic analysis on migration migrant labor in urban China*, Beijing: Social Sciences Academic Press 2003. Figures of 2008 and 2009 are from *Annual Report* of the National Bureau of Statistics of China.

resource distribution by the market, due to their market capabilities, such as human capital. However, the state has an important impact on the market, too, because the state is the regulator and supervisor of the market. The biggest players in the market, such as big private enterprises, are willing to share their profits with the state and seek a position in the state organisation. Individuals or groups are easily able to profit from the market if they hold an advantageous position within a state organisation.

As well as the state and the market, there is a third domain – the society – represented by NGOs or other similar grass roots organisations. This sector is underdeveloped in China, even though the number of NGOs is increasing very quickly. In 1988, the number of 'social organisations' registered with the Ministry of Civil Affairs was 4446. By 1996 the number had soared to 184,821, an increase of more than 40 times. During the late 1990s, the government made an effort to rectify and control these organisations, which resulted in a decrease in their number. In 1999, there were 142,665 social organisations. Since the beginning of the twenty-first century, social organisations have again started to develop. The number increased to 386,916 in 2007, namely 2.7 times the number in 1999. However, most of these social organisations are not independent NGOs. The majority of them have certain relationships with the government or are actually a part of government departments. At the same time, there are many small grass roots organisations that are not registered. The number of these not entirely legitimate organisations was estimated at about 758,700 in 2007.[78] Grass roots organisations have developed rapidly in recent years, but there is a legitimacy problem for these organisations and their activities are severely limited by the government. The government sometimes incorporates a few of these organisations if they develop well and show that, in the eyes of the government, they have a positive function. Many of these NGOs indeed prefer to be co-opted by the government in order to gain more support and legitimacy.

Different elite groups, based on the state organisation, have been forming an 'elite coalition', which dominates the decision-making of important policies of the country. Political elites (higher party-government officials, leading cadres) are the ones with the most organisational and power resources because they are located in the key position of state organisation. Economic elites (larger entrepreneurs) would be in a difficult situation if they lacked government support. Letting the government and its officials share their profits is a major way for economic elites to gain government support and protection. That brings about the prevalent phenomenon of 'trade power for money', which is considered to be the main origin of corruption. However, this is a two-way relationship, as political elites also need support from the economic elites in order to attain the main target of the state – economic growth. This coalition between the political and economic elites is most evident at the local and regional levels. Governors of local governments, in particular, need support from large local entrepreneurs because the achievement assessments of these governors depend upon the economic efficiency of these enterprises. Entrepreneurs who provide economic results and thus help the government to reach its goals may enjoy favourable treatment and interest protection from the government side. This local and regional practice is repeated at the national level. A coalition has emerged between the political elites and the CEOs of large state-owned enterprises, joint ventures between state and private or foreign investors, and state-protected private enterprises.

Most cultural elites and influential intellectuals in China are, in general, working in institutions controlled or financially supported by the state. Important parts of cultural industries, such as major media, universities, hospitals, and so forth, are more or less affiliated with the state. This affiliation makes those cultural and intellectual elites dependent on the state, at least to some extent. Many cultural–intellectual elites become government advisors with significant influence in policy-making, while the government rewards the respective cultural elites with favourable treatment. At the same time, cultural–intellectual elites gain a lot from the market, because some of their representatives often become spokespersons for the interests of large entrepreneurs or CEOs of certain industries.

The elite coalition

The current 'elite coalition' was formed during the late 1990s. Before that there were, to some extent, conflicts among different groups of elites, especially between political and economic elites. In the 1980s and early 1990s, conflict at the local level between cadres and private entrepreneurs was not unusual. There was also much discontent among intellectuals over government policies. Conflicts of interest among different groups of elites destabilised the socio-political balance and led to the political turbulence of 1989. The 'elite coalition' has provided a foundation for political stability since the 1990s. However, it has simultaneously resulted in the possibility of a 'cleavage society', in which members of the society are separated into two groups: the elite minority and the mass majority. The elite minority monopolises most of the resources while the mass majority's interests are ignored.[79]

Yet this possibility, predicted by some sociologists, seems not to have become a reality because, since the beginning of the 2000s, the central government has taken a series of steps to balance the interests of the elite groups and the mass majority. Although the elite groups possess the most organisational resources and thus often dominate the policy-making of the state, the one-party state, in a more abstract or holistic sense, has its own ultimate goal of maintaining socio-political stability. Increasing criticism from the middle class and the intensive grievances of the underclass have threatened socio-political stability, and in order to ease the criticism of the elite groups the state sometimes plays the role of arbitrator among the conflicts of interest between the classes. Indeed, it argues that it represents and protects the interests of the majority, especially those of the underclass and vulnerable groups, although the policy-making of government is actually dominated by the elite groups.

Because of a lack of representative democracy and class-based politics, interest contests among the classes or groups takes place mainly through bargaining between governmental departments and organisations. Negotiation between the central and local governments is one of most important means of interest contest in today's China, with bargaining among ministries and departments of central government the other main venue for contesting interests. Industrial associations and professional organisations, most of them having an affiliation to the government, are also major institutional means of bargaining. Different parts of the elite groups and the middle class claim their interests and contest with other groups within the organisational system of the government. The state becomes an arbitrator between the conflicting group and class interests.

Trade unions in China, as nominal spokespersons for the working class, are organised into a large bureaucratic system. The National Trade Union is equivalent to a department of the central government. It has branches in each level of government including provincial, municipal, district and county governments. Trade unions in enterprises or institutions are affiliated to these branches. A few trade unions in large-scale enterprises or institutions are directly under the National Trade Union. Before the economic reforms, all enterprises and institutions had their own trade union, which effectively made all workers members of a trade union before 1978. However, most of the private and foreign enterprises which appeared during the economic reform did not set up trade unions in the 1980s and 1990s. The large-scale privatisation of state-owned enterprises in the late 1990s brought about a decrease in the number of trade unions and in the size of their membership. Since the beginning of the 2000s, the National Trade Union has launched a rebuilt trade-unionism movement which requires private and foreign enterprises to set up trade unions. Both the numbers of trade unions and of their membership have been increasing sharply (see Figure 3.8). In 2006, there were 1,508,376 trade unions with 204,524,207 members. The National Trade Union and trade unions of local governments are departments that represent the interests of the working class within the government system.

They usually are in a weak bargaining position in relation to other departments which represent the interests of the owner and leadership of the enterprises (such as the Entrepreneurs Association, China Federation of Industry and other industrial associations). However, the National Trade Union has also been protecting the rights and interests of the working class through legal changes. The Labour Contract Law, adopted in 2008, was a great victory in bargaining with employers. According to the new law, the National Trade Union required local governments to establish special labour dispute arbitration institutions to protect labour rights. At same time, trade unions in China have never played an active role in collective negotiation at the enterprise level. Trade unions in enterprises more resemble leisure associations. To change this, in 2010 the National Trade Union started a campaign to encourage trade unions at the enterprise level to become involved

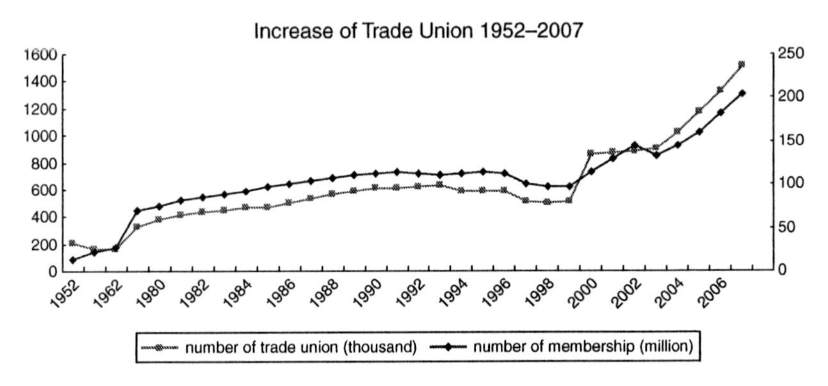

Figure 3.13 Numbers of trade unions and their membership, 1952–2007

Source: *Yearbook of Labor Statistics of China*, Beijing: China Labor Press.

in collective negotiation in labour market disputes, which has led to a sharp increase in labour union activities (see Figure 3.13).

The collapse and rebuilding of the welfare system

Before the economic reform, China had a huge welfare system which provided comprehensive social security and welfare for all urban workers in enterprises, institutions and governmental organisations. The social security and welfare included pensions, free health care, and almost free education and housing. This welfare security was provided by the work-units (enterprises, institutions, organisations) themselves. The government adopted a universal employment policy and almost all the urban labour force had a job in work-unit organisations. In other words, the social welfare system covered all urban residents. However, rural residents, which were about 80 per cent of the total population, have been excluded from the social welfare system. In rural areas, the government provided almost free education and very cheap health care. Peasants were employed in People's Communes (collective economy), which offered peasants with an income, means of production, and subsistence.

In the first 20 years of the economic reform, China's welfare system experienced a transition from the socialist welfare model into a liberal welfare model. Reform of welfare system in the 1980s and 1990s was actually a steady shrinking of the system. On the one hand, the government stopped providing some parts of social welfare such as practically free housing and education, as well as free health care. On the other hand, the government excluded gradually more and more social groups from the welfare system. First, all employers and employees in the private economy were excluded from the system. Second, through the reform of state-owned enterprises in the late 1990s, most employees in state-owned enterprises and the collective economy were excluded. Third, some employees in institutions financed by the government have also been excluded. Now only a few privileged persons still enjoy significant social welfare benefits, including formal employees of the central and local governments, and managers and professionals in state-owned enterprises and large-scale institutions. Most people have to acquire housing, health care and education on the free market.

At same time, the government has been trying to establish a new system of social security, an insurance-based system including five major parts: an old-age pension, medical insurance, unemployment insurance, work injury insurance, and maternal and childcare insurance. In addition, in the urban areas an institutionalised system of social protection based on a minimum standard of living and basic salaries has been established. Poor families in urban areas who have a lower income than the minimum standard of living can receive subsidies from the government. However, rural families are not included in the system.[80]

Figure 3.14 shows the percentages of social expenditure in relation to how gross domestic product has changed over time. The percentage of

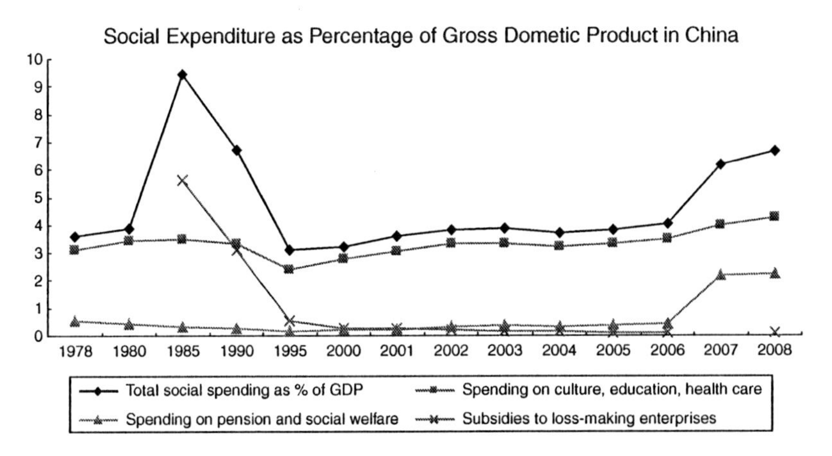

Figure 3.14 Percentages of social expenditure in GDP in China
Source: China Public Finance Yearbook; Beijing: China Financial Press.

GDP spent on culture, education, health care, pensions and other social welfare decreased slightly in the 1980s and 1990s although the country's economy grew quickly during that period. A major part of social expenditure between 1985–1995 was subsidies to loss-making state-owned enterprises. These enterprises had been privatised or bankrupted in the late 1990s. Tens of millions of workers from these enterprises had lost their jobs and correspondingly had lost their social protection, security and welfare because these benefits (pension, health care, labour security and other welfare provision) were originally derived from these enterprises. Some of these citizens fell into poverty and became dependent on help from their parents and relatives.

Economic reform and the shift towards a liberal model of welfare provision brought about a series of social problems. Poverty rates in urban areas increased and rural poverty remained at a high level. Protests over the unbearable costs of medical care, education and housing were frequent. Unequal access to welfare for different social groups also aroused strong and widespread discontent against the government. Since around 2000, the policy of China's government has been shifting from the focus on economic growth alone towards the combination of economic growth and social development. The newly-declared aim is to construct a 'harmonious society', including the rebuilding of the social security system. Indeed, in recent decades the government has adopted a series of social policy measures to rebuild and expand the social security system, such as increasing the coverage of social insurance, especially in regard to medical care and pensions, upgrading minimum living standards and increasing coverage of social protection, increasing government budgetary expenditure on education and health care, and so on. At the same time, the costs of social insurance have moved from being borne by individuals to a shared responsibility of the government, enterprises, and individual insurance holders. Social classes and groups such as employees in the private economy, rural residents and migrant workers, who were excluded from social security in the 1980s and 1990s, have returned to the social security system. Figure 3.14 and Table 3.10 reveal a significant increase in social expenditure in relation to GDP, as well as the extent of the coverage of social insurance. Social expenditures vis-à-vis GDP increased from 3.25 per cent in 2000 to 6.66 per cent in 2008. The increase has been especially prominent since 2006. The coverage of social insurance is also increasing. In 2008, the total size of the labour force was about 792.4 million. About 64.5 million among the total labour force are employees in the public sector who enjoy social welfare from government.

Table 3.10 Number of participants in the social insurance system in China (million persons)

Year	Basic old-age insurance	Basic worker medical insurance	Unemployment insurance	Injury insurance	Maternity insurance	Rural cooperative medical insurance	Urban citizen medical insurance	Rural old-age insurance
1989	57.10							
1995	109.79	7.46	82.38	26.15	15.00			
1998	112.03	18.79	79.28	37.81	27.77			
2000	136.17	37.87	103.26	43.50	30.01			
2001	141.83	72.86	103.55	43.45	34.55			
2002	147.37	94.01	101.82	44.06	34.88			
2003	155.07	109.02	103.72	45.75	36.55			
2004	163.53	124.04	105.84	68.45	4384	80.00		
2005	174.88	137.83	106.48	84.78	54.09	179.00		
2006	187.66	157.32	111.87	102.69	64.59	410.00		
2007	201.37	180.20	116.45	121.73	77.75	726.00	42.91	51.71
2008	201.37	199.96	123.99	137.87	92.54	815.00	118.26	55.95
2009	235.50	219.37	127.15	148.96	108.76	833.00	182.10	86.91

Source: Ministry of Civil Affairs of China.

Notes: The authors thank MA Markus Kainu for considerable assistance and Professor Linda Cook for valuable comments.

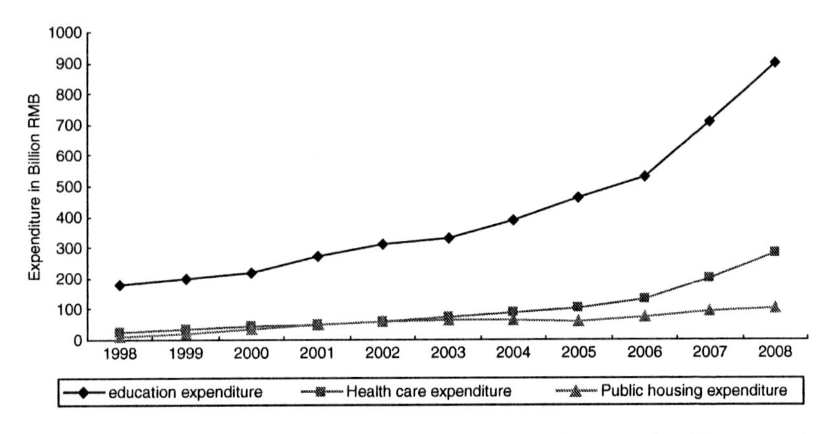

Figure 3.15 The increase in social expenditure on education, health care and public housing

Source: *China Public Finance Yearbook*, Beijing: China Financial Press.

Among the other 727.9 million, about 44.9 per cent had basic old-age insurance, a much higher percentage than in 1989. In addition, most urban and rural residents have medical insurance. Figure 3.15 clearly illustrates the expansion of the social security system. Education expenditure in 2008 was about 4.5 times greater than it was 1999. Health care expenditure is almost 8 times greater than in 1999.

Thus, the new government policy implies a new trend in Chinese social welfare reform – a clear shift away from the liberal model of social welfare, and towards a more regulated model. In recent decades, analysts and experts from the government have reflected upon the negative consequences of the marketisation of housing, health care and education. The conclusion is that the previously adopted liberal welfare model, mostly associated with the United States, is not the best choice for China. Social problems caused by this kind of liberal model would probably threaten political stability and undermine the political legitimacy of the Communist Party. The social protests and riots that have been increasingly occurring in the country function as empirical proof of this conclusion. The new generation of leadership and political elite thinks it is time to shift away from the liberal model and towards adopting a more balanced welfare model. The government, with the new discourse of constructing social harmony, has proposed a new development strategy in order to establish a fine balance between economic development and social development; this includes a slow but continuous rise in social expenditures in general and in government health care expenses in particular. The new trends in welfare system reforms focus on increasing the coverage of social security, more equal access to social welfare, and the institutionalisation of the social security system.

To conclude, China's welfare regime is still evolving. What kind of welfare model will the new trend lead to? It is not clear yet. Recently, policy-makers from the Chinese government and their advisors have paid a lot of attention to the conservative model of continental Europe, especially to the German system of medical care. Some socialist theorists in the Communist Party prefer the Scandinavian model of social welfare instead. However, they admit that this model is currently a utopia for China.

A rapid expansion in social welfare and social security are indeed helpful to maintain the stability of the existing social and political system and ease conflicts of interest among different classes, but it cannot completely solve the problems. Discontent over the income gap and corruption has continued to increase. Various forms of protest against the poor performance and abusive administration of some local governments have occurred, with increasing frequency. Undoubtedly, these protests have created much pressure on the government to improve its performance. However, it is not yet clear whether they will expand enough to truly shake the government into action. At present, the greatest protests come from the bottom of the society – the unemployed, peasant workers or land-expropriated peasants – who are called the 'biggest losers' of the market-oriented transition. The government's programme of expanding welfare is trying to put an end to this discontent. The middle class has benefited greatly from the transition and is less motivated towards a radical reform of the system, even though many members of this class criticise the unfair government policies which have resulted in elite and privileged groups gaining too much and becoming the biggest beneficiaries. Currently, the critical trigger for vast socio-political change is economic conflicts of interest, rather than a political democracy movement.

Alliances of political, economic and cultural elites under the authoritarian state system now dominate the strategic choices on socio-political development, and these alliances then guide the direction of reforms towards benefiting themselves. Top leaders in central government and the Communist Party have gradually recognised that unfair distribution is becoming a serious threat to political stability. They have implemented a series of social policies to adjust the distribution of welfare, termed the *Construction of a Harmonious Society*. These policies include providing more welfare and subsidies to poor and vulnerable groups, raising the minimum wage and poverty line, increasing investment in rural areas and underdeveloped regions, increasing taxes on wealth, and so on. Positive effects from these policies have become apparent over the last five years. The average wage of a manual labourer and peasant worker has increased significantly since 2003. In 2010, the growth in per capita income of rural residents exceeded that of urban residents for the first time in almost 30 years. More and more members of the lower classes enjoy health insurance and pensions. Some optimistic experts predict that the income gap will begin to decrease and the social security system will soon cover all citizens. However, widespread discontent against bureaucrats and the wealthy has not reduced. Conflicts of interest between different social groups have not eased either. The future direction of class relationships and their impact on political stability still remains uncertain, and the attitudes of the rising middle class will probably become a decisive factor in the outcome.

Conclusions

The chapter has discussed the emerging class structure and social stratification in Russia and China. As the old class structures and respective institutions have been eroded and new ones have emerged, in both countries the socialist welfare system has also given way to a new system. The main question this chapter has discussed is: what are the main characteristics of the newly-emerging welfare models in Russia and in China?

Starting with Russia, we first discussed the rather chaotic privatisation process which first, through so-called spontaneous privatisation, allowed the old managerial elite or nomenklatura to capture most of the property that was privatised. This was followed by a deliberate policy by the government to create a new entrepreneurial class of capitalists, who took over the biggest natural resources and related production facilities and created financial institutions to manage this stage of privatisation. A partial renationalisation or bureaucratisation of property took place when the strategic parts of the Russian economy were put under the control of hand-picked members of the elites which surrounded President Putin. Through this process, however, a kind of a new entrepreneurial middle class was created, which was adapted to the new market economy conditions. However, the actual entrepreneurial middle class in Russia is still rather small when compared with the middle classes in the West. It is also considerably smaller than that of China. As far as a wage-earning middle class is concerned, a striking feature in Russia is the large share of the potential middle class consisting of doctors, teachers, lawyers and engineers who have no autonomy at the level of the 'politics of production'. We also argued that the trade union organisations representing the working class are weak. The new market economy has eroded their traditional Soviet role as providers of social benefits, and the trade unions have had difficulties in implementing their new role as defenders of their members' interests against employers. This development was mainly an unintended result of uncontrolled development, and not so much the result of systematic reform processes.

The strengthening of the middle class under current Russian conditions seems not to have reinforced public services, but rather to have put the emphasis on private ones, and the middle class seems to be organising itself politically as the party of power in the form of *United Russia*. The working class is too weak in its representation of interests and seems to have insufficient resources to put forward its own model. The new system is taking shape, and although it has not been stabilised yet, our analysis leads us to conclude that eventually the outcome will be a liberal model welfare state, a poor man's version of the US model.

In the Chinese case, when the step-by-step privatisation started, there was, in the name of stability, pressure upon the policies of the government concerning welfare distribution. Unlike in Russia, the transition did not create any new classes of poverty and economic oligarchies did not appear in China during the broad-scale privatisation in the same way that they did in Russia. Unlike Russia, which started its transition when it was already a fully industrialised and largely urbanised society, China's transition has been characterised by large-scale industrialisation and urbanisation. This has resulted in a significant reduction of the peasant class, an increase of the working class in the 1990s, and an expansion of the middle class during the 2000s. The privatisation process has led to the emergence of the capitalist and middle-class entrepreneurial classes, members of which had previously worked for the public sector. Most or all people have improved their economic situation; however, the rising income gap has become the main source of social discontent and cause for criticism of government policies. As in Russia, in China the role of the middle class is an issue. Some regard it as a potentially destabilising group which needs to be controlled, whereas others see it as a socio-political stabiliser which defends political conservatism because it benefits most from the economic reforms and rapid economic growth, while at the same time it is strongly dependent upon the state. In general, since the beginning of the 2000s, the central government has taken a deliberate series of measures to balance the interests of the elite groups and the mass majority. Although the trade unions are generally weak bargaining parties within the vast bureaucratic machinery, the state has been rather successful in functioning in its role as an arbitrator of interest conflicts. Moreover, within the elites, it can be noted that an 'elite coalition' formed during late 1990s, which seems to have found a balance between the different elite interests and solved potential major conflicts, especially between the political and economic elites.

First, the economic reform in China meant shifting towards a liberal, US-inspired model of welfare. While China's welfare regime is still evolving, it seems that the government has already turned in another direction. The liberal model brought about a series of social problems, which were understood as producing instability and thus threatening the current power constellation. Due to this policy shift, many social classes and groups that were excluded from social security in the 1980s and 1990s have returned to the social security system. One can tentatively conclude that since around 2000, the policy of China's government has been moving towards a new model with stronger corporatist elements. In this system the costs of social insurance has been shifting from individuals to a shared responsibility between the government, enterprises, and individual insurance holders.

All classes are weak in Russia as well as in China. Systematic interest representation is not developed within the political systems. There seems to be a complex tension between the concepts of structure and process. What are the basic processes that actually create the structural features of societies? Many 'commonly understood' mega-processes seem to be quite shallow when they are put into the context of real historical events in transitional societies. If there were a universal tendency towards class *fragmentation and decomposition,* post-socialist societies would be far more advanced than the advanced capitalist countries in this respect. Europe could look at them and see in them the future of its own class structure. This is, of course, highly paradoxical. In fact, structuration towards a more defined class society is a distinct process in Russia as well as in China.

However, the most commonly defined processes of class relations are out of place here. Neither the theory of *embourgeoisement* nor the theory of *proletarianisation* can provide an adequate explanation of either the past or the future of Russia or China. We have shown that growing inequality does not mean a straightforward *polarisation* of society. The role of the middle classes is growing in both countries. However, we have argued against expectations which are too straightforward with regard to the benign interests of the middle classes. In China as well as in Russia, the economic transition towards market-based societies, including elite and mass privatisation, has fundamentally transformed social structures. The transition has created new capitalists as well as small employers and petty bourgeois social groups. However, these groups remain a minority in a wage-labour based society. In Russia, the new wage-labouring middle class positions have grown stronger during the Putin regime, having previously been in decline during the first ten years of transition. There are more entrepreneurs in urban China than in Russia. On the other hand, the wage-labouring middle classes are larger in Russia. In both countries the working class situation has also improved in economic terms over the last ten years. *This may be more significant for the working class experience and consciousness than the growth of relative differences.* In urban China, both the working class and middle class positions have increased and general standards of living have improved considerably. The remarkable economic growth has increased the real incomes of the Chinese working class. This has paradoxically maintained the legitimacy of the hegemonic project, which in fact means an implicit erosion of the "sacred" working class.[81] Communist regimes always declare themselves as representatives of the working class, and the growth of the middle classes emerges as an unintended result of their modernisation efforts. In contemporary China the working class has grown, while deep internal segmentation has emerged. It should also be noticed that *neither in Russia nor in China can inequality be reduced to class differences.* In Russia huge regional differences prevail, whereas in China the class structure is to a large extent dualistic. Upper classes are almost non-existent in rural China.

The emergence of entrepreneurial class groups and the growth of the wage-labouring middle classes in both countries is the product of strategic choices made by the ruling elites in response to the consequences of economic transition. The Soviet type of welfare regime has been wound up and there is no strong welfare sector in the economy in either country. If trade unions are relatively weak in promoting the interests of the working class in the formation of the welfare regime (although in China their role seems to be growing), that is, if classes do not have systematic interest representation, then market capacities play the crucial role in the formation of the service sector and the welfare regime. The upper and middle classes are inclined towards a liberal model of the welfare state. In the formation of welfare, both state bureaucracies and professional organisations are significant stake-holders because of the weakness of class forces. Both countries have an obvious need to create a new welfare system. *Both the entrepreneurial and wage-labouring middle classes will have the market resources to live with private institutions of welfare and education and there will be a strong tendency towards a liberal model of the welfare state.*

However, in both countries, a counter-tendency also exists which favours state-run social welfare, and it seems probable that the welfare model in each country will comprise elements from several welfare regimes. What the real substance of these state elements in the welfare regime is remains to be seen. In principle both countries have the potential to make use of the late-comer's advantage in creating the institutional forms of their welfare regimes. Presidential programmes in Russia and the growing social and economic rights in Chinese legislation represent new tendencies. So far it seems most probable that the liberal model will dominate, with limited elements of redistribution through taxation or state-run welfare. In China, informal security similar to the South Asian model might also play a significant role.

As it now stands the dominating liberal model does not automatically challenge the hegemonic project of the elites in either country. The working class is not willing to mobilise in opposition because of rising living standards and weak organisation. Because of their stronger market capacities and incomes, the middle classes are served well under the liberal model of welfare. Additionally, the prospect of building a career in the ruling parties (the Communist Party in China and *United Russia* in Russia) is tempting to the middle classes.

Notes

1. When discussing the structural preconditions for this choice, the focus of our analysis is placed on the emerging social structure and its interplay with the state, as the basic source of explanation. The theoretical starting point is the idea of the structuration of classes. We link this to the conceptualisation of the welfare state in a way that is not common in the discussion of models of welfare. Aspalter argues that explanatory theories of social welfare may be characterized either as actor-based (conflict) theories, or structural (functional) theories. Actor-based theories suggest that it is the power and the programmes of different actors that are the key to the formation of welfare regimes. These actors are classes and the state, corporatist institutions, political parties, labour unions, but also ruling elites, governing administrators, activists, and professional organisations. In many cases the role of international bodies, such as the IMF, the World Bank, the United Nations, or the

OECD has to be taken into account. Actor-based explanatory theories seem to imply *a diversification of welfare regimes based on different power resources of various actors in particular societies.* On the other hand, structural theories are apt to predict a convergence on social policies based on common structural determinants such as, for example, the degree of economic development, urbanisation, modernisation, or the advance of capitalist market economy. *Our analysis here adheres to an action-based explanation.* If structural theories based on modernisation were correct, the elements of Russian and Chinese welfare regimes might indicate a convergence on a universal welfare mix based upon the global hegemonic project of neoliberalism. To anticipate our argument, we hold that both in Russia and in China the choice of welfare models is still open. Starting from the class structure, we intend to analyse the structural conditions of this choice. Our argument is not based on some kind of ahistorical class interests grounded on mere theoretical constructions. Rather, we intend to analyse the interests based on concrete analysis of class structure and class situation. Christian Aspalter, 'The welfare state in cross cultural perspective', *International Social Work* Vol. 51, 2008/6, pp. 777–789; Christian Aspalter, 'New Developments in the Theory of Comparative Social Policy', *Journal of Comparative Social Welfare* Vol. 1, 2006/1, pp. 3–22, (2006a); Christian Aspalter, 'The East Asian Welfare Regime', *International Journal of Social Welfare* Vol. 15, 2006, pp. 290–301, (2006b).

2. Michael Burawoy, *The Politics of Production: Factory Regimes Under Capitalism and Socialism*, London and New York: Verso 1985.
3. World Bank, *Transition. The First Ten Years: Analysis and Lessons for Eastern Europe and the Former Soviet Union*, Washington DC, 2002.
4. Simon Clarke, 'The contradictions of 'state socialism', in Simon Clarke *et al.*, *What about the Workers. Workers and the Transition to Capitalism in Russia*, Cheltenham: Edgar Elgar 1993.
5. Simon Clarke and Veronika Kabalina, *Privatisation and the Struggle of Control of the Enterprise in Russia*, Paper for the conference: Russia in Transition Elites, Classes and Inequalities, Cambridge 15–16 December 1994.
6. *Ibid.*
7. Minxin Pei, *From Reform to Revolution: The Demise of Communism in China and the Soviet Union*, Harvard University Press 1998, p. 129.
8. Pekka Sutela, *The Road to the Russian Market Economy: Selected Essays, 1993–1998*, Helsinki: Aleksanteri Institute 1998, p. 129.
9. *Ibid.*, p. 158.
10. For a detailed and critical description of this era, see David E. Hoffman, *The Oligarchs: Wealth and Power in the New Russia*, New York: Public Affairs 2003; for a sympathetic picture of these new 'entrepreneurs' and their political allies, see Anders Åslund, *Russia's Capitalist Revolution: Why Market Reform Succeeded and Democracy Failed*. Washington DC: Peterson Institute For International Economics 2007, p. 157*ff.*
11. Åslund, *Russia's Capitalist Revolution*, pp. 250–9.
12. Ibid., pp. 277, 280.
13. Gil Eyal, Ivan Szelenyi and Eleanor Townsley, *Making Capitalism without Capitalists: Class Formation and Elite Struggles in Post-Communist Eastern Europe*, London: Verso 1998.

14. Gil Eyal, 'Anti-Politics and the spirit of capitalism: dissidents, monetarists and the Czech transition to capitalism', *Theory and Society* Vol. 29. No. 2000/1. February, pp. 50–92, here p. 50.
15. Ivan Szelenyi, *The New Grand Bourgeoisie under Post-Communism: Central Europe, Russia and China Compared*, UNU-Wider Working Paper No 2010/63.
16. See, for example, M.G. Gorshkov *et al.*, *Srednij klass v sovremennom Rossiiskom obschestve*, Moscow: RNISNiNP 1999; Leonid Grigoriev and Tatyana Maleva, 'Srednii klass v sovremennom rossiiskom obshchestve', *Voprosy ekonomiki* 2001/1, pp. 40–50; M.G. Gorshkov *et al.* (eds), *Srednij klass v sovremennoj Rossii*, Moscow: Institut sotsiologii RAN 2008; E.B. Golovljanitsina, 'Innovatsionen li rossijskij srednij klass? Osobennosti professional'noj struktury i trudovyh tsennostej srednego klassa nakanune krizisa', *Mir Rossii*, Vol. 18, 2009/4, pp. 19–36; *cf.* O.I. Shkaratan, 'Vozproizvodstvo sotsialno-ekonomitsheskogo neravenstva v postsovetskoj Rossii: dinamika urovna zhizni i polozenie sotsialnyh nizov', *Mir Rossii*, Vol. 17, 2008/4, pp. 60–89; O.I. Shkaratan, S.A. Injasevskij and T.S. Ljubimova, 'Novyj srednij klass i informatsional'nye na rossijskom rynke truda', *Obchshestvennye nauki i sovremennost'*, 2008/1, pp. 5–27.
17. Cf. especially Grigoriev and Maleva 2001, 'Srednii klass v sovremennom rossiiskom obshchestve'; M. G. Gorshkov, 'Rossijskoe obschestvo v sotsiologitsheskom izmerenii', *Mir Rossii*, Vol. 18, 2009/2, pp. 3–21; for a more developed view, see V. V. Radaev, 'Obytshnye in innovatsionnie praktiki', in T.M. Maleva (ed.), *Srednie klassi v Rossii: ekonomitsheskie i sotsialnye strategii*, Moskva: Gendal'f 2003.
18. *Cf.* Gorshkov 'Rossijskoe obschestvo v sotsiologitsheskom izmerenii', pp. 10–11; V.A. Anikin, 'Tendentsij izmenenija sotsialno-professionalnoj struktury Rossii v 1994–2006', *Mir Rossii*, Vol. 18, 2009/3, pp. 114–131.
19. E.g. S.G. Kordonskij, 'Soslovnaja struktura postsovetskoj Rossii (Chast II)', *Mir Rossii*, Vol. 17, 2008/4, pp. 3–36.
20. Markku Kivinen, *Progress and Chaos. Russia as a Challenge for Sociological Imagination*, Helsinki: Kikimora Publications 2002; Markku Kivinen, 'Classes in the Making? The Russian Social Structure in Transition,' in Göran Therborn (ed.) *Inequalities of the World, New Theoretical Frameworks, Multiple Empirical Approaches*, London, New York: Verso 2006, pp. 239–286.
21. See Markku Kivinen, *Parempien piirien ihmisiä*, Jyväskylä: Tutkijaliitto 1987, p. 195; and Markku Kivinen, *The New Middle Classes and the Labour Process – Class Criteria Revisited*, Department of Sociology, University of Helsinki 1989, pp. 295–296.
22. In both versions of Erik Olin Wright's theory these people would represent marginal middle class groups, whereas in our approach (in which the accent is on autonomy) they belong to the working class.
23. Kivinen 2002, *op. cit.* pp. 84–160.
24. Kivinen 1989, *op. cit.*
25. See Kivinen, 'Classes in the Making?'
26. See e.g. Markku Kivinen, *The New Middle Classes and the Labour Process – Class Criteria Revisited, Department of Sociology*, University of Helsinki 1989. Erik Olin Wright, *Class Counts*, London, New York: Verso 1997.

27. Erik Olin Wright, 'The new middle classes and the labour process: class criteria revisited by Markku Kivinen. Huomautuksia Kivisen luokkateoriaan,' *Tiede ja edistys*, Vol. 15, 1990/2, pp. 142–146, and 1997, *op. cit.*; Michael Hout, 'Economic Change and Social Mobility', in Göran Therborn (ed.), *Inequalities of the World*, London: Verso 2007, pp. 119–135.
28. Markku Kivinen, 'Russian Societal Development – Challenges Open', in Hiski Haukkala and Sinikukka Saari (eds), *Russia Lost or Found*, Helsinki: Edita 2009. *Cf.* Olli Kangas, *Well-being in Comparison: Evidence from European Social Survey.* Paper presented in Aleksanteri Conference 2008: Welfare and Agency in Russia and Eastern Europe. Stakes, Helsinki, 11 December 2008; T.V. Merkulova, 'Ekonomitsheskij rost i neravenstvo: institutsionalnyj aspect i modelirovanie vzaimosvjazi', *Mir Rossii* Vol. 19 2010, pp. 59–77.
29. Ulrich Beck, *Risikogesellschaft. Auf dem Weg in eine andere Moderne*, Frankfurt am Mein: Suhrkamp 1986.
30. Simon Clarke, 'Post-socialist trade unions: China and Russia', *Industrial Relations Journal*, Vol. 36, 2005/1, pp. 2–18; Tim Pringle and Simon Clarke, *The Challenge of Transition: Trade Unions in Russia, China and Vietnam*, Basingstoke and New York: Palgrave Macmillan 2010.
31. S. Klimova, S., 'Na rasput'e, ili samoopredelenie rossiskih profsojuzov', in A.E. Oslon *et al.* (eds), *Grazhdanskoe obchshestvo sovremennoj Rossii*, Moscow: Institut Fonda Obchshestvennoe Mnenie 2008.
32. Clarke 'Post-socialist trade unions'; Klimova 'Na rasput'e, ili samoopredelenie rossiskih profsojuzov'.
33. V. Il'in, *Vlast' i ugol: shahterskoe dvizhenie Vorkuty (1989–1999 gg.)*, Syktyvkar: SGU 1998.
34. Linda J. Cook, 'Russian Labour', in Graeme Gill (ed.), *Handbook of Russian Politics and Society*, London: Routledge, forthcoming, 2011.
35. Simon Clarke (ed.), *Management and Industry in Russia: Formal and Informal Relations in the Period of Transition*, Cheltenham: Edward Elgar 1995.
36. Clarke, 'Post-socialist trade unions', pp. 1–4.
37. S. Klimova and K. Kleman, 'Rol' novogo Trydovogo kodeksa reglamantatsii trydovyh otnoshenij v Rossii', in *Stanovlenie trudovyh otnoshenij v postsovetskoj Rossii*, Moscow: Akademitsheskij Projekt 2004 pp. 18–20.
38. Cf. Klimova, 'Na rasput'e, ili samoopredelenie rossiskih profsojuzov'.
39. *OPFR: O sostojanii grazhdanskogo obshchestva v Rossiiskoi Federacii*, Moscow: Obshchesvennaia palata Rossiiskoi Federacii 2008; Cf. Meri Kulmala (2010a), '"Women Rule this Country": Women's Community Organizing and Care in Rural Karelia', *The Anthropology of East Europe Review* 28 (2), November 2010; Meri Kulmala (2010b), 'Rethinking State-Society Boundaries in a Small-Town Context of Russian Karelia', in Maija Jäppinen, Meri Kulmala and Aino Saarinen (eds), *Gazing at Welfare, Gender and Agency in Post-socialist Countries*, Newcastle upon Tyne: Cambridge Scholars Publishers, pp. 170–198.
40. Alfred B. Evans Jr., V*ladimir Putin's Design for Civil Society*, in Alfred B. Evans Jr. et al. (eds), *Russian Civil Society. A Critical Assessment*, Armonk, NY: M.E. Sharpe 2006, pp. 147–160.
41. Richard Sakwa, *Russian Politics and Society*, London: Routledge 2008.
42. Olga Matich, *Erotic Utopia: the decadent imagination in Russia's fin-de-siecle*, Madison, Wisconsin: University of Wisconsin Press 2005; cf. Kivinen 2002, *op. cit.*, pp. 181–223.

43. Robert N. Bellah, 'Civil Religion in America', *Dædalus*, Winter 1967, Vol. 96, No. 1, pp. 1–21; Kivinen 2009, *op. cit.*
44. Geof Wood and Ian Gough, 'A Comparative Welfare Regime Approach to Global Social Policy', *World Development*, Vol. 34, 2006/10, pp. 1696–1712, here p. 1699.
45. Gösta Esping-Andersen, *The Three Worlds of Welfare Capitalism*, Cambridge: Polity Press and Princeton University Press 1990; see also Walter Korpi, *The Democratic Class Struggle*, London: Routledge and Kegan Paul 1983.
46. Christian Aspalter, 'New Developments in the Theory of Comparative Social Policy', *Journal of Comparative Social Welfare*, Vol. 1, 2006/1, pp. 3–22; Christian Aspalter, 'The East Asian Welfare Regime', *International Journal of Social Welfare*, Vol. 15, 2006, pp. 290–301.
47. Wood and Gough 2006, *op. cit.*; Nita Rudra, *Globalization and the Race to the Bottom in Developing Countries: Who Really Gets Hurt?* Cambridge: Cambridge University Press 2008. Rudra focuses on India, Brazil and Korea to develop new 'productivist' and 'protectivist' typologies for successful developing states' welfare regimes.
48. Clarke et al., *What about the Workers*. About the realities of Soviet social policy, see Elena Yarskaya-Smirnova (ed.), *'Sovetskaya sotsialnaya politika, Stseny i dejsvujuschschie litsa'*, Moskva: Variant 2008.
49. Joe C.B. Leung, 'Dismantling the "Iron Rice Bowl": Welfare Reforms in the People's Republic of China', *Journal of Social Policy*, Vol. 23, 1994/3, pp. 341–361; Aidi Hu, 'Reforming China's social security system: Facts and perspectives', *International Social Security Review*, Vol. 50, 3/1997, pp. 45–65.
50. Ka Lin and Olli Kangas, 'Social Policymaking and its institutional basis: Transition of the Chinese social security system', *International Social Security Review*, Vol. 59, 2/2006, pp. 61–76.
51. Lin and Kangas, 'Social Policymaking and its institutional basis'.
52. Neil C. Hughes, 'Smashing the Iron Rice Bowl', *Foreign Affairs*, Vol. 77, No. 4, July/August, 1998, pp. 67–77.
53. Alfio Cerami, 'Socio-Economic Transformations in Post-Communist Countries: Central and Eastern Europe and Russia Compared', *Romanian Journal of Political Science*, Vol. 9 No. 1, 2009, available at http:///www.sar.org.ro/polsci/. See also Linda J. Cook, 'Eastern Europe and Russia', Chapter 46 in Frances Castles, Stephan Leibfried, Jane Lewis, Herbert Obinger and Christopher Pierson (eds), *Oxford Handbook of Comparative Welfare States*, Oxford: Oxford University Press 2010.
54. Linda J. Cook, *Postcommunist Welfare states: Reform Politics in Russia and Eastern Europe*, Ithaca and London: Cornell University Press 2007.
55. Cook 2007, *Postcommunist Welfare states*.
56. V.V. Petuhov, 'Ot monetizatsiya l'got k natsionalnym projektam', *Sotsiolgicheskie issledobaniya* 2006/12, pp. 22–27.
57. G.I. Osadchaya, 'L'goty v kontekste reformirovaniya socialnoj politiki', *Sotsiolgicheskie issledobaniya* 2006/11, pp. 38–42; John B. Williamson, Stephanie A. Howling and Michele L. Maroto, 'The political economy of Pension reform in Russia: Why partial privatisation?', *Journal of Aging Studies*, Vol. 20, 2006, pp. 165–175.

58. As an overview of the contemporary situation see Linda J. Cook, 'Welfare State Development', *Oxford Bibliographies On-Line: Political Science* (Rick Valelly, Editor-in-Chief), 2011, available at http://www.aboutobo.com
59. See Meri Kulmala's studies on Karelia: Kulmala a and b, *op. cit.*; Meri Kulmala, 'Kansalaisyhteiskunta ja valtio Venäjän Karjalassa', *Futura* 2/2008, 43–61; Meri Kulmala, *Russian State and Civil Society in Interaction: An Ethnographic Approach*, unpublished manuscript 2011.
60. Oxana Gaman-Golutvina, 'The Changing Role of the State and State Bureaucracy in the Context of Public Administration Reforms: Russian and Foreign Experience', in Anton Oleinik (ed.), *Reforming the State without Changing the Model of Power?*, London: Routledge 2009.
61. Luc Boltanski and Laurent Thévenot, *On Justification: Economies of Worth*, Princeton, NJ: Princeton University Press 2006.
62. On charity and the third sector in contemporary Russia see Rosalinde Sartorti, 'Looking back, Looking ahead: Charity and Philanthropy in the New Russia', in: Elina Kahla (ed.), *Between Utopia and Apocalypse: Essays on Social Theory and Russia*, Jyväskylä: Aleksanteri Series 1/2011.
63. As an example, see Harri Melin, 'Towards New Paternalism in Kondopoga', in Harri Melin (ed.), *Social Structure, Public Space and Civil Society in Karelia*, Helsinki: Kikimora Publications (B 64), pp. 61–75.
64. Theodor Geiger, *Die Klassengesellschaft in Schmelstiegel*, Köln: G. Kiepenheuer Verlag 1949; Hans Speier, *German White Collar Workers and the Rise of Hitler*, New Haven: Yale University Press 1986.
65. Hout, 'Economic Change and Social Mobility'.
66. Scholars have proposed distinctive perspectives on labour's future in Russia. Paul Kubicek sees organized labour as permanently disempowered by the forces of economic globalisation. By contrast, David Ost anticipates a qualified revival of post-communist labour unions. See Paul Kubicek, *Organized Labor in Postcommunist States: from Solidarity to Infirmity*, Pittsburgh: University of Pittsburgh Press 2004; David Ost, 'The End of Postcommunism: Trade Unions in Eastern Europe's future', *East European Politics and Society* 23 (1), pp. 13–33. *Cf.* Pringle and Clarke, *The Challenge of Transition*, pp. 147–202 and Cook 'Welfare State Development', pp. 13–14.
67. Vesa Oittinen, 'Marxismi-leninismistä valtiopatriotismiin – Venäjän kommunistien aatteellinen kehitys', *Venäjän ja Itä-Euroopan Instituutin tiedonantoja ja katsauksia* 2, Helsinki 1995; Sakwa, *Russian Politics and Society*.
68. Göran Ahrne and Erik Olin Wright, 'Class and Social Organisation in the United States and Sweden: A Comparison', *Acta Sociologica* 3–4, 1983, Vol. 26, pp. 211–236.
69. *Cf.* Pekka Sutela, 'The Economic Future of Russia', *International Journal of Economic Policy in Emerging Economies*, 2007/1, pp. 21–33.
70. Li, Chunling, 'Expansion of high education and inequality in opportunity of education', *Sociological Research*, 147(3), 2010, pp. 82–113.
71. Li, Chunling, 'The Composition of Middle Class of the Contemporary China', *China Population Science*, 99 (6), 2003, pp. 25–32; see also Li, 'Expansion of high education and inequality in opportunity of education'.
72. Shi Li, *Positive Analysis on Distribution of Income in China*, Beijing: Social Science Academic Press 2000; Chunling Li, 'Income Inequality of Social

Groups: Polarization or Pluralization?' *Strategy and Administration*, 2004, No.3, pp. 45–53; Chunling Li, *Cleavage or Fragment: An Empirical Analysis on the Social Stratification of Contemporary China*, Beijing: Social Science Academic Press 2005.

73. Li, Chunling, 'Evolvement of Chinese Urban Social Stratum', in Nu Fenrui, Pan Jiahua and Liu Ziyan (eds), *Urban Development in China: 30 Years (1978–2008)*, Beijing: Social Sciences Academic Press, pp. 228–242.
74. Xueyi Lu, *A Research Report on Social Classes of the Contemporary China*, Beijing: Social Sciences Academic Press 2002; Li, Chunling, *Cleavage or Fragment: An Empirical Analysis on the Social Stratification of the Contemporary China*, Beijing: Social Science Academic Press 2005.
75. It must be noted here that in Chinese academia, *class* is a term lacking a clear definition. Because of the tremendous changes in social structure and stratifying mechanisms, it is difficult to describe clearly the process of the change based on a class categorisation with a certain class theory such as traditional Marxist class theory, Neo-Marxist class theory (Erik Olin Wright's class schema) or Neo-Weberian class theory (John Goldthorpe's class schema). The problems in these approaches are two-fold. First of all they do not have proper concepts for a society where the capitalists and the cadres coexist as upper classes. Secondly, these theories do not have concepts for processes of class relations in post-communist societies. Having said that, it should be emphasised that most of the empirical results presented here are not very sensitive to the operationalisation differences linked with particular theoretical models. Most of the results would be either exactly the same or very much in the same direction if we were using different models of class schemas (Markku Kivinen 'The difficult road to welfare', in Jouko Nikula & Mihail Chernysh (eds): *Social Class in the Russian Society*, Saarbrücken: Lambert Academic Publishing AG & Co. 2010, pp. 125–139.). Consequently, we argue that the basic analysis of class structuration on this synthetic level would be relevant whatever model we would use. This does not mean that there would not be open issues as far as interests and consciousness are concerned. Chinese researchers usually prefer to use *Jieceng* (*stratum* in literal translation) instead of *Jieji* (*class* in literal translation) to refer to different social or class groups. In this context, class categorisations adopted by Chinese researchers usually have more detailed categories in order to reflect changes of social, economic and institutional transformation.
76. Li Chunling, *Formation of Middle Class in Comparative Perspective: Process, Influence and Socioeconomic Consequences*, Beijing: Social Science Academic Press 2009.
77. Li, Qiang, 'Middle class and Middle stratum', *Transaction of Renming University*, No.4, 2001; Zhou, Xiaohong, *Survey on Chinese middle class,* Beijing: Social Science Academic Press 2005.
78. Lu Xueyi (ed.), *Social Structure of Contemporary China*. Beijing: Social Sciences Academic Press 2010, p. 362.
79. Sun, Lipin, *Cleavage: Chinese Society since 1990s*, Beijing: Social Science Academic Press 2003.
80. Studying welfare in rural China, Lily Tsai argues that differences in public goods provision are consequences of informal village-level institutions that enmesh officials in webs of obligation and responsibility. Based on a

combination of in-depth case study research and an original survey of 316 villages in rural China, Tsai shows that even when formal accountability is weak, local officials can be subject to unofficial rules. These are provided by encompassing and embedding solidary groups. Lily L. Tsai, 'Solidary Groups, Informal Accountability, and Local Public Goods Provision in Rural China', *American Political Science Review*, Vol. 101 (2), May 2007, pp. 355–372. Cf. discussion on Meri Kulmala's studies on Russia above.

81. Markku Kivinen, *Progress and Chaos. Russia as a Challenge for Sociological Imagination*, Helsinki: Kikimora Publications 2002, pp. 207–221; Kivinen 2007 *op.cit.*, pp. 248–257. Analysing post-communist labour in comparative perspective, Chen and Sil argue that while organised labour may be weak in both Russia and China, this can be explained by fundamentally different mechanisms. Russian labour, while more autonomous from the state, has been too fragmented to organise widespread protest, whereas Chinese labour, while organisationally unified, is not autonomous enough from the state to even consider challenging it. Calvin Chen and Rudra Sil, 'Communist Legacies, Postcommunist Transformations and the Fate of Organised Labor in Russia and China', *Studies in Comparative International Development*, Vol. 41 (2), pp. 62–87. See also Pringle and Clarke, *The Challenge of Transition*, p. 202.

4
Authoritarianism or Democracy?

Christer Pursiainen and Minxin Pei

The Freedom House comparison, which measures 'freedom' as the opportunity for citizens to act spontaneously in a variety of fields outside the control of the government and other centres of potential domination, listed both Russia and China as 'not free' in 2011. In a separate evaluation of 'political rights' and 'civil liberties', on a scale of 1 to 7, Russia receives 6 and 5 and China 7 and 6 respectively, thus ending up in the worst class of countries. According to this data and interpretation, while China has remained authoritarian, the Russian authoritarian turn took place in 2005; until then Russia had been 'partly free' since the early 1990s.[1] This evaluation might be open to question, but it reflects rather well the picture drawn from the perspective of liberal democracy as a model. The tumultuous reforms in Russia under Boris Yeltsin in the 1990s initially generated enormous hopes for the country's transformation into a liberal democracy based on a market economy. However, the optimism of the 1990s turned out to be unfounded when Vladimir Putin, handpicked by Yeltsin, assumed the presidency and proceeded to install a new form of authoritarian rule. In the Chinese case, the post-1989 era has also ushered in a more distinctive form of post-communist autocracy, which has demonstrated an enormous capacity for adaptation and survival.

The post-communist experiences of Russia and China, though different in many crucial aspects, raise important theoretical questions. What are the factors responsible for the re-emergence of post-communist authoritarian rule in Russia, and what has led the transformation of China's post-Maoist regime into an adaptive autocracy that has successfully delivered impressive economic performance and consolidated its hold on power against strong odds? What are the defining characteristics of these regimes? How do these regimes maintain legitimacy and their hold on power? What are the internal political dynamics of these regimes? What ideological forces animate the thinking of the ruling elites and inform their policy choices? What are their institutional weaknesses and political vulnerabilities? What are the prospects of fundamental change in these two regimes? This chapter addresses these crucial questions vis-à-vis Russia and China with a comparable but flexible set of arguments arising from both structural and process-related approaches.

Russia

Analysing Russia's political system has never been an unambiguous task. There were fundamentally different ways to interpret the Soviet political system, and there are even more disagreements about post-Soviet developments and Russia's present political system. While Russia has established formal democratic power institutions, most scholars agree that Russia does not deserve to be labelled a genuine democracy; there is no consensus about how democratic it was in the 1990s, or how exactly it should be labelled today.[2] Put into the wider context of democratisation studies, Russia is seen at best as a perfect example of the more general trend of "democracy with adjectives",[3] without, however, any clear, shared criteria for describing this kind of mixed system. Russia's current political system has been characterised as *managed, manipulated, imitated, partial, imperfect, semi-, illiberal, pseudo-, virtual, oligarchic*, or, in the preferred term of Russia's current leaders, a *sovereign democracy*. If the focus is placed on the authoritarian features, we encounter such concepts as *electoral, competitive, soft, moderate, bureaucratic, new, non-repressive, non-ideological, 'user-friendly', 'zombie'*, or even *'vegetarian'* authoritarianism. Some authors prefer to avoid the value-laden words 'democracy' and 'authoritarianism' and use concepts such as *grey zone system, mixed system*, or *hybrid regime*. Often the emphasis is placed on political economy, or on the intertwined system of political and economic elites, and then concepts such as *bureaucratic capitalism, oligarchic capitalism, crony capitalism*, or *petro-state* are used, to name but a few.[4]

These concepts nevertheless give us a few hints about how the Russian political system is perceived. The majority, or at least a very visible part, of the scholarship has so far interpreted Russia explicitly or implicitly from the perspective of a failed transition, and treat it. more or less. as an anomaly. The explanation for this anomaly is looked for either in the underlying structural determinants, which are emphasised by the modernisation school; in the political processes, agency and institutions, which are emphasised by the transition school; or in the characteristics of Russia's political and economic elite and their internal power struggles, which are emphasised by the neo-Kremlinologian school based on investigative journalism. Thus, issues such as biased socioeconomic development, the lack of democratic political culture, the underdevelopment of civil society, the under-institutionalisation of the party system, 'superpresidentialism', over-personalised political processes, or simply such characteristics of Russia's leadership as greed or intolerance, have all been marshalled to explain why Russia does not match the picture of a liberal Western democracy. Let us discuss these and related issues in more detail, adopting, however, an a priori open-ended approach to Russia's transformation, where both structural preconditions and process-related factors intertwine and affect each other.

What was the essence of the Soviet political system?

In order to analyse Russia's political transformation, it is useful to look at the situation it started from. Much of the discussion on the essence of the Soviet system resembles the current discussion on Russia. Besides Kremlinology, which concentrated on the power struggle at the top levels of party and government while trying to break 'the code of Soviet jargon',[5] the more theoretical and dominating Sovietological school of thought was the so-called totalitarian model, which tried to grasp 'the essence of the Soviet political system'. According to that model, the Soviet system was defined by six major characteristics: an official ideology, a single party, a police force willing to use terror, a centrally directed economy, a party monopoly on the media, and a party monopoly on the armed forces.[6] Others put this totalitarian model more simply, merely stating that the essence of the system was the centralised control of political power, or a command system. While being theoretically very simplified, the importance of this model was that in order to recognise change, it was necessary to define the essential nature of the system, and then one could conclude that changes in this essence affect all other parts of the system.[7]

Some scholars eventually started to consider that perhaps it would be possible for the Soviet Union to evolve in a more instrumental direction, namely from a totalitarian and ideological system, under the pressure of the social forces emerging from modernisation.[8] It had already been argued, in the 1960s, that the source of change in the

Soviet system lies in the immanent systemic crisis of totalitarianism, which would ultimately lead to a decline in effectiveness, legitimacy and stability. In order to manage the crisis, the Soviet Union would be soon forced to become more tolerant of the expression of diverse opinions, and therefore, should the regime want to survive, it should allow for a certain amount of competition for power among rivals, and the possibility of the formation of at least temporary informal coalitions.[9]

From the early 1960s onwards however, this totalitarian model was criticised for misinterpreting the whole nature of the Soviet political system. It was challenged by different bureaucratic models which emphasised the organisational and corporative character of the Soviet system. From the late 1960s onwards, pluralistic models emerged, which paid attention to the diffusion of power between different interest groups. This school claimed that the interest groups can and do exercise influence and share political power in the Soviet policy process. The empirical source of this new interpretation was naturally the perceived change of the post-Stalinist political system. However, representatives of this school reminded their readers that the top Soviet leaders are not only articulators of group interests, but at the same time are also leaders in their respective fields of responsibility and can force the groups to follow certain policies.[10]

In fact, we argue here that both views were correct. The totalitarian school focused on the few main features of the system that made it different from the liberal democracies. The interest group school could draw a more precise picture of the realities: it opened the Soviet 'black box' and found in it, perhaps not surprisingly, many features common to most political systems. To some extent these two models were incompatible as they worked on different levels of interpretation.

After the collapse of the Soviet Union, these schools blamed each other for not having been able to understand the change. The representatives of the totalitarian school were the more aggressive, arguing that the totalitarian school, for all its faults, kept the focus on the central and unique features of the system and offered the basis for measuring change. The new models, losing any basis for measuring, they argued, had gone too far and mistaken the direction of change as evolution towards a liberal system. Therefore the new models could not recognise that the old system had to collapse before such liberal development became a serious possibility.[11] To be fair though, one should mention that the representatives of the totalitarian school also failed to forecast the fate of the Soviet system in late 1980s.

Civil society in embryo

From the point of view of holistic social change, it is important to understand the social realities of the Soviet Union, especially the issue of civil society, which was discussed in the previous chapter from the point of view of the autonomy and influence of social classes. This issue was a neglected area of study in Western Sovietology, and unsurprisingly even more so in the Soviet social sciences, but since the collapse of the communist system it has received some attention. The mainstream argument is that there was no civil society in the Soviet Union; that in Russia the short period of civil society development, about half a century, was interrupted by the October revolution of 1917 and was renewed only at the end of the 1980s.[12] Of course, there were also organisations and associations in the Soviet Union which were not only party organisations, or oppressed clandestine opposition or dissident organisations. For instance, the ecological movement in Russia dates back at least to 1924 when the All-Russian Association for Nature Conservation was established.[13] Nevertheless, the mere existence of organisations was not enough for the existence of a civil society; after all, some elements of civil society (family, working community, social organisations) can – and do – appear under totalitarian regimes. Nevertheless, the lack of the necessary conditions which could ensure their independence from political power and their right to self-governance and independent activity makes it impossible to consider such a society a civil one.[14]

Nevertheless, in contrast to the notion of the total absence of civil society in the Soviet Union, some scholars have put forward a somewhat broader view, or definition, of civil society.[15] This view starts from the remark that the disappearance of civil society is a typical technocratic utopia, which cannot ever completely materialise. Instead, the paradox of totalitarianism was exactly located in the fact that it could never destroy the roots of civil society. Within totalitarianism itself, there remained the seeds of an alternative social-economic project. However, totalitarianism did succeed in thoroughly changing the nature of civil society. It was able to push civil society to the edge of the public sphere, and often far beyond it. When access to the public sphere was blocked, civil society managed to seek a way into the kind of power structures in which the articulation of individual and group identities could be secured. This kind of sphere was found on the margin of the public sphere – in one's family and one's circle of friends. This constituted a 'civil society in embryo'. In the absence of open, public engagement, this kind of a civil society found its expression in stories, narratives, songs, jokes, anecdotes and rumours. This strategy – an escape into micro-groups – enabled criticism of political practices in a special way, with the help of semantic, coded communication forms, which were widely popular in some social groupings.

When one looks at Soviet society, it is easy to find examples of those kinds of civil society practices as described above, based on informal human links and initiatives.[16] One could go further by arguing that it was not only a question of informal micro-groups but also subcultures with some informal – but still, to some extent, institutionalised – social patterns that developed independently of, or often as a reaction to, the official Soviet culture and its institutions, rules, and norms. In a way, an alternative, unofficial public sphere was developing in the Soviet Union under the conditions of modernisation. Spontaneous convergence and the transnationalisation of values, consumption, popular taste and cultural habits took place in spite of the repressive actions of the regime.

From above *and* from below

Emphasising the existence of a kind of a silent protest and the existence of a shadow civil society in the Soviet Union raises the question of whether the communist system collapsed from above or from below. In most analyses, the Gorbachevian *perestroika* period has been understood as a typical revolution from above,[17] opposing an interpretation that stresses the role of popular opposition to the system from below. The collapse of the old system should be interpreted so that those 'democratic forces', which overthrew the ruling Communist Party of the Soviet Union (CPSU), had grown from within the nomenklatura itself, not from grass roots level movements. By the end of *perestroika,* the majority of the political and economic elite – though not all – would have concluded that their own well-being, as well as Russia's modernisation, would best be served within a capitalist – and perhaps, a democratic – system. This section of the nomenklatura was willing to get rid of the CPSU, because the party failed to adopt a cohesive modernisation strategy and had ceased to satisfy the needs of the elite. Regional elites also had an important role in the process of dismantling the party structures. For this majority of the elite, the coup d'état in August 1991 proved that the CPSU could not serve as the vehicle for the fundamental social change that would enable Russia's modernisation, or 'catching up with the West' which had proved its superiority in dealing with the post-industrial phase of modernisation.

However, another school interpreted this period in quite the opposite way – as a *perestroika* from below[18] – focusing on late-Soviet grass roots developments, and offering a much more complex interplay between the state elite and non-state actors than is suggested by the revolution-from-above interpretation. Given the two-level nature of Soviet society (the official and the unofficial), it was not long before an alternative public sphere, beyond state control, had stealthily come into being. Several kinds of groupings came out of kitchens and basements and into the public sphere, if not always literally then at least mentally. As control and punishment rules concerning anti-Soviet propaganda were loosened in the spring 1987, many groups that were anti-system in spirit became more visible and began to use the language of politics. On the semi-official side, public 'discussions' and '*perestroika* clubs' in the spirit of *glaznost* (openness) were organised. At that time, many dissidents returned from their punishment institutions, and utilised the situation to organise seminars and movements which, unlike *perestroika* clubs, went beyond the internal criticism of the socialist system.

Naturally we can find a school of thought that combines these two perspectives. This in fact, to our mind, seems to be the most reasonable description, or even explanation, for the collapse of the old system. From this point of view, the developments during the phase of transition "included cycles of reforms and cycles of protest".[19] Gorbachev's *perestroika* consciously adopted a policy that opened up opportunities for public discourse and organisational development. In this sense, the institutional revolution came from above, though the real mobilisation of society took place independently within these new conditions. The common enemies of the newly mobilised civil society of the *perestroika* period were the nomenklatura and Stalinism. Also the Slavophilism-inspired national patriots, who advocated new versions of the century-old 'Russian idea' and Russia's corresponding global–political entitlements, re-emerged during these years.[20]

At this stage of the Soviet Union's transformation, as has been noted by some scholars, there was only a negative consensus in society – a consensus strong enough to create the preconditions for the demolition of the old system but not strong enough for defining the basic characteristics of the new one, let alone its final goals. Ultimately this means that any further reforms were possible only from above.[21]

Market reforms and democracy – interrelated, but how?

If accepted, the interpretation put forward above would explain the rather authoritarian path of the original reform process in the Russian

Federation, combined with the rather anarchic and non-institutionalised civil society and poor state–society relations. However, many of the current representatives of Western(ised) Russian studies are not satisfied with the rather vague notions produced by much of the sociological and historical analysis. Therefore the issue has often become to measure, in the spirit of positivism, the 'cause' of Russia's 'anomaly'. The potential structural factor in this context which is usually discussed first, the relationship between democracy and socioeconomic development, is a debate where one can find not only several answers, but also several possible interrelationships.[22] In our case the issue is not whether or not democracy has a positive causal effect on socioeconomic development – a contested issue in itself – but is, rather, the other way around: whether socioeconomic development levels have a causal effect on democratisation. It has been argued that because most of the consolidated democracies seem to do rather well in terms of socioeconomic development, it is reasonable to suggest that this factor would also have a positive causal effect for the consolidation of democracies after their break with authoritarian or totalitarian rule.[23] Empirical evidence seems to prove that there is indeed a positive correlation.[24]

This issue has been studied with regard to Russia, and the conclusion is that "Russia is an underachiever in democratisation for its level of economic development".[25] Basically this is an argument which posits that there is nothing in the general economic development level of Russia that would preclude it from becoming democratic. Another related issue is the nature of this wealth, especially the causal effect of natural resources – n the case of Russia, most notably oil and gas – on democratisation. Scholars have found a positive correlation between a country's dependence on natural resources and a low level of democratisation. While there are several plausible causal links explaining this correlation, in Russia's case the effects of, firstly, corruption, which undermines public and elite support for open politics, and, secondly, distorted economic liberalisation and economic statism, have been put forward as explanations.[26]

Another relevant argument in the Russian context is that a relatively egalitarian income distribution would have a positive effect on democratisation,[27] which naturally would mean that in Russia the case is the opposite, characterised as it is by economic inequality. Both of these issues lead the discussion to Russia's market reforms and their effect on Russia's political system.

Some theorists consider a market economy as a precondition for democracy and its basic elements such as civil society, and even as a precondition for a transition process towards democracy. The absence of a market economy, "which is the real basis for civil society", would have made the existence of civil society in the Soviet Union virtually impossible.[28] In general, the idea that private property and a market economy is a precondition of civil society, and that the functioning of these institutions in turn necessitates a functioning civil society, is as widespread in Russian political thought as it is in Western political thought.[29] It has been argued that the lack of economic liberalisation in Russia "retarded the development of independent social organisations and the socioeconomic bases for the development of such groups, and circumscribed the autonomy of the organisations that did emerge".[30]

While this 'no market economy means no democracy' formula prevails in many political studies, the issue is nonetheless contested. Indeed, it is sometimes noted even in mainstream Russian debates (and not only in leftist debates and debates on alternative civil society)[31] that under certain conditions a free market economy can create real obstacles to the effective realisation of the principles of pluralistic democracy, or might even undermine those principles.[32]

In classical Western political science on democracy, there is kind of a compromise argument which states that there is no unambiguous connection between democracies, democratisation, and a market economy.[33] The close empirical link between twentieth-century democracy and the presence of an advanced market economy is, obviously, quite clear. However, the exact nature of the relationship of a market economy to democracy, or especially democratisation, is puzzling. The market economy and democracy facilitate and favour each other in multiple ways, but the sequence in which they emerge is not determined: which comes first? The Western world has followed a modernisation path where democratisation precedes and ultimately favours socioeconomic market-oriented developments. On the other hand, the market economy can precede democracy, or the developments can take place more or less simultaneously.

The latter was supposed to be the case for Russia, but there is no clear consensus on how the market economy reforms have affected democratisation. It is, however, difficult to claim that the market reforms in Russia would have been democratic in themselves. A more contested issue is whether their outcome has enhanced or hindered democratisation. This issue is difficult to evaluate, not only because ideological and moral values are involved, but also because Russia's market reforms were not transparent. Only the very best investigative journalism, or neo-Kremlinology, has actually been able to get a hint of what was and is happening. Obscuring this is the fact that Russia's road to a market economy has included several phases; this theme was discussed in Chapter 3 in some detail. To be sure, it has not evolved 'naturally' from the socioeconomic conditions, but has been closely connected to politics and those in power, and therefore the causal arrows between the 'market economy reforms' and 'democratisation' are difficult to analyse. The 'West', with its advices and political and financial support, has tried to affect this development, often with a poor understanding of, and influence on, what was really happening.

Some scholars have argued that post-communist change has its own limitations, compared to, for instance, Latin American dictatorships which already had a market economy. Economic change can occur without political change in a post communist state, as China has demonstrated, but the "very organisation of communist regimes meant that political change could not occur without economic change".[34] Should we agree with that, we would exclude the possibility that some kind of a democratic socialism could have been developed from Soviet Communism, which was perhaps the goal of Gorbachev at some point during *perestroika* – "not less but more socialism, not less but more democracy!" as the slogan went. From this point of view it has quite rationally been concluded that

> the limited success of democracy in the post-communist world keeps alive the hypothesis that simultaneous economic and political change is less likely to succeed [to reach liberal democracy] than regime changes undertaken in capitalist economies in which the fundamental organisation of the economy is not subject to negotiation.[35]

In more detailed studies, it has been proposed that the causal effect of this 'dual transition' is that the elites in power, having accumulated economic benefits during the market reforms, fear democratic accountability and therefore hinder further democratic developments from above.[36]

Does Russia have a democratic political culture?

Most radical or liberal democracy theorists agree with the statement that "if the political institutions of a country are not supported by a strong democratic political culture, they may give way to authoritarianism when the country faces a severe crisis".[37] So, does Russia have a democratic political culture, and if so, how would we know that? While in principle the majority of analysts confirm that the emergence of a democratic political culture would be needed, the degree to which this goal had been realised in Russia creates great scepticism. There is no consensus among scholars about the present state of Russian political culture. As early as the 1990s some commentators took the view that it would not be possible to transplant the type of democratic political culture developed in the West into the conservative Russian soil for a long time to come.[38] To the contrary, others believed that Russia has always had – in addition to, or parallel with its authoritarian political culture – an alternative, democratic political culture.[39] A third school of thought suggested that the latter view is partly true, but with the qualification that the authoritarian political culture has always been dominant and the democratic political culture has, at best, been expressed as a periodic social reaction against certain acts of the state.[40] Looking at the current situation, empirical evidence can be marshalled to support any of these views, and none of them can easily be rejected.

Currently, the obvious puzzle for any Western-minded observer is why Russia's authoritarianism, unlike the Chinese regime, "survives even though elites and ordinary people alike view it as dysfunctional and uninspiring".[41] Would it have something to do with the political culture, its lack of 'democrativeness'? One way of evaluating the 'democrativeness' of Russia's political culture has been to consider 'public attitudes'. There are some comparative large-N case analyses on mass attitudes concerning phenomena such as trust or intolerance. It has been concluded that Russia is clearly an underachiever compared to other countries if we look at public attitudes and the real level of democracy; that is, with the existing level of trust and tolerance that its population demonstrates in opinion polls, Russia would quite well match many democratic countries, whereas its political system does not mach these civic virtues.[42] One qualitative review of Russian attitudes about democracy from the 1990s to the early 2000s argued that the public at large had never questioned the need for transition towards a democratic system of governance and political freedom. At the same time there was a clear decline in the importance that the general public attached to various democratic institutions and rights from the late 1990s onwards. Not surprisingly, the public ranks such social and legal rights as equality before the law, public safety, the right to a job and education, and so forth, higher than political rights. The majority thinks that effective means of influencing the authorities do not exist: only about one-fifth of the population considers taking part in elections to be such a means, and even less would put their hopes in taking part in the activities of parties or public organisations. At the same time there is overwhelming trust in the argument that only leaders and experts and those with experience ought to govern the country and find the correct path. In a poll conducted in 2000, almost half thought that the cause of social transformation was President Putin.[43] More recent surveys, taken in Russia on rather a regular basis, give similar yet also somewhat contradictory answers. For instance, while most Russian seem to think that elections are important as a political instrument, simultaneously the prevailing opinion has been that elections do not reflect public opinion.[44]

Nevertheless it remains difficult, if not impossible, to measure the 'democrativeness' of Russia's political culture with any unambiguous parameters. And it is even more difficult to 'scientifically' evaluate its causal effect on the political system in ways other than including qualitative, culture-informed considerations in the empirical interpretations. However, it should be mentioned that, contrary to many observers who see the emergence of the Putin regime only in terms of manipulation and high-level power struggles, some researchers have studied the origins of this regime: they emphasise that it was also deeply rooted in social networks, though not at the level of ordinary people's civic organisations but rather at the level of a wide-range of business and administrative elites.[45]

A mass society or a civil society?

The question of the absence or weakness of a democratic political culture has often been dealt with while making reference to the differences between a monolithic mass society and a pluralist society. In the previous chapter, it was argued that Russia belongs to the former type of society: "Mass society is the naked society, a society without collective action organisations that clothe and protect individuals from excesses of government."[46] Even where formal channels based on popular representation do exist – such as the right to vote in elections – a mass society is not capable of controlling the exercise of power by the state, or its political and economic elites. The basic components of the rule of law – such as adequate legal protection against arbitrary decisions by public officials, or the equality of citizens before the law – may be guaranteed in theory, but in practice they will still be infringed. In contrast, a pluralist society, characterising a more participatory model of democracy, is more effectively organised into a variety of material and ideological interest groups and the society participates through these groups in promoting its own interests and criticising and controlling the exercise of power by the administrative and other elites. In discussing countries where civic traditions are weak, it is exactly a functioning of this kind of a civil society that is usually seen as constituting the hitherto missing key to successful democratisation.[47]

What is the state of Russian civil society today in practice? Is there an institutionalised civil society in the first place, and if so, what kind of a civil society it is? It seems very clear to us that an institutionalised civil society developed in Russia in the 1990s. According to one analysis, four periods of the formation of the new Russian civil society could *already* be identified during the very first years of the new Russia. The first period would have been 1990–1992, largely based on volunteers' activities and new relations with Western non-governmental organisations (NGOs). The second period (1992–1994) was characterised by new methods in new conditions, and was already largely influenced by learning from Western examples. The third period (1994–96) saw a more robust civil society with extended self-sufficiency, an emerging legal framework on NGOs, as well as some dialogue between parts of civil society and parts of the state. During this time, the theme also became a popular subject of study by Russian and foreign social scientists. The fourth period, from 1996 onwards, was seen as an era of potential stabilisation.[48]

We agree with this analysis to the extent that although new periods can be added, the question is no longer about whether there is or is not a civil society in Russia. It already emerged during the 1990s, it has grown steadily in terms of the number of organisations, and in some issue areas or territorial areas parts of it have been and continue to be grow and be very active. The 'non-commercial organisations' (NCOs) are registered with the Ministry of Justice and the official statistics are held by the Federal Taxation Agency and the Federal State Statistics Service. In 2005 the official figure was 480,183 NCOs,[49] whereas in January 2009 it was 731,240. This is not a lot compared to the population of Russia vis-à-vis Western societies. However, these official figures do not support the popular view that Russian civil society is again dying or shrinking, but rather suggest the opposite. Yet, a closer analysis has shown that only half of them belong to the non-profit sector as an institution of civil society in the sense of a 'genuine' NGO. Moreover, every new official investigation, usually made on a regional or local basis, reveals a number of 'dead souls', which are then deregistered. Nevertheless, there is no non-ambiguous data on active NGOs in the Russian Federation available, since the definition of a 'public organisation' or NCO or NGO vary from one year, estimation, or register to another. [50]

However, it has been roughly estimated that about two-thirds of Russian non-commercial organisations could be genuine NGOs and, of these, perhaps only 25 per cent are active in different parts of Russia.[51] Because in official statistics the NGOs or NCOs are registered according to their legal status, it is difficult to estimate their sphere and level of activity. While interest, leisure, and different types of social welfare organisations make up the majority, less than 10 per cent work in fields that are directly political or are political pressure organisations. In any case, all of this suggests that the picture is not as gloomy as one might conclude after the rather pessimistic evaluations of many analysts and politicians who claimed that there is no civil society in Russia. Also, random empirical investigations, in the field or on the internet, can assure anyone that there are plenty of civil society activities taking place in Russia. Russian civil society may be shallow and fragile, but it does exist.

Before late-2011 it was easy to conclude that the nature of this activity was different from that of the turbulent years of the late 1980s and early 1990s. However, the large-scale public anti-regime protests that started in Russia in connection with the national elections show that a large-scale mobilisation of the population is possible at the grass roots level, especially by utilising social media. Whether this will bring about a deeper change in Russia civil society, or the political system at large, is hard to predict, however.

Against the state or within the state?

As to the civil society coordinated into formal organisations, the question then becomes that of what kind of relationship has developed between civil society and the Russian state machinery. It might be more reasonable not to define one exact relationship, but rather to try to identify the dominant model. During the later years of *perestroika*, one could already differentiate between several kinds of civil society–state relations, depending on the nature of the group in question. One type of relation was cooperation, the opposite complete antagonism. In between these alternatives one could find such relationships or strategies as, for instance, attempted pre-emption: the respective state organ adopted some of the goals of the association in question and tried to deny its legitimacy. Another strategy was an attempted co-option: if the respective state organ had to eventually accept the existence of the association, it tried to subordinate it under official control. A more modest approach was benign tolerance, meaning that state agencies paid little, if any, attention to the existence of the association or group.[52] After twenty years, the picture of the civil society–state relationship remains as complex as ever, and all of the above forms of relationship or state strategies (and perhaps many more) can be found in contemporary Russia.

Nevertheless, looking the same issue from the civil society point of view, it can be claimed that a certain institutionalised development from the 'against the state' pattern towards the 'with(in) the state' pattern can be identified. The rights and duties of these public associations are already defined in various federal and regional laws and regulations. This development had already started in the mid-1990s: many then acknowledged that the legislative base had been improved, and politicians slowly developed a better understanding of the fact that NGOs have a certain impact and influence on voters and can thereby affect the popularity of political leaders. We can argue that, in the 1990s, a great part of Russian civil society perceived the development as a process of gradually moving towards a less antagonistic civil society–state relationship. This was especially so in relation to the socially-oriented civil society, which was ready to function as the third sector, taking care of many of the functions that the Russian state was unwilling or economically unable to manage. Whereas NGOs in more sensitive issue areas such as human rights, whose direct objects of criticism were the deeds and practices of the authorities, or in any foreign-related activities where some perceived hostile political purposes were involved, did less well with the authorities.

In principle, this trend, where the active civil society was divided into 'constructive' and 'non-constructive' parts by the authorities, was institutionalised when Russia entered the new century. A new development in civil society–state relations started in 2001, when the then President Putin introduced a new approach to civil society. This policy change, which culminated in a Civic Forum organised in the Kremlin in November 2001, with over 5000 representatives of Russian NGOs, divided into 21 working groups in the very spirit of civil society–state dialogue. At the time, after his first year in charge, this move was interpreted as Putin choosing a new model of development for Russia. He would have faced a choice between two models for modernising Russia. In the first, authoritarian, model, bureaucracy would serve as the primary instrument of government while society would be passive and subject to manipulation. The second model would be one of more democratic modernisation based on active partnership between the state and society. Putin, it was claimed, began his presidency with the first model, but he realised that it was not working and started to seek new resources and supporters for a more stable and effective modernisation – yet still within the conditions set by the political elite.[53]

At the same time it was claimed by more critical voices that, from the very beginning, this new approach was only a matter of political tactics, carried out in order to imitate a developed civil society–state relationship, supporting the ruling authority while discriminating against a critical civil society that put forward alternative ways of development.[54]

In any case, the Kremlin's new attitude finally found institutional expression in a new body aimed at connecting the state and civil society, the so-called Public Chamber. It started activity in 2005. The idea was that this body, formally based on the representatives of Russian NGOs, particularly monitors the State Duma's activities by having a formal right to be heard when new legislation is adopted. However, it is clear that the body cannot be regarded as an independent institution. The president has the right to nominate 42 members – one-third of the total – who will in turn nominate another 42 members from NGOs, and these members will then select the final one-third of the chamber.[55] Early on, critics of these developments pointed out that the approach that was started in 2001 was actually nothing more than building a "Potemkin civil society", thus "letting the NGOs tell the Russian leaders what they want to hear".[56]

However, we argue that it was, and remains, easy to find examples of how the Russian state apparatus, including federal, regional, and local executive and legislative bodies, is not a coherent, unitary actor. Rather it can be understood as a complex bureaucracy, including several rivalries, conflicting interests, overlapping roles, and consequently different attitudes towards civil society actors. Given this, in many or perhaps even in most cases, civil society agents may have both allies and enemies within the state or more local administrative apparatus. In most cases the authorities lack the ability to form a cohesive strategy towards the civil society. Furthermore, civil society–state relations also vary across regions: some regions seem to have a more-developed and others a less-developed political culture. Given that the Russian decision-making and political system today is a battlefield of several interests and ideas, even an imitated institutionalisation of civil society–state relationship might produce some promising opportunities for civil society actors for a more participatory role in policy-making. Perhaps, as time goes on, the current approach and top-down state-society institutions cooperating only with the 'constructive' part of the civil society, could serve as a more democratic platform for a genuine civil society–state relationship, allowing civil society to also put forward alternative ways of development.

So far this seems not to be the case. The critical civil society has been left outside of any institutionalised dialogue and formally its situation has worsened. In 2006 a new law on non-governmental organisations increased the power of the Justice Ministry to monitor NGOs, which in practice has turned out to be a way of attacking critical civil society groups. The law stipulates particularly high criteria for organisations receiving foreign funding. Additionally, in 2008, the tax-exempt status was removed from most foreign NGOs by a presidential decree. A partial step towards a more tolerant approach was taken in July 2009, when President Medvedev signed into law amendments to simplify registration and reporting procedures for the NGOs and to make inspections less frequent.[57]

While, during the current regime, there have frequently been rather small-scale and spontaneous demonstrations against the authorities' decisions in issues which usually concern people's lives in concrete terms, such as income or neighbourhood building projects, a more principles-focused opposition has been organised in an unexpected alliance of 'dissident march' (*marsh nesoglasnyh*); these have gathered together small groupings, reaching from ultra-communists to liberal human rights watchers. Referring to the 31st article of the Constitution, which allows demonstrations and free expression of opinion, the group has regularly organised public gatherings on the 31st day of the month, especially in Moscow. The fact that these gatherings were usually not allowed, were pushed into the outskirts, or even suppressed by the police, showed that the Russian state genuinely fears this bottom-up discontent. The threat scenario is clearly what happened in Ukraine during the 'Orange Revolution'. As this was interpreted in the Russian leadership as a bottom-up minority revolt manipulated by and with the encouragement of the West, organisations with foreign contacts and funding in particular have become the object of legislative restrictions and punishment measures.

The 2011/2012 mass anti-regime protests which gathered together tens of thousands (or more) demonstrators in the capital and many other major cities – many of them previously completely inexperienced in this kind of activity – shows that the 'colour revolution' scenario has some potential in Russian society, even if there is no obvious political elite or leadership alternative on the opposition side. While originally interpreted as a West-inspired and manipulated movement by the Russian leadership, when faced with a multitude of demonstrators it soon adopted a more moderate tune, partially opening the door for dialogue.

The 'authoritarian turn'

When and how, then, did Russia's political system become what it is now, a semi-democratic or semi-authoritarian regime? While there are a variety of ways to define democracy and its various real life expressions,[58] Dahl's eight classic criteria for liberal democracy are usually taken as the zero definition of democracy in the majority of transition literature and also in Russian studies: the right to vote; the right to be elected; the right of political leaders to compete for support and votes; elections that are free and fair; freedom of association; freedom of expression; alternative sources of information; and institutions that depend on votes and other expressions of preference.[59] Many others have developed these criteria by adding some procedural and operative principles and conditions.[60] From these rather 'minimalist' democracy definitions, located within the Schumpeterian tradition which puts competitive elections at the centre of the democracy definition, one can naturally move far towards 'maximalist' definitions that focus on participatory models of democracy.[61]

While Russia's 1993 Constitution has a democratic pathos and undoubtedly includes all the classical criteria of liberal democracy and much more, by the end of the 1990s there was a rather widespread consensus among scholars that in practice Russia was not following a linear road from authoritarian rule towards a Western type of liberal democracy. The general spirit among scholars – in the Anglo–American political science discourse, and that part of the Russian domestic political science discourse that has adopted the same mainstream vocabulary and approaches – is that Russia has experienced a change of political system since the Soviet era but has not 'reached' a genuine democracy, or has perhaps even turned 'back' after the initial democratisation of the 1990s. That said, scholars do not agree upon where Russia is now, or where it is going. The title of a 2007 book, *Russia – Lost in Transition*,[62] is a good expression of the current state of affairs not only in Russia itself, but in the scholarship as well. There have been efforts to classify the rival views on Russia's degree of democracy or authoritarianism.[63] There are those who argue that Russia has endured a failed democratisation, and those who hold a democratic evolutionist view, putting their cautious optimism in the institutional potential of the existing constitutional order. Each side can marshal enough evidence to make their case.

A typical narrative of the authoritarian turn starts from around 2000 and goes as follows: it all started with the crushing of the independent media, beginning with television and later extending to increased state control over print and online media. After that came the reduction of the autonomy of regional governments and the taming of the Federation Council, the upper house of the parliament, by removing elected governors and heads of regional legislatures from their seats and replacing them with appointed representatives; this was followed by the abolition of the system of elected governors. Further, the autonomy of parliament was weakened by utilising the state-controlled media and the support of the now-tamed regional leaders to ensure Putin's own party, *United Russia*, an overwhelmingly dominant position in elections and consequently in parliament. At the same time, other political parties and their representatives were unfairly discriminated against in political processes. During Putin's second four-year term – from 2004 onwards – civil society and critical NGOs became the object of increased state control with new legislation that allowed them to be marginalised. This increasing authoritarianism was accompanied by a weak judicial system and nationalist propaganda which blamed the West for Russia's problems.[64] It has therefore been concluded that Russia today displays all the facets of limited political pluralism, and even if there still exists a system of formal multi-party electoral competition, Russia's authoritarianism can no longer be regarded as genuinely competitive.[65]

Very often, however, Putin and Medvedev's Russia has been presented as a truly, full-fledged authoritarian regime. In the less academic genres of Russian studies in particular, the definition of Russia's political system may sound rather harsh, almost Stalinist: "It is a brute force model, the main aspect of which is the use of force unfettered by any restrains – legal, traditional, or moral. That is the essence of brute force politics."[66] In this context, Russia's political system is understood as an extremely authoritarian regime that "rests on personalized power".[67] Put into more academic language, although political institutions are established in Russia, "political processes remain underinstitutionalized", focusing on "personalized ties rather than administrated procedures".[68] Some have argued that Putin's leadership, continued in the tandem regime with President Medvedev, represents a "distinctive type of neo-authoritarian stabilisation that did not repudiate the democratic principles of the constitutional order in which it existed, but which did not allow the full potential of the democratic order to emerge".[69] The 'sovereign democracy' – the term advanced by Russian leaders themselves, especially during the first decade of the millennium – is a "tutelary democracy", in which the free play of societal political competition is restrained, but the principles of pluralism are not repudiated. This regime is non-ideological in its spirit. Krastev has put this nicely: "The ease with which Russian elites recently shifted their slogan from 'sovereign democracy' to 'modernisation' exemplifies the post-ideological character of the current regime. It presents itself as a variant of, and not as an alternative to, Western democracy, and it has managed to adapt some key democratic institutions – most notably elections – for its own purposes."[70]

This kind of a hybrid regime can be seen as unstable. As Putin's power-base rests on mere patronage networks, bureaucracy, the security apparatus, and official state parties, and is not rooted in organised interests in society, it has been argued that this system of governance is clearly unsustainable in the long run. Therefore, Putin's (as it now has become clear, temporary) successor Medvedev "will either have to allow greater political pluralism and a deeper institutionalisation of constitutional processes, or make a radical turn towards overt authoritarianism".[71]

Yet in these debates it is often forgotten that when referring to Yeltsin's era the explanation for why the state did not democratise was also often said to be due to extremely personalised rather than institutionalised political processes, keeping the state almost completely detached from society. In this social scientific discursive context, it is not surprising that the less scientific Kremlinology, as a way of studying Russia's political system, has also had a renaissance. Neo-Kremlinology emphasises the need to study the Moscow power struggles closely in order to better understand Russian politics. Instead of the Communist Party top level, the focus is now on *oligarchs* (especially during the Yeltsin era) or *siloviki* (especially during the Putin–Medvedev era): who they are, where they came from, what their interests, relationships, and influence on political decision-making in different fields are?[72]

'Superpresidentialism' – the reason for failure?

Some scholars of Russia's political system have identified poor 'institutional design' as the main reason why democracy does not work or has not been consolidated in Russia.[73] Some see the *timing* of establishing these institutions as the main explanation, and in Russia the "brief window of opportunity when a democracy could have been built was missed" – meaning right after the failed August 1991 coup.[74] Let us take a closer look at these institutions. Representative democracies are usually divided between presidential and parliamentary models. The roots of Russia's 'superpresidentialism' are found in Russia's 1993 Constitution. This Constitution was born of the conflict between the reformist president and the conservative – or perhaps nationalist and communist – legislative body. Against the then-current Constitution, President Yeltsin forcibly dissolved the country's legislature, claiming public support on the basis of an earlier referendum that had supported his reform programme. The legislature responded by impeaching Yeltsin and proclaiming Vice President Aleksandr Rutskoy as acting president. The leaders of the anti-Yeltsin legislature were planning to establish a parliamentary republic with rather weak presidential power – something that the current critics of the Russian political system would mostly support – but this project was replaced by its opposite when President Yeltsin won the struggle by ordering tanks to shell the parliament. The West generally supported Yeltsin without hesitation.[75] A new Constitution was quickly drafted and confirmed by referendum, now emphasising the power of the president over parliament, with the aim of avoiding similar stalemate situations which could block reforms.

While some statistical studies focusing on other countries suggest that "presidentialism and party system fragmentation do not seem to affect consolidation",[76] in Russian studies the idea of 'superpresidentialism' is today often put forward as one of the main issues that hinder democracy.[77] In principle one can agree with the claim that parliamentary democracy, with its collective discussions and votes, is more transparent and therefore more easily monitored and controlled by the citizens than decision-making by the president in his cabinet surrounded by advisors, even if he has been elected democratically. Though the motivation for the presidential system may be, as was perhaps the case with Yeltsin, to stabilise the situation in order to democratise the political system afterwards, the weakness of the authoritarian, top-down model of democratisation or modernisation is the weak state–society link. In this context personal relations, corruption, and corporatist elites can easily take over the real decision-making power, leading to oligarchy instead of democracy.

This seems to have happened in Russia. According to analysis of elite recruitment patterns in Russia, the country is not led by politicians but by a technocratic elite. The leaders at different government levels, including the very highest level – namely the government itself – have only rarely entered office with previous experience as elected officials. Almost a third of them have earlier experience in uniformed services (that is, the *siloviki* structures), and most of the elite has spent their entire career in state service. The conclusion is that governance in Russia is characterised more by technocratic administration than by representing the diverse interests contained within society. [78]

Shrinking the alternatives

One of the characteristics of Soviet totalitarianism was a single-party system, whereas liberal democracy presupposes a multi-party system. Russia is, by any criteria, formally a multi-party system. The party system in Russia has been the subject of extensive study, though scholarly interest in these issues has eroded with the development towards a less competitive model of the system during the Putin–Medvedev regime. Issues such as fragmentation of the party system, weak partisanship among the citizenry, the nature of the parties as vehicles for single leaders rather than for a social movement, weak party organisations, the limited role of parties in influencing government policies, and the weak regional roles of parties, have usually been marshalled to support the argument for the undemocratic or non-consolidated nature of Russian democracy.[79] During Putin's first and second presidency terms, the scholarly argument of the limited penetration of parties into governance has been turned the other way round, and it has been claimed that the Putin administration's institutional reforms point towards more, rather than less, encroachment of the state into party politics, making Russia less than a fully-fledged multi-party democracy.[80] Surveys show that, to a large extent, the Russians themselves are rather sceptical about elections as a tool to affect politics.[81] Some scholars have tried to balance these claims by putting them into a more comparative perspective, for instance, by arguing that party politics not only in Russia but in general (or at least in Europe), is in crisis, and for many, parties appear obsolete as vehicles of popular mobilisation, identity, and interest formation.[82]

If one tries to characterise the development of the Russian party system, one striking feature is that the number of parties rose rapidly up until the mid-1990s, but since then has come down drastically. This development concerns both the parties that have been registered and those who actually have taken part in elections. This development is shown in Table 4.1.

This obvious trend clearly results from the conscious efforts of the Russian leaders to stabilise the party system, as well as the parliamentary processes. In 1995 the State Duma passed the 'Law on Parties', but it was never approved by the upper house Federation Council and the party system was regulated under the legislation regulating 'public organisations'. After Putin's rise to power, the work on a party law started anew and in 2001 a 'Law on Political Parties' was approved. The opponents of this law argued that it would give the administration too much power

Table 4.1 State Duma elections, 1993–2011: number of parties

State Duma elections	1993*	1995*	1999*	2003*	2007	2011
Eligible (registered) parties	91	258	139	73	15	7
Parties taking part in elections	13	43	26	23	11	7
Parties elected to the State Duma (from the party list)*	8	4	6	4	4	4
Participation rate %	54.81	64.4	61.85	55.75	63. 78	60.1
Election threshold %	5	5	5	5	7	7

Note: *Up until 2003 elections, additionally 50% of candidates (225 of 450) were selected from single-candidate districts with majority principle, who might or might not be party members, or join a party fraction, or establish their own fraction.

to discriminate against parties in the registration process, whereas its supporters saw it as a precondition for finally creating a working party system based on perhaps two or three major parties, following the example of Western democracies such as the US and UK. In principle, the Putin–Medvedev administrations have done exactly as was encouraged by the classic theorist of liberal democracy, Dahl, in this type of situation:

> [...] to reject this possibility of social engineering seems to me equivalent to the medical profession refusing to use antibiotics because they have been so widely abused. Aside from purely partisan manipulation, it is difficult to see why the deliberate attempt to reduce potential fragmentation through electoral engineering is inherently 'undemocratic,' or, even if it were, undesirable in a liberalizing hegemony.[83]

The requirements for registering a party were defined as rather strict, and since then the approval of the law has been subject to amendments, which have aimed to find a solution that would lead to the goal of diminishing the number of parties. In the current version, a party has to have a regional organisation in at least half of the constituent subjects (regions, and so on) of the Russian Federation, it has to have at least 40,000 members nationally, and 400 members in regional organisations.[84] According to these regulations, there were only 7 such parties that are registered by the Ministry of Justice and thus were in principle eligible to take part in the State Duma election in 2011,[85] whereas in 1995 the figure was 258! The recent amendments mean that the number of parties has continued to diminish, as compared to the 2007 elections.

Furthermore, the law regulating elections has been modified, a move which was officially motivated in order to achieve the same declared goals: a more effective and stable party system. Some scholars had argued that the mixed system of national State Duma election, where 225 candidates were chosen from party lists and 225 candidates from single-mandate districts with a majority principle, undermined the development of the party system as it allowed non-party popular candidates to enter the State Duma.[86] If this was so, the new election law approved in 2005 was a move towards a more consolidated party system as it abolished the single-mandate system. It has been argued that the previous single-mandate system would in fact have been beneficial for United Russia, the ruling party, in terms of its share of State Duma seats. But as the loyalty of these single-mandate parliamentarians was directed more towards the regional leaders and elite, they were difficult to manage and undermined the federal centre's power; thus it was better to abolish the system.[87] By increasing the election threshold from 5 to 7 per cent for parties entering the State Duma, the new law again aimed at moving towards a smaller number of parties. If one looks at the number of parties that have been selected (from the party list) to the State Duma, one can however see that the number has been stable since the mid-1990s.

It is a challenging task to draw the ideological map of Russia.[88] Russia is full of movements and small groupings, from anarchists to monarchists, and among them strange combinations such as liberal anti-Semites or socialist monarchists. Russia is truly a pluralistic society in this sense. Looking only at the party system, one could classify the Russian parties that emerged from the breakdown of the one-party system into four broad ideological categories. The *'centrist wing'* has been steadily growing in power and its current flagship *United Russia* is the clearly biggest party in the State Duma. In 2007 it received 64.3 per cent of all votes and 315 of the 450 seats; in 2011 it lost, but according to the official figures (which were heavily questioned by the opposition) it still received 49.3 per cent of all votes and 238 of the 450 seats, that is, over half of the seats. It has also managed to bring most of the regional leaders into party politics. This is the current 'party of power', the party of the Kremlin, and actually the first to manage to create an electoral majority for the sitting president and government.

The *'left wing'* includes communist parties of different kinds, who represent various degrees of yearning for the past, opposing market reforms in particular, and demanding more equality and a just social policy. Of the current parties represented in the State Duma, the anti-Kremlin *Communist Party of the Russian Federation* most clearly represents this orientation. The other leftist party in the State Duma, *Just Russia,* is a rather recent amalgam of some smaller leftist and national-patriotic parties that were apparently established with the consent of the Kremlin in order to create a more 'constructive' leftist variant.

The third ideological category, the *'reformist wing'*, includes a variety of movements from social–democratic to liberal or neo-liberal orientation, looking (to some extent) to Western societies as a model for the political and economic system. The anti-Kremlin *Yabloko* has ideological horizons reaching from social–democratic to liberal wings within the party. The *Right Cause,* established in 2008 from more right-wing and market-oriented neo-liberal parties (with perhaps the support of the Kremlin) can be seen as representing the reformist parties. Neither *Yabloko* nor the parties preceding the *Right Cause* managed to pass the 7 per cent threshold in the 2007 and 2011 elections.

The fourth category, the *'national-patriotic wing'*, stands for specific Russian traditional values and is seeking to reclaim the traditional great power status. The *Liberal Democratic Party of Russia* represents an opportunistic national-patriotic line in the State Duma, but perhaps more true to national-patriotic ideas is the small *Patriots of Russia,* which is the smallest of the currently-registered parties but does not have any seats in the State Duma.

Parties in post-communist Russia tend to come and go, merge and fragment. Nevertheless, the four *categories* outlined above seem to be rather stable, and the main parties, whatever they represent or are called, can be classified in these terms presumably for the next decade or so to. The overall tendency, besides the diminishing number of registered (eligible) parties and especially those represented in parliament, is that the 'centrist' forces have become the overwhelming majority and the 'reformist' forces have been marginalised and pushed, at least temporarily, out of parliament. The success of *United Russia* among the electorate (even if there was falsification of the electoral results) can be seen not only in its connection to the (diminishing) personal popularity of Putin, but also in the fact that this party has adopted popular elements from other main political forces. From the national patriots it has borrowed its nostalgic great power vocabulary and the Slavophile communitarian urge towards wholeness; from the communists it has adopted the pathos of paternalistic state-led development and anti-oligarch rhetoric; and from the Westernisers it takes the slogans of the market economy and civil society. Thus the huge success of the centrist *Unity of Russia* is partly due to the fact that it has managed to balance between, or perhaps create a workable compromise from, the main ideas of the other ideological orientations.

Free but not fair?

However, it is often argued that the core of the 'managed democracy' is precisely the fact that those in power are able to manipulate the election results. Indeed, while elections are the core of any theory of Western democracy, most of the analysts who try to understand the failure of Russia's democratisation do so precisely by looking at 'failures' in its party and election systems.[89] Since 1989 a great number of competitive national elections, referendums, regional and local elections have been organised in Russia. Should we apply Huntington's 'two-turnover test', we would conclude that Russia is not a consolidated democracy. This test means that:

> a democracy may be viewed as consolidated if the party or group that takes power in the initial election at the time of transition loses a subsequent election and turns over power to those election winners, and if those election winners then peacefully turn over power to the winners of a later election.[90]

This seems to be the case when considering, for instance, individual State Duma deputies: a great number of new candidates have been elected in each election. But the problem is that the results of Russian elections are more or less predetermined, especially in presidential and regional elections. The fact that presidential elections have "never produced a change in 'party'" is "curious, if not alarming". The elites have learned to reduce uncertainties and utilise administrative resources, and consequently "elections are likely to perform a quasi-democratic function in post-communist Russia".[91] Some scholars argue that the role of the media in elections is to act as a propaganda tool to ensure that the ruling elites stay in power, with the ruling party controlling most of the important media, especially television.[92] The only obstacle is the extent to which the Kremlin feels it needs to project the image of democracy to the world. Sakwa complains that Russia's electoral politics and electoral outcomes seem to be relatively disconnected from power relations: "Parties fight elections, but in Russia they do not fight elections to form the government."[93]

From the very beginning, there have been accusations about the undemocratic nature of the Russian elections. The main accusations have concerned falsification, unfair use of administrative resources, manipulation of the media, and unfair treatment of some candidates. The Parliamentary Assembly of the Council of Europe (PACE) concluded that the 2008 presidential "election repeated most of the flaws revealed during the Duma elections of December 2007". The criticism mostly focused on candidate registration, "putting into question the degree of how free the election was", and on the equality of the access of the candidates to the media and the public sphere in general. Nonetheless, the delegation concluded that "even if those concerns had been addressed, the outcome of the vote – amounting, in effect, to a vote of confidence in the incumbent President – would have been the same". The Organization for Security and Cooperation in Europe (OSCE) has monitored most of the Russian national elections. The reports have usually found the elections to be well-organised but not completely fair, focusing on the above-mentioned issues. With regard to the 2011 State Duma elections, it focused its principal criticism on the convergence of state and the ruling party, which was reflected in the lack of independence of the media and the election administration. Within Russia, opposition forces have been more straightforward in their criticism, accusing the regime of large-scale falsification, whereas the authorities claim that the accumulated effect of reported falsification does not concern more than 0.5 per cent of the total votes.

While the current leadership seems inclined to use any methods to stay in power, they have also signalled that they are not aiming at returning to a single-party system, but that the Russian multi-party system will have some peculiarities. In 2008, President Putin put it in a way which could be understood as a threat to some parties:

> Russia's future political system will be centred on several large political parties that will have to work hard to maintain or affirm their leading positions, be open to change and broaden their dialogue with the voters. Political parties must not forget their immense responsibility for Russia's future, for the nation's unity and for our country's stable development. [...] Irresponsible demagogy and attempts to divide society and use foreign help or intervention in domestic political struggles are not only immoral but are illegal. They belittle our people's dignity and undermine our democratic state. [...] Finally, Russia's political system must not only be in accordance with our national political culture but should develop together with it.[94]

Vladislav Surkov, the "chief regime ideologist" of contemporary Russia, and apparently the mastermind behind Putin's political speeches, put this idea as follows:

> The proportional model of parliamentary elections ensures the merging of disparate politically active groups into large national parties. The ban on the creation of political parties on a regional, religious, or occupational basis, emphasizes that parties must not only divide voters in accordance with their views and convictions but also unite them around shared values. To divide the electorate but unite the nation – such might be the principle of a Russian multi-party system.[95]

Medvedev's public statements during his presidency tended to be more liberal, and disagreements between him and Putin, and also between him and Surkov, were reported, especially on the concept and contents of 'sovereign democracy'. As to the party system, in his September 2009 *Go Russia!* vision,[96] he noted:

> As in most democratic states, the leaders of the political struggle will be the parliamentary parties, which will periodically replace each other in power. The parties and the coalitions they make will choose the federal and regional executive authorities (and not vice versa). They will be responsible for nominating candidates for the post of president, regional governors and local authorities. [...] The political system will be renewed and improved via the free competition of open political associations. There will be a cross-party consensus on strategic [...] goals. A similar consensus exists in all modern democracies. This year we started moving towards the creation of such a political system.

A year later, apparently due to the results of the autumn 2009 regional elections, one could sense a tone of frustration that things did not develop in that direction: "If the opposition hasn't the slightest chance of winning in an honest fight, it degrades and becomes marginal", Medvedev said in November 2010. "But if the ruling party has no chances to lose anywhere at anytime, it becomes 'bronzed' and ultimately degrades, too."[97] The expected changes on the basis of this kind of statement were thought to include that the ruling party will become weaker and the opposition will gain in strength and, instead of four parties, perhaps five will be represented in the next State Duma.

However, an opposite tendency was again created on the eve of the 2011 State Duma elections. Around ten parties were not able to register themselves according to the rules. Some of these developments have been seen as fabricated legal motivations. For instance, instead of increasing the possibilities for political competition, the Ministry of Justice announced in June 2011 that it was refusing to register the *People's Freedom Party* (PFP), a liberal-minded coalition whose leaders included such well-known figures as the former Prime Minister Mikhail Kasyanov and former minister Boris Nemtsov, leading figures in post-election demonstrations. The official reason, according to the ministry, was that some listed members were under-age, some were 'dead souls', and some did not live at the addresses provided in documents filed by the party.[98]

As the result in the December 2011 State Duma elections turned out, *United Russia* remained as what has previously been called a 'dominant' party in the cases of Japan and Mexico. Those who have put forward this analogy argue, however, that as one can study the mechanisms through which these countries' dominant party systems survived for such a long time, one can also draw lessons from the breakdown: "[...] political opportunities and optimum strategies for opposition forces do exist, even in electoral authoritarian systems such as Russia's."[99]

Failed federalism?

Russia currently consists of 83 constituent subjects (previously 89), of which 21 are 'republics', 9 are districts (*krai*), 46 regions (*oblast'*), 2 cities, 1 autonomous region, and 4 autonomous districts (*okrug*). Furthermore the country is divided into 8 federal districts (*federal'nye okrugi*), which aim to coordinate federal policies in the regions. This list quickly reveals that the federal system is not very clear; moreover, it has been in constant turbulence in terms of its centre versus constituent subjects relationship.

What, then, is the essence of centre–region relations in Russia? One can find two alternative interpretations, very much resembling the earlier Sovietological arguments between the totalitarian and interest group schools. The first interpretation sees Russia as a very centralised, Kremlin-led polity where Moscow gives orders to the regions. This interpretation was given particular emphasis after Putin came to power in 1999 and started to implement his 'power vertical', establishing a much stronger top-down link between the federal and regional governance systems compared to that of the Yeltsin era. These centralisation efforts were understood as an undemocratic move by most analysts and scholars – indeed, as one of the major signs of the authoritarian turn in Russia. It has been said that "superpresidential federalism" has led to instability and undermined true federalism "involving significant real local autonomy".[100] Some analysts have put this slightly differently, arguing that the reforms were initiated from above, and that even when amendments to laws seemed to be steps towards more autonomy for local governance, the rationale had much less to do with democracy or public approval than with the need for a more rational system of government in order to enhance economic growth.[101] However, in this context, it is often forgotten that the fact that the federal state was previously unable to implement its policies in the regions, and often the regional governments passed laws that conflicted with the national laws, was also seen as a sign of unconsolidated democracy by many scholars.[102]

The other interpretation is more nuanced and focuses on regional elites and their relationship with Moscow. In this interpretation institutional equilibrium between the regions and Moscow was found only when highly personalised elite preferences were satisfied. Therefore the Russian federal system is the product of short-term, institutional solutions suited to elite survival strategies developed under conditions of economic, political, and social uncertainty.[103] This interpretation does not make the picture of Russia's realities any prettier in democratic terms, but it does not see Russia as a monolithic unity; rather, it emerges as a battlefield between different elites and their respective interests, where sooner or later some kind of a balance of interests is usually reached based on power relations.

How stable is the current federal system? In President Putin's *Strategy 2020* from 2008[104] it was acknowledged, in a way, that the current administrative and federal system does not work towards innovative high-tech developments through enhancing human capital – the main drive of the strategy. Although Putin's message was that this innovative system cannot be achieved without further administrative reforms that move towards decentralisation, he did not frame this failure in terms of the unintended consequences of the centralisation of his own making. The problem, according to Putin, was excessive and time-consuming bureaucracy, and therefore more responsibility and initiative should be taken by individual authorities, regional and local actors. However, in saying this, he refers not to decentralised innovation in terms of more autonomous governance of regional and local actors. In this scheme it is still the government that "should be the centre for coming up with ideology and strategic plans", whereas the *implementation* should be more decentralised, leading to much more efficient governance.

When Medvedev took over in 2009, the question was whether he would put his own stamp on regional policy and, if so, whether it would mean that a more decentralised type of federalism would emerge.[105] No clear signal about Medvedev's aspirations on this can be identified following the end of his presidential period, except that he has used the centralised tools that his predecessor created when replacing a number of governors. The reasons for these replacements, which have created a lot of media coverage and speculation, have been connected to personal power struggles and the central government's urge for more efficient policies at the regional level. As noted earlier, these political nominations seem to be based upon "informal bargaining rather than administrative procedures".[106]

China

China's transition from communism can be dated back to 1979, when Deng Xiaoping acquired political supremacy and began his market-oriented economic reforms. Had the Soviet Union not collapsed in 1991, a comparison based on this chronology would not have been controversial. This comparative exercise is also made more complicated by the 1989 Tiananmen Square incident, which led to a purge of the liberals among the ruling elites and turned China's transition in a very different direction.

Recognising that structural preconditions significantly strained the choices of the elites in the immediate aftermath of the Cultural Revolution, we should analyse how these preconditions may have influenced China's transition in the 1980s. However, as the post-1989 development of China has a considerably more important impact on the emergence of the current autocratic crony-capitalist order, the pre-1979 structural factors should be considered as having no meaningful impact on the post-1989 transition process. Instead, the new political and socio-economic dynamics unleashed by the post-1989 transition process are the most important variables in explaining and understanding the strategic choices of the ruling elites and the defining characteristics of the new political and economic order.

The era of balancing and power struggles

In the literature on democratic transitions, there is lively debate on whether the nature of the old regime has had any impact on the course of transition itself. Huntington, for example, believes that the nature of the old regime has at best a modest influence on the mode of transition, even though he concedes that personal dictatorships are more likely to be replaced than transformed.[107] On the other hand, scholars such as Juan Linz, Alfred Stepan, Terry Lynn Karl, Michael Bratton and Nicolas Van de Walle assign much greater importance to how the nature of the old regime affects the transition process.[108] Specifically, to the extent that the nature of the old regime determines the distribution of power within society and the regime, it almost certainly affects the probability of a negotiated or non-negotiated transition, as well as the ability of the ruling elites of the old regime to manage the transition process.

In the Chinese case, the nature of the old regime is quite unique in comparison with that of most authoritarian regimes that were transformed or replaced during the third wave of democratisation. Like the former Soviet Union, the pre-1979 Chinese regime was a state-socialist system completely dominated by a Leninist party-state. Political power and economic resources were far more concentrated in the hands of the ruling elites and the state than in any non-state–socialist authoritarian country. Thanks to the regime's repression, civil society either did not exist in any meaningful sense or it was extremely weak. Such a lopsided balance of power between the state and society makes it almost impossible for negotiated transitions to occur in indigenous communist revolutionary regimes such as China and the former Soviet Union.[109] As a result, transitions in such systems tend to produce two outcomes. In the most likely scenario, the ruling elites dominate the transition process and determine its direction and pace. However, in cases where the initial opening triggered a fundamental split among the ruling elites and, subsequently, a massive upsurge in political mobilisation of previously excluded groups, the discredited old regime would not be able to exit power via negotiation. In fact, it is most likely to be replaced, as the collapse of the former Soviet Union showed.[110]

Compared with the former Soviet Union, China's post-Mao leadership enjoyed several important advantages on the eve of transition. The Cultural Revolution unleashed by Mao had not only discredited Maoist extremism and brought tremendous suffering to ordinary Chinese people, it had also shaken the foundations of Maoist totalitarian rule. The communist party-state, itself a target of the Cultural Revolution, had been severely weakened during a decade of political chaos. Many of its elites were physically abused, or even eliminated. Most were demoralised. The political mass mobilisation during the Cultural Revolution, although fuelled by leftist radicalism and responsible for horrific human suffering, performed a valuable role by severely undermining the cohesiveness and credibility of the old regime – in the same way that an upsurge of mass mobilisation at the beginning of a democratic transition weakens an old regime. More importantly, since most transitions, political or economic, are initiated by the elites of the old regime, the legacy of the Cultural Revolution greatly facilitated the formation of a pro-reform grand coalition which encompassed conservatives, moderates, and liberals from within the regime because they had all been victims of Mao's radicalism.[111]

While this grand coalition easily ousted the beneficiaries of the Cultural Revolution, such as the interim leader Hua Guofeng, it soon began to fall apart over the direction of reform. The members of the grand coalition agreed on the need to reverse Mao's disastrous policies, but little else. The conservatives, led by Chen Yun and Li Xiannian, advocated a return to the pre-Cultural Revolution status quo, a more rationalised form of post-totalitarian rule within the frameworks of a state-socialist economy and the political supremacy of the Chinese Communist Party (CCP). Pragmatist reformers, led by Deng Xiaoping, agreed with the conservatives on the objective of maintaining the CCP's rule, but differed on the economic strategy by which such an objective could be achieved. The pragmatists understood that only pro-market reforms could deliver the improved economic performance required to bolster the CCP's legitimacy and sustain its rule. The liberals within the CCP, although a tiny minority represented by Hu Yaobang, believed that pro-market economic reforms could not be successful without some limited liberalising political reforms. Even though it is doubtful whether the liberal wing inside the CCP ever intended to bring about genuine democratic reforms, their support for more tolerance and openness in political debate clearly set them apart from the moderates.[112]

Such division among the ruling elites unavoidably led to serious conflict over policy during the 1980s. On economic reform, the pragmatists and liberals formed a winning coalition against the conservatives. On political reform, the pragmatists and conservatives worked together to defeat the liberals. The political dynamics of the conflict over the direction and pace of reform were complex and unpredictable. However, by and large, the combined political strength of the pragmatists and liberals ensured that pro-market economic reforms would proceed against persistent conservative opposition. At the same time, the overwhelming political dominance of the pragmatists and conservatives doomed any possibility that even limited democratising political reforms could be carried out that decade.

The three-way division among China's ruling elites was conclusively ended only with the Tiananmen Square massacre in June 1989.[113] The liberals were purged after the downfall of Zhao Ziyang. For a brief period between late 1989 and 1991, the conservatives held the power and attempted to roll back economic reforms. Soon afterwards, a rapid series of events fatally weakened the conservatives and enabled the pragmatists to become the dominant political force inside the CCP. First, the conservatives' attempt to roll back the economic reforms proved a spectacular failure in reviving China's stalled economic growth and encountered strong resistance from local governments, which were worried about losing their newly-acquired autonomy. Second, the collapse of the former Soviet Union in 1991 caused panic among China's ruling elites and imparted a sense of urgency in seeking a strategy to avoid the fate of the Soviet Communist Party. Finally, clearly frustrated with the conservatives and fearful that his historical legacy was at risk, Deng himself expended all his political capital and led the charge to revive economic reform in early 1992 with his famous southern tour.[114] The post-1992 transition in China is thus fundamentally different from the transition in the 1980s – it is has greater political coherence and a clearer direction. The post-1992 ruling elites were unified around a survival strategy centred on establishing a system of autocratic capitalism.

Did the level of economic development matter?

As indicated above, China's transition process should be divided into two distinct phases: the 1980s and the post-1992 period. It would be difficult to argue that structural factors could have influenced the elites' strategic choices in such starkly different ways within one decade. If structural factors played a decisive role in China's transition process, it is most likely that they had a much greater impact on the elites' decision to launch economic reform in the early 1980s than on their decision to accelerate economic reform in the direction of an autocratic capitalist order following Deng's historic southern tour in 1992.

Measured in terms of per capita income, urbanisation, educational attainment, communications infrastructure, and the structure of labour force, China in the late 1970s was a typical low-income country (Table 4.2). Based on modernisation theory, countries at low levels of economic development, such as China in the late 1970s, possess unfavourable structural factors for democratic transition.[115] However, recent scholarship on democratic transition challenges such a view, finding that levels of income have no influence on the timing of the transition to democracy (although this variable affects the durability

Table 4.2 China's key socioeconomic indicators in the 1970s

GDP per capita (1978/yuan)	315
Urbanisation (1979 / %)	18.9
Population with a higher education (1982 / %)	1
Enrolled college students (1978)	856,000
Non-agricultural labour force (1979 / %)	24.6
Fixed telephone lines (1978)	1.93 million
Number of television sets (1978)	3.04 million
Contribution of agriculture to GNP (1978 / %)	33

Source: Statistical Yearbook of China 1990, pp. 34, 37, 294, 561; China Social Statistical Yearbook 2006, p. 3; Statistical Yearbook of China 1991, pp. 79 and 95.

Christer Pursiainen is responsible for the parts concerning Russia and Minxin Pei for those parts concerning China.

of democracy).[116] In the Chinese case, its relatively low level of socio-economic development in the late 1970s may not have provided the most favourable conditions for transition to democratic rule, but it certainly influenced the post-Mao grand coalition's strategic choice as to where to make the breakthrough in economic reform.

For the post-Mao grand coalition, the most important political imperative was to demonstrate the efficacy of their economic policy and create a new source of political legitimacy that was fundamentally different from the personal character of the late dictator. This political consideration heavily influenced their thinking on where to initiate economic reform. In a society where more than 80 per cent of the population resided in the countryside and where radical agrarian policies had suppressed individual initiatives, a breakthrough in agricultural reform was not only highly feasible, but also most likely to create, within a short period of time, beneficiaries from, and thus constituencies for, reform. In contrast, attempting a breakthrough in the urban-based state-owned industrial sector was much less promising. Technically it would be a lot more difficult to accomplish because reforming the modern sector required a package of far more complex and comprehensive policies and institutional reforms (such as financial sector reform, social safety net reform, administrative restructuring, foreign trade reform, tax reform and ownership reform).[117] Politically, this approach was almost certain to encounter fierce resistance and risk splitting apart the post-Mao grand coalition. The privileged bureaucratic interests of the party-state, deeply entrenched in the state-owned sector, would be motivated to forestall reforms threatening to undermine their power and privileges. Urban industrial workers, though victims of the poorly performing state-socialist political economy, nevertheless enjoyed certain perks, such as job security and state-provided fringe benefits, as was discussed in more detail in the previous chapter. Reforming state-owned enterprises by reducing trade barriers, increasing competition from the private sector, eliminating redundancy, and hardening budget constraints would definitely have made many members of this group worse off.

In terms of socioeconomic equality, the situation in pre-reform China was marked by overall relative income equality but severe regional and urban-rural disparities. The national Gini coefficient in 1978 was roughly 0.30, making China a relatively equal society in terms of income;[118] however, rural residents were much poorer than their urban counterparts. Based on official per capita consumption data, an average urban resident consumed three times more than the average rural resident in 1978.[119] It is difficult to determine whether the relatively high level of overall income equality in China on the eve of its transition away from communism played any role at all. The disparity between the welfare of urban and rural residents could conceivably have had some (undetermined) effects on the source of economic entrepreneurship. In addition to their exclusion from the welfare benefits provided by the pre-reform system, the relative deprivation of China's rural population could be one explanation for why private entrepreneurship originated in rural China and spread across the country in the 1980s.[120]

The decisive turn toward autocratic capitalism in 1992

The near-death experience of the CCP during the Tiananmen crisis in 1989 traumatised the party's leadership. The temporary ascendance of the conservatives also brought the economic process to a halt. However, the combination of the deep economic recession which followed the Tiananmen crackdown and the anti-market policies adopted by the conservatives led to widespread discontent, among both the elites and the public, over the direction in which they were taking the country. The pivotal event which fundamentally altered China's domestic political dynamics and rallied the CCP around Deng's vision of an autocratic capitalist system was the collapse of the Soviet Union in December 1991. To be sure, the fall of communism in Eastern Europe in 1989, which immediately followed the Tiananmen crackdown, seriously demoralised the CCP. But it was the sudden and dramatic disintegration of the Soviet Union that caused a sense of panic among China's ruling elites. If the Chinese elites were divided over whether capitalism could save China before the Soviet collapse, such a debate was over by early 1992.

The consensus, as articulated by Deng, was that only market-oriented reform could save the CCP regime.[121]

In theory China's decisive turn toward autocratic capitalism was not predetermined. In terms of preconditions, in 1991–92 China enjoyed much more favourable structural conditions than in 1978–79. Its per capita income had more than doubled since reform began. The level of educational attainment had risen; telecommunications, the media, and social mobility had all grown at a rapid pace. In the 1980s, civil society also blossomed.[122] However, these supposedly favourable structural preconditions for a democratic transition had no effect on the CCP leadership's strategic choice in 1992. Several factors precluded the adoption of a different strategic choice, one that would embrace *democratic capitalism*, not autocratic capitalism. For one thing, the liberal wing inside the CCP had by then been almost completely purged, at least at the top level. It would be impossible to launch political liberalisation from within without liberals at the top. Another factor that weighed heavily on the Chinese ruling elites was their reading of the causes of the Soviet collapse. Instead of attributing the collapse to the inability of a decayed political system to adapt to change, Chinese leaders were deeply convinced that poor economic performance had fatally undermined the Soviet regime! In order to prevent such a fate, the CCP itself had to completely embrace the more productive capitalist system. Finally, the immediate chaos following the Soviet collapse appeared to have caused deep anxiety among ordinary Chinese, who remained traumatised by the catastrophic Cultural Revolution and maintained a strong sense of national pride, a sentiment adroitly exploited by the CCP elites who used state-owned propaganda machines to play up the post-collapse chaos in the former Soviet Union.[123] To be sure, the decisive turn toward autocratic capitalism was widely hailed as the revival of China's economic reform. In a narrow sense, that was true. After Deng's southern tour, China's march toward capitalism entered a new and irreversible phase. What was not understood at that time was what kind of regime this 'capitalism without democracy' would create.[124]

Representative institutions in a one-party state

The idea that a one-party state can have truly representative institutions that embody popular sovereignty may sound fanciful. By definition, a one-party state, such as the People's Republic of China, allows no such institutions to exist, let alone compete for power against the ruling CCP. Yet, despite the fundamental incompatibility between the representation of popular sovereignty through a competitive process and the monopoly of political power enjoyed by a post-totalitarian party, representative institutions in a one-party state not only exist, but also perform certain political functions crucial to the operation and maintenance of a one-party regime.

In the Chinese case, the rehabilitation of representative institutions was actually given top priority by the post-Mao leadership.[125] Even though leaders such as Deng did not intend to establish genuinely democratic representative institutions that could undermine the CCP's political supremacy, they apparently understood the useful functions that such representative institutions could play in China's march toward a market economy and a more effectively governed society. Thus, the initial political considerations of the top elites were primarily pragmatic. The restoration of China's most important representative institution, the National People's Congress (NPC), could significantly contribute to political stability, economic reform, and effective governance.

First, by restoring a national political institution which normally enjoys constitutional supremacy, the CCP leadership could achieve the goal of dispersing authority *within* the party-state and preventing the rise of another totalitarian ruler like Mao. It is important not to confuse the *dispersion of power among the ruling elites* with the emergence of *institutional pluralism*. In the case of the former, the checks and balances produced would curb, if not altogether prevent, the political hegemony of an individual leader or a particular faction without undermining the overall monopoly of the one-party state. Obviously, the dispersion of power among the ruling elites does not require the granting of genuine institutional autonomy to the representative institutions in question. To the extent that these institutions are staffed by members of the ruling elites whose primary political identity lies not with these institutions but with the CCP, the risks of institutional pluralism and genuine checks and balances are minimised.

Second, representative institutions in a one-party state can perform specific functions more efficiently. In the Chinese case, the NPC, as the sole legislative organ of the state, gradually acquired greater technical and organisational capacity for law-making. By separating the legislative function from the CCP's central political apparatus, the ruling party gained significant benefits in terms of the specialisation and division of labour without conceding much real power because the legislative or policy-making initiatives continued to flow from the CCP.

Third, to the extent that the NPC creates the appearance of a transparent and competitive policy-making process, the post-Mao regime could distinguish itself from the Maoist regime as being more 'democratic' and inclusive. Of course, to achieve the right balance in making the NPC more apparently representative and democratic without actually encouraging it to be genuinely so is difficult. In reality, the CCP has opted to err on the side of caution: it has preferred the control of the NPC to the potential benefits of having a slightly more autonomous representative institution.[126]

The CCP's determination to maintain its hegemony has prevented China's NPC, as well its local representative institutions such as local people's congresses, from acquiring politically meaningful capacity in policy-making. To be sure, compared with the Maoist era, the NPC is not a completely docile political institution. Occasionally it functions as a powerful political forum for venting complaints against the policies of the CCP and holding individual CCP officials accountable.[127] Organisationally, the staff of the NPC has also become more professionalised. The procedures of law-making are now better established as well. Despite all these technical and organisational gains, however, China's transition from Maoist totalitarian rule to a Dengist autocratic capitalist order has had, at best, a limited impact upon the country's representative institutions because China's one-party state sees these institutions as potential threats to its monopoly and has thus pursued a strategy to marginalise them within the political process.

Participatory institutions within a non-democracy

The persistence of autocratic rule in post-Mao China has precluded the establishment of meaningful institutions for *democratic* political participation at all levels of government. Village elections, which have received a huge amount of scholarly attention, may be considered the only institution for democratic participation, even though the body elected by these elections, the villagers' committee, is legally a civic self-governing organisation, not a local government.[128] The story of village elections provides an excellent illustration of the promise of reform in the 1980s and the limits of the autocratic capitalist order that has prevailed in China since the early 1990s. Despite unfavourable structural conditions for democratic experiments in the Chinese countryside, the Chinese leadership managed to pass a law in 1988 which allowed this limited experiment with democracy to proceed in villages. Without doubt, the explicit objective of the CCP leaders at that time was to use village self-government to maintain rural stability and make the countryside more governable. However, over time, village elections became the most important regularised channel of participation for rural residents. The effects of such participation on rural governance are ambiguous because of the diversity of implementation of this new institution in China and the CCP's own worries about the democratic potential of village elections.[129] A delicious irony of the village elections is that such limited democratic participatory rights are denied to China's relatively privileged urban residents since the equivalent of village committees in urban areas – neighbourhood committees – are not competitively or semi-competitively elected.

Experimental grass roots democracy has not gone beyond the village level despite calls for the expansion of this experiment to rural townships, which would constitute the foundations of local governance. After ruling out the direct election of township officials on the grounds that existing election laws do not allow them, the Chinese government nevertheless permitted various pilot programmes which used indirect electoral methods to choose township officials. The effects of such experiments on local governance are hard to measure. In any case, such experiments are simply too occasional to make a real impact on local governance.

Beyond the villages, formal electoral institutions have remained essentially unchanged.[130] The members of local legislatures and delegates to the NPC are appointed by the CCP and not elected through free or competitive contests. While formal participatory institutions in China do not exist or function in any meaningful way, and mass political participation through regime-sponsored campaigns has virtually disappeared since China entered its post-totalitarian era, semi-formal or informal channels of participation not only exist, but also provide the most important and direct means of participation for ordinary Chinese citizens.

What is notable about these semi-formal or informal means of participation is that they allow *individual* Chinese citizens to voice their demands and air their grievances in many creative ways, though with limited and unpredictable effects.[131] China's *xingfang* system (petition through letters and visits) is one such example. A relic from the imperial times, *xingfang* allows millions of ordinary Chinese citizens to lodge complaints against local officials with higher government hierarchies. However, scholarly research indicates that most petition efforts fail.[132] Filing administrative lawsuits against local government organs, made possible by China's post-Mao legal reform, also offers limited judicial relief to tens of thousands of Chinese citizens each year who go to the courts to seek to redress the wrongs inflicted by abusive local officials. The effectiveness of this approach is limited due to the high risks of retaliation by local officials and the low probability of success.[133]

In the absence of effective and meaningful channels of political participation, the most popular current forms of political participation in China are informal. Two of these deserve special attention. One is political participation via cyberspace. The advent of the internet has permitted millions of ordinary Chinese citizens to voice their demands of the government via virtual online communities. Despite determined efforts by the CCP to control the web, political participation via cyberspace has become perhaps the most important form of participation in China.[134] The other form of participation is collective protest. Fuelled primarily by rising social frustrations and an irresponsive state, aggrieved individuals are taking part in spontaneously organised collective protests against specific violations of their rights and property.[135] The rapid increase in the number of such incidents since the mid-1990s should be taken as a reflection of the failure of the CCP to create meaningful formal participatory institutions to accommodate a citizenry with diverse interests and rising political assertiveness.

The challenge of governance

The transformation of China's governance institutions in the post-Mao era has been substantial and far-reaching despite the lack of democratic transition. Both in terms of the formal restructuring of these institutions and the substantive manner in which these institutions operate, China's governance institutions at the national, regional, and local levels have adapted to the country's top priority of maintaining high-speed economic growth. As it is impossible to describe these changes in the limited space of this section, I will focus on the two most important developments in this area since the late 1970s.

At the national level, one might be tempted to identify the resurrection of the NPC as the most important change in China's national governance institutions. Actually, this is not the case because of the severely limited political potency of the NPC. Arguably, the critical change at the national level is the transformation of the central economic bureaucracy from an apparatus designed to manage a command economy to one that attempts to govern a transition economy. This change has been accompanied by the abolition of ministerial agencies no longer relevant to the Chinese economy and their subsequent replacement by new agencies and ministries with more clearly identified missions which are staffed by more capable technocrats. Technocratic competence, sorely lacking during the Maoist era, has undeniably become the second-most important qualification for positions in central ministries (next to political loyalty and contacts). The ascendance of competent technocrats is especially pronounced in the financial sector. The rising level of technical competence at the central position has been accompanied by another important development in the national governance institutions: a systematic attempt to build a regulatory state.[136] In the reform era, the promulgation of hundreds, if not thousands, of administrative rules and regulations has laid the ground, at least on paper, for a more rule-based mode of governance, in spite of the uneven record for the enforcement of these rules and regulations.

The governance institutions in provinces and municipalities may not have changed significantly in form, but they have acquired unprecedented autonomy and power as a result of the devolution of power (particularly fiscal power) during the reform era. Beijing's strategy to incentivise local leaders to become stakeholders in the economic reform process by granting them significant administrative and fiscal autonomy has delivered the desired results. However, such devolution of power has come at a great cost. During the 1980s, the central government was starved of fiscal resources because the tax-farming system which was introduced immediately after reform began allowed provincial authorities to keep most of the extra revenues generated by economic growth. Even after the re-centralisation of fiscal revenues in the mid-1990s remedied this problem, local leaders have resorted to extracting revenues from land seizures and sales to make up the short-fall in their fiscal resources, and this has greatly exacerbated social tensions.[137] In addition, the exclusive focus on GDP growth as the sole measure of performance has led to a reduction in the social services provided by local governments.

The devolution of administrative and fiscal power without political accountability has produced another far-reaching consequence in terms of governance: local elites have become unaccountable in terms of their policy and behaviour. Due to the prohibitive costs of monitoring this vast bureaucracy, the central government has few effective institutional mechanisms for enforcing accountability on the local ruling elites. The lack of democracy or a free press further allows local ruling elites to engage in predatory activities with impunity.[138]

The Communist Party – beyond recognition?

Of all the political changes in the post-Mao era, the transformation of the CCP from a radical revolutionary party into a conservative right-wing elitist ruling party is, without doubt, the most important for an understanding of the nature of the existing Chinese regime. To be sure, the CCP was uncertain about its future direction in the 1980s because, as discussed earlier, the post-Mao grand coalition was engaged in a bitter internal ideological fight over the direction of China's transition. This fight was decisively settled by Tiananmen (which led to the ousting of the liberals from the top) and later by Deng's southern tour (which fatally weakened those conservatives opposed to market reforms). Consequently, the CCP's transformation into a right-wing elitist party occurred during the 1990s under Jiang Zeming's reign.

But several important institutional and normative changes had occurred within the CCP during the 1980s. Although these changes did not directly affect the party's turn to the right, they played an important role in establishing more binding rules and norms within the CCP. As a result of these changes, pushed through mainly by Deng, the CCP managed to institute a mandatory retirement system, which allowed younger and more educated party members to rise to positions of power. More importantly, the party greatly enhanced the mutual security of the elites by eschewing Maoist-style purges. Although such security was not absolute – as can be seen in Zhao Ziyang's dismissal and subsequent long-term house arrest, and in the corruption convictions of two Politburo members under Jiang and Hu Jintao – by and large the top CCP elites have enjoyed a level of security unimaginable during the Mao era.

The CCP has also managed to improve its succession process as well. Despite its failure to establish a competitive process for selection of its top leaders, the post-Deng leadership has nevertheless avoided any destabilising or debilitating power struggles surrounding succession. The bargaining among the top elites may be opaque and full of intrigue, but the results of the bargains that have been struck have apparently endured. It may be an exaggeration to claim that the CCP has completely solved its succession problem by establishing a durable institutional arrangement, but the degree of unpredictability over the choice of the top leader and his political viability has fallen measurably in the post-Deng era.[139]

China's transition has altered the membership of the CCP almost beyond recognition. The party's policy of promoting younger and better-educated members to positions of responsibility has produced a classical technocracy, which is homogenous in its ideological outlook (politically conservative but economically pragmatic), educational attainment (mostly college-educated), and career patterns (gradual promotions in the state and party bureaucracies). As part of its strategy of co-opting social elites, the CCP began to open its doors to the intelligentsia, college students, professionals and even private entrepreneurs.

The combined impact of this process of promoting technocrats and incorporating social elites has fundamentally altered the composition of the party, turning it into an elitist ruling party. Some analysts believe that the CCP, instead of decaying, has actually transformed itself through adaptation.[140]

Despite the CCP's myriad efforts to adapt to China's rapid socio-economic changes, there is one area in which the party's attempt to transform itself has made little progress: making the party itself more democratic and transparent. The cry for "inner-party democracy" has been a constant refrain in the CCP's rhetoric. During the Maoist era, political life inside the totalitarian party was, to quote Hobbes, "brutish and short". In the reform era, top leaders have instituted modest reforms to avoid the excessive concentration of power in the hands of one individual. At the top level, the selection of the Central Committee members has become more competitive, with typically 5-10 per cent more candidates than positions. The post-Deng leadership, in both the Jiang and Hu administrations, has become genuinely collective. But a consensus-driven decision-making process at the top is hardly democratic. At best, it is competition within an oligarchy. At the grass roots level, reformist leaders in the 1980s tried to institute some form of representative institutions within the CCP so that ordinary party members could monitor, and hold accountable, local party officials. But the practical difficulties encountered by local party organs rendered numerous proposals impractical. Out of fear of losing control of the appointment of the nomenklatura, encouraging open factionalism and splitting the party, the CCP has steadfastly resisted holding competitive elections to fill the positions of local party chiefs.

Poor interest representation

China's transition has produced rapid economic development, unprecedented urbanisation, and rising social mobility. Although Chinese society has grown more diverse and complex as a result of these changes, the persistence of autocracy has greatly constrained the development of formal and effective institutions for interest representation and articulation. Ever fearful that the emergence of such institutions could potentially challenge its political supremacy, the CCP has attempted to convert those institutions of representation and articulation controlled by the regime into the components of a post-totalitarian form of state corporatism.[141] In form, if not in substance, the CCP-controlled institutions of interest representation and articulation, such as the All-China Federation of Labour, the All-China Federation of Industry and Commerce, the Chinese Women's Association, and the China Writers' Union, certainly resemble classical models of state corporatism. But whether these institutions actually perform the political functions of connecting major social groups with the CCP regime remains an open question. While there is little doubt that the CCP appoints the leaders of these pillar groups and the Chinese state funds their activities, it is doubtful that these groups have the support of their grass roots members. It is not even clear whether the leaders of these groups actually bargain with the regime to press for policies beneficial to their groups.

Outside the officially sanctioned channels, such as those identified above, no formal autonomous institutions of representation and articulation exist. This does not mean, however, that societal interests are not represented or articulated in China today. They are, but via informal channels, mostly through public opinion and collective protest. The absence of legitimate, autonomous, and societal institutions of representation and articulation presents a serious challenge to the CCP even though, ironically, that is precisely the consequence of the regime's strategy of preventing the formation of such institutions. On the one hand, a Chinese version of state corporatism gives the regime a sense of security but, in all likelihood, the regime's control of societal interests through this model of interest representation and articulation is highly fragile and unreliable because these institutions are not viewed as legitimate by the social groups they purport to represent, their leaders are politically beholden to the party-state and, most critically, many of China's new social groups, such as peasants, migrant labourers, professionals working in foreign-owned corporations, and owners of small- and medium-sized private firms, have no institutions that represent or articulate their interests.

The political consequence of this institutional lacuna is two-fold. First, members of those social groups that are either illegitimately represented or unrepresented are bound to feel a strong sense of alienation from the regime, thus depriving the regime of a source of political support. Second, the members of these groups will attract sources of support for potential opposition in the future when circumstances are potentially more favourable for mounting a serious political challenge to the ruling elites.

Civil society in China?

The space for civil society was severely restricted during the Maoist totalitarian period. Civil society groups were practically non-existent at the end of the Cultural Revolution and could not have been a relevant factor in China's rural breakthrough in the 1980s. Although economic reform and the relaxation of social control by the post-Mao regime later created more public space and allowed a limited resurgence of civic groups in China, they remain weak in terms of size and access to resources, they operate under severe restrictions imposed by the state, and they have demonstrated their modest capacity in only a small number of arenas (such as environmental protection and public health).[142]

If the Maoist totalitarian rule succeeded in completely smothering China's civil society, the post-Mao transition away from communism has not only created space for a modest revival of Chinese civil society, but has also transformed state–society relations in important and complex ways – despite the lack of a democratic breakthrough. The revival of civil society, though modest in scale due to continuing restrictions on autonomous associational life in Chinese society imposed by the regime, ranks among the more encouraging developments in post-Mao China.[143] The principal manifestations of this revival can be found in the emergence of non-governmental organisations (NGOs), the growth of religious groups, and the formation of business interest groups. Although the political effects of the revival of Chinese civil society are not measurable at this point, this development has, at a minimum, enriched civic life in Chinese society. NGOs specialising in leisure, artistic, and recreational activities, as well as purely professional associations, have blossomed because of the relative tolerance of the regime toward these 'apolitical' groups. NGOs that perform a useful social function, such as environmental protection and public health, can also operate with some degree of freedom (although the regime remains suspicious of these groups and occasionally limits their operations).[144] As for religious groups, the regime's long-standing policy is to subject them to direct state control. However, the rapid expansion of various religious groups throughout China, particularly the so-called underground church (religious groups unaffiliated with the state-controlled religious organisations) has rendered such a policy all but ineffective. Despite the regime's persistent efforts to turn back the tide and resort to repressive tactics, independent religious groups have become so deeply entrenched in Chinese society that it would not be possible to destroy them without a full-scale reversion to Maoist totalitarian rule.[145] Of course, in 1999 the post-Deng regime did use brutal totalitarian tactics to suppress the Falun Gong, a nationwide spiritual movement which had emerged in the 1990s. The attempt was successful, but extremely costly because it required nothing short of the complete mobilisation of the regime's repressive capacity to accomplish it.[146]

Economic modernisation, attitudinal and structural changes within Chinese society, and the relaxation of social control characteristic of post-totalitarian regimes have driven this revival – and fundamentally redefined the boundaries of state–society relations in the process. If such boundaries were completely blurred during the Maoist era because of the intrusiveness and repressiveness of the state, they have become more clearly drawn and defined in the post-Mao era. In setting the boundaries between the state and organised groups of society, the post-Mao regime has apparently followed an implicit rule: it grants greater space to those that possess less *potential* capacity to challenge its political monopoly, while restricting those with greater potential.[147] In this sense, the political are separated from the non-political. Of course, such boundaries are set, not by formal institutional guarantees (since they lack credibility), but by a set of political realities – such as the perceived legitimacy of state intrusion into these organised civic activities, the level of resistance against such intrusion, and the political priorities accorded to such intrusion by the ruling elites. As the costs of overt repression of civic life of a non-political nature rise (because of the illegitimacy of such repression), the regime has learned to adapt to this reality by economising on the use of repression in defending its power. It has thus progressively ceded control of those arenas considered less vital to its survival. In this sense, the boundaries between the Chinese state and society are highly fluid. But, for average Chinese citizens, the constant redrawing of state–society boundaries has meant a gradual expansion of personal freedom. If the Chinese public has a higher tolerance for the regime's repression of organised civic groups, its tolerance of the regime's repression of personal freedom has steadily decreased, to the point where, for individual Chinese citizens, the risk of state intrusion into their sphere of personal freedom is negligible.[148]

A harmonic political elite?

The formation of the interests and identity of the political elites – in this case members of the CCP and the party-state – has gone through two stages during the transition. It is reasonable to distinguish between the pre-1989 and post-1989 periods as there is a qualitative difference in the nature of the Chinese regime in these two periods in terms of the homogeneity of ideological outlook, socioeconomic background, and political incentives. If the pre-1989 political elites were more heterogeneous in these critical factors which influence the formation of their identity and interests, the post-1989 political elites were far more homogeneous.[149] One of the reasons for this difference, as we explored earlier, is the nature of the coalition formed by the political elites. In the immediate aftermath of the Cultural Revolution, the winning coalition was nearly all-inclusive, comprising conservatives, pragmatists, and liberals. Their socioeconomic backgrounds and career paths were also extremely diverse, despite the fact that a large majority of the survivors of the Cultural Revolution were veterans of the Chinese Communist Revolution. The political incentives which motivated the elites in the 1980s were diverse as well, ranging from idealism for the liberals, preservation of the CCP's rule through better economic performance for the pragmatists, and preserving the state-socialist economic system for the conservatives.

In the post-1989 era, the political elites have become far more homogenous. Ideologically, they are mostly pragmatists, following Deng's neo-authoritarian strategy of saving the CCP with capitalism. Their socioeconomic backgrounds and career paths are much less diverse: most were educated in the post-1949 Chinese education system and socialised in the post-Cultural Revolution nomenklatura system. Their incentives are nearly identical, thanks to the CCP's exclusive focus on economic growth. In order to get ahead in the system, they must deliver satisfactory performance records in growth in their jurisdictions.[150]

To understand the process of identity and interest formation of the current Chinese political elites, it is critical to examine the factors that influence this process. Theoretically, the identity and interest of the political elites are a product of the values they attach to the political system in which they control hegemonic power, the privileges such a system grants to them, and the costs of losing their ideological hegemony and practical privileges in the event of a regime change. Thus, the political elites tend to identify most closely with a political system that embodies their values, provides them with privileges, and demonstrates durability.

If we examine how these three factors have influenced the process of the formation of identity and interests of China's political elites in the post-1989 era, it is apparent that the values embodied by the current Chinese political system may have the least powerful effect. To the extent that the official communist ideology has been all but totally discredited, it is impossible to argue that traditional ultra-leftist values continue to form the ideological basis of the collective identity of the political elites.[151] The interesting question is: do the political elites identify with the underlying values of capitalism? This question is almost impossible to answer because of the variety of forms of capitalism. But if the continuing heavy presence of the state in the economy is any evidence, it is clear that the political elites do not identify with *liberal* capitalism that seeks to minimise the state's economic role. It is very likely that China's political elites share the values embodied in a different variety of capitalism, such as bureaucratic capitalism, which gives the state enormous, if not dominant, influence in the economy, or crony capitalism, which is centred on access to political power in gaining competitive advantages in the economy. Of course, a transition economy such as China's is more likely to exhibit characteristics of both bureaucratic and crony capitalism. To be sure, the value the political elites attach to bureaucratic and crony capitalism was not apparent until well into the 1990s – after the CCP's turn towards autocratic capitalism began to yield much improved macroeconomic performance (high growth rates) and unprecedented rent-seeking opportunities for political elites themselves (as a result of the decentralisation of administrative authority and property rights).[152] In this sense, the formation of the collective identity of the political elites, at least on the ideological dimension, was due to both the intrinsic appeal of bureaucratic or crony capitalism (since it grants an oversized role to the state and allows the ruling elites to convert power into wealth) and to its instrumental value to the regime and its members.

The privileges for the political elites are by far the most important factor in the formation of their interest and identity. In the post-1989 autocratic capitalist order, Chinese political elites, it may be argued, have enjoyed privileges unimaginable in the Maoist era. Rising economic prosperity in general, and their privileged access to the resources controlled by the state in particular, allowed the political elites at all levels of the hierarchy to monetise the value of their power almost effortlessly. The monetisation of power occurs in two forms: direct appropriation and proxy appropriation. At the lower levels of the party-state, the political elites tend to prefer direct appropriation, either legally or illegally. Legally, local elites can give themselves fancy office buildings, luxury official cars, unlimited expense accounts, heavily subsidised houses, and all sorts of official junkets. Illegally, they take bribes in exchange for providing favours to businessmen or private individuals. Direct appropriation is necessitated by the circumstances in which local elites operate. In many instances, they directly control the allocation of privileges, resources, and rents, and can conduct insider transactions with minimal transaction costs.

In contrast, the political elites at higher levels prefer proxy appropriation for shrewd political reasons. The official privileges that they can enjoy legally are typically extremely generous, obviating the need to expand such privileges at greater political risk. Since the political elites at the higher levels of the hierarchy have already invested heavily in their political career (including much bigger sunken costs), they have a greater incentive to protect their investment through discretion and self-discipline. To the extent that the competition for power grows more fierce at the higher level of the party-state, those political elites harbouring ambitions for higher office are motivated to eschew ostentatious displays of privilege, as they can been seen as a political liability. The marginal utility of additional privileges at the higher levels of the Chinese party-state is limited (since such privileges are already substantial), but the political cost of getting caught abusing such privileges can be significant – disastrous, even – for elites aspiring to higher office. Yet, even top political elites need to monetise their power (which is the return on the cumulative investment they have made in the regime). They resolve this dilemma by opting for a strategy to appropriate the rents by proxy – typically through their spouses, children, and relatives.

As a result, senior elites (at the provincial level and above) have used such proxies to amass wealth. Their control of the power of personnel appointment and rent allocation gives their proxies privileged access to the huge rents in China's transition economy. One question we might ask is whether proxy appropriation poses any risks to the political elites. The answer is no. Senior Chinese political elites have apparently resolved the coordination problem by agreeing among themselves that such appropriations should be allowed. Of course, such agreements are not public, and may even not be explicit, yet since practically all senior leaders are engaged in proxy appropriation, it is hard to imagine that there is no implicit pact sanctioning this privilege. The privileges granted to the political elites are clearly the powerful glue that holds the system together. As ideological values no longer bind the political elites to a collective identity, only enormous privilege can provide the incentive for them to remain loyal to the regime.

Yet, it would be wrong to ignore the fear factor in the formation of interest and identity. While privileges provide positive incentives for the political elites, the fear of losing power in the event of a regime change exerts a powerful influence on their interest and identity. Opinion surveys conducted among elites routinely show a widely shared sense of insecurity.[153] Some of this stems from social instability and economic difficulties during transition (such as riots, crime, inflation, and unemployment). But it is also reasonable to argue that most of the insecurity comes from the elites' own sense of the uncertain future of the regime, which lacks a more reliable source of legitimacy and, in spite of its post-1989 economic successes, continues to face enormous odds in building a durable form of capitalist autocracy.

The infusion of fear as a source of interest and identity formation produces a complex effect. On the one hand, the fear of the loss of power and the disastrous consequences of such a loss tends to motivate the political elites to strengthen their collective identity as the ruling elites. But, on the other hand, the same fear tends to motivate those same elites to value their individual interests over the corporate interests of the regime. The reason is fairly simple: if members of the ruling elite are uncertain about the future of the regime, they are more likely to increase the rate at which they cash out their investment in the regime. This can mean more corruption, a process that, ironically, is likely to accelerate the regime's political decay and make the political elites' fear of regime change a self-fulfilling prophecy.

A new equilibrium – but how stable?

Two decades after China's ruling elites made their decisive – and fatal – turn towards autocratic capitalism, a new equilibrium or order has been established. China-watchers are deeply divided over this issue. Some scholars fundamentally reject this thesis, arguing instead that China is moving towards a more politically open and rule-based system.[154] Differences of opinion exist even among those who agree with this thesis. Some believe that the post-1989 order is durable as a result of the CCP's enormous success in institutionalising its rule. But others scholars reject the view that China's autocratic capitalist order is resilient. They point to the fundamental flaws embedded in this order and argue that its misaligned incentive structure renders the system highly vulnerable.[155] In this paper, we pursue the argument that the post-1989 order may have exhausted its potential as a durable equilibrium. While many of the policies and institutional experiments adopted in the aftermath of the dual shocks of Tiananmen and the collapse of communism in 1989 have effectively worked to preserve the CCP's political monopoly, they can no longer address the new challenges created by the flaws embedded in the autocratic capitalist order itself.

In any case, the contours of the new equilibrium are quite visible today. China's autocratic capitalist order rests on four interconnected pillars of support: (1) legitimacy based on economic performance, (2) co-option of social elites, (3) selective repression of societal and political opposition, and (4) a patronage system underpinned by the CCP's control of vast economic resources.

The most important source of support for the post-1989 equilibrium is, without any doubt, performance-based legitimacy. A combination of fortuitous factors and policy since the early 1990s has allowed the CCP to maintain rapid economic growth. The resultant increases in the standard of living for the Chinese public seems to have formed the basis of an implicit deal between the CCP and Chinese society: acquiescence to the regime's monopoly on political power is contingent on its continued ability to deliver the economic goods. The centrality of satisfactory economic performance for the CCP's survival cannot be over-estimated. Internal surveys of the CCP's elites consistently show they connect economic growth with social stability.[156] If social peace is threatened by declining growth, rent-seeking by the elites could not be sustained without growing prosperity, either. Aware of the danger of its dependence on performance-based legitimacy, the CCP has recently attempted to diversify its sources of support within Chinese society. One experimental approach is to increase the regime's responsiveness to the voices of the public. Consequently, the top leadership has adopted populist rhetoric and attempted to make local ruling elites more accountable. But, at the same time, the CCP is deeply wary of introducing liberalising measures that might mobilise the public in support. As a result, such experimental efforts, attempted exclusively under Hu Jintao's rule, have not succeeded in developing alternative sources of support for the regime.

The second pillar of support for the new equilibrium is the alliance between the CCP and the social elites (such as the intelligentsia, professionals, and businessmen). The CCP invested enormous energy, efforts, and resources in the building of this alliance in the 1990s, initially targeting the intelligentsia and the professionals and eventually expanding the alliance to include China's private entrepreneurs.[157] Several considerations drove the CCP's co-option of social elites. One was the lessons learned from the 1980s, when the intelligentsia, led by the liberals, constantly pressured the regime to adopt democratising reforms. Opposition from the intelligentsia culminated in the Tiananmen debacle for the CCP. In order to pre-empt similar challenges to the CCP's rule, the most effective strategy is to co-opt the key elements of the intelligentsia into the regime and improve the material benefits for the rest so that they have a direct personal stake in the regime's well-being. Finally, successful co-option of the social elites would deprive the masses on the lower rungs of the sociological ladder. Despite the CCP's success in co-opting the social elites, questions remain as to the actual degree of support from the co-opted social elites for the CCP. Co-option is not conversion: aside from receiving practical benefits from the ruling party, these social elites do not necessarily identify with the regime. And, in return, the regime does not necessarily trust the co-opted social elites.

The use of repression, albeit on a much smaller scale, helps maintain the post-1989 equilibrium. While the benefits of economic growth and co-option provide positive incentives for the public and the social elites to acquiesce to the CCP's political monopoly, repression is perhaps the most important and reliable instrument of rule for the CCP. Of course, all autocratic regimes rely on repression for survival. What is notable in this case is the selective, and apparently quite efficient, application of repression by the CCP in the post-1989 era. First, while continuing to suppress political dissent and curtailing civil liberties, the regime has almost completely withdrawn from the private sphere of the individual's life. As a result, personal freedom in China has flourished even as political rights have deteriorated. This enables the CCP to avoid needlessly antagonising the majority of the Chinese public while concentrating its repressive resources on a relatively small number of political dissidents and social activists (labour leaders and rural organisers). Second, the regime has been highly effective in strengthening its capacity for repression by investing in manpower and technology. Compared with the 1980s, the Chinese state today possesses an impressive array of repressive instruments, ranging from well-trained anti-riot police, a network of informers, and specialised internet police units. Under the post-1989 order, the use of selective repression should be credited for two remarkable achievements: (1) the maintenance of social stability in the face of rising popular resentment and protest, and (2) the elimination of organised opposition.

If performance-based legitimacy, co-option of social elites, and selective repression allows the CCP to maintain its political hegemony over Chinese society, political patronage underwritten by bureaucratic capitalism constitutes the principal means for the regime to sustain internal unity. One distinguishing characteristic of the post-1989 order is the relative unity exhibited by the ruling elites. Part of this may be explained by the political homogeneity of the regime after the purge of the liberals following Tiananmen. The most probable explanation, however, is an informal system that allows the ruling elites to use the rents controlled by the state to reward the elites and help resolve their conflicts. Two developments necessitated the use of rents to maintain the internal unity of the regime. The demise of communist ideology has forced the regime to seek an alternative means of motivating its members. As the post-1989 elites have no strong ideological commitments, the most effective method to maintain their loyalty is to make them genuine stakeholders in the current system. This requires rewarding their loyalty with materials perks that would not have been possible in a competitive system. Since these perks are inherently costly, the only way that the CCP can afford them is to use the rents controlled by the state to fund them. This is perhaps one of the most important reasons why the Chinese state continues to control a significant and lucrative portion of the Chinese economy. A second development in the post-1989 order is the use of those same rents as a means of managing intra-elite conflict. As the political struggles over ideology have disappeared, the current conflicts among the ruling elites are over the allocation of rents. Settling such conflict becomes impossible without the CCP's control of rents being embedded in China's bureaucratic capitalist system. Therefore, the nature of the CCP as a regime comprised of non-ideological rent-seeking individuals dictates that it perpetuates the dominance of the state in the economy. Recent trends for strengthening the control of the economy by the state reinforce this analysis.

This new equilibrium may have been stable for the two decades after Tiananmen, but its dynamism and durability have possibly been exhausted. Performance-based legitimacy is the least reliable form of legitimacy for a one-party state. For the CCP, maintaining high rates of growth may become more difficult due to a host of adverse factors that threaten to slow down China's economic engine (such as demographics, environmental degradation, rising inequality, and structural imbalances).[158] Co-option of social elites may soon become too costly since the modernisation process itself is now producing millions of new social elites (mainly college graduates) whom the CCP will have no financial means for co-opting.[159] Social elites left outside the system tend to become the core of a potential counter-elite. The patronage system itself can also become extremely costly since its maintenance requires generating – and tolerating – enormous waste, inefficiency, and corruption. Such a system can come unstuck in two ways. Politically, the ostensible privileges it bestows upon the ruling elites can become a source of public resentment, galvanising populist protest and opposition which could become a broader anti-regime movement. For those elites that have been the beneficiaries of the patronage system, conflict over the distribution of rents could become irreconcilable and thus lead to internal disunity, especially in the event of an economic downturn (which will significantly reduce the rents available for distribution). Economically, the patronage system itself can distort the economy to such an extent that it threatens economic growth, thus undermining performance-based legitimacy.

Conclusions

This chapter has discussed the transformation of the political systems of Russia and China, starting from the communist periods and ending with the present day. To begin with Russia, what is its current political system like? If one compares Russia with the six characteristics that the totalitarian school model of the Soviet Union described, it is easy to conclude that Russia has undergone a major political change. There is no official ideology, there is no single party, there is no centrally directed economy. If, on the other hand, one compares today's Russia with the pluralistic, interest group models used in Soviet studies, one could perhaps see that, close up, the political systems of the Soviet Union and contemporary Russia resemble each other, especially in terms of how the decision-making takes place. In this sense, the country has not come very far, and decision-making is still characterised by rather centrally defined overall objectives, while bureaucratic struggles and conflicts of interest take place within these limits. Should one compare Russia to the criteria of Dahl's 'polyarchy', instead? It is easy to conclude that Russia in theory, or in its Constitution, fulfils all the criteria for a liberal democracy, but in practice often fails to match them. On the other hand, it is easy to see that Russian (civil) society is truly pluralistic and transnationalised, in spite of the tensions between the political leadership and the critical part of civil society. Thus, while these notions draw an approximate picture of Russia's political system and change, it seems that the exact definition of Russia's political system greatly depends upon the level of analysis. In essence this system is a hybrid regime.

It can be argued that Russia's socioeconomic situation and political culture has conditioned the actions that have led to this regime, but these structural factors have also been shaped by those very actions. Because of the complexities involved in this structure/agency relationship, Russia's political change has been an a priori open-ended, uncertain process. Thus, in abstract terms, instead of interpreting Russia from the teleological perspective of failed democratisation, its political change during the past two decades should be understood as a temporal period of systemic change from one political system or regime type to another, originally with a high degree of institutional instability or uncertainty over the political power relations and related political outcomes.

This said, however, it can be asked whether at this point Russia's political system has already consolidated or whether further radical changes are to be expected. Consolidation in this context could be understood as institutionalisation of a new balance of power and respective rules of the game: that is, shared understanding and voluntary or forced acceptance of formal and informal rules under which the state and societal actors can take part in political exchanges and decision-making. Here we might find two rival interpretations, both of which could be supported with as much evidence as one wants to collect. There are those scholars who would say that the ownership structure of the economy and the political elite constellations have finally found a balance that seems safe in the sense that there are no social forces which could challenge the current elite equilibrium. Even if the population at large does not regard the current ownership system as fair, and feels that the privatisation process was nothing more than a big theft of state property, it seems not to be willing or capable of organising another period of turmoil in order to reorganise ownership and power structures; a large part of it already has too much to lose. But there would also be those who would note that, in any case, the state–society relationship of the current model is too weak to be considered stable, and it therefore includes tensions that sooner or later will lead to another period of protests from below. Both might be correct, the first in the short run of, say, ten years, whereas the latter perspective may materialise in some kind of revolt if state–society relations do not evolve either towards a more authoritarian or a more democratic relationship. In any case, the further transnationalisation of Russian society and economy will certainly mean that Russia's modernisation process is bound to change and adapt to whatever direction global developments are going.

Turning to China, the consequences of the CCP's decisive turn toward autocratic capitalism have now become blindingly clear: the party has succeeded beyond its wildest dreams. The productive potential unleashed by the post-1992 strategy has generated economic gains that few inside the CCP's top leadership, including Deng himself, could have imagined. The party has not only survived the post-Tiananmen trauma and the shocks of the collapse of communism: it has prospered. Organised domestic opposition groups are non-existent. Individual dissidents are firmly under control. Riots and protests by disgruntled peasants, workers, and urban dwellers may be frequent, and occasionally difficult to contain, but they do not constitute a genuine threat to the party's capacity to govern. If the post-Tiananmen era has been good to the party, it has been even better for its members, many of them having successfully converted their political power into enormous personal wealth.

In retrospect, however, the emergence of the post-1989 autocratic capitalist order was not predetermined. It was the result of a deliberate and strategic choice made by the ruling elites. After its near-death experience in June 1989 and the fall of communism later on, the CCP saw the light and rallied around Deng's call, "Development is the cardinal truth." But Deng's overriding priority was not, as most people believe, economic development itself, but rather the objective of economic development – the survival of the CCP. Post-1989, Deng correctly concluded that only capitalism could save the CCP's autocratic rule. Thus, in China's case, instead of producing favourable social and political dynamics for democracy, capitalism has in fact strengthened autocracy, at least temporarily.

However, this form of autocratic capitalism is not without internal contradictions. Ideologically, the CCP is a hostage to its nominal allegiance to communism even though its policies are obviously pro-capitalist. Economically, its pro-growth policy is based upon incentives adverse to long-term sustainability. Politically, an elite-based ruling coalition finds itself increasingly under attack from rising populism. So, it is too early to conclude that the CCP has found a durable alternative to democratic capitalism in the transition from orthodox communism. Analysts will make no bigger mistake than to claim that the CCP regime has managed to overcome the fundamental weaknesses that have afflicted, and caused the downfall of, countless autocracies around the world.

Notes

1. *Freedom in the World 2011. The authoritarian challenge to democracy. Selected data from Freedom House's annual survey of political rights and civil liberties.* Available at http://www.freedomhouse.org/images/File/fiw/FIW_2011_Booklet.pdf
2. 'Reading Russia', *Journal of Democracy*, Volume 20, Number 2, April 2009.
3. David Collier and Steven Levitsky, 'Democracy with Adjectives: Conceptual Innovation in Comparative Research', *World Politics*, 49:3 (1997): pp. 430–451; see also the themed issue of *Journal of Democracy* on 'hybrid regimes': Volume 13, Number 2, April 2002.
4. For an overview of this literature, see Archibald Brown, *Problems of Conceptualizing the Russian Political System.* Paper prepared for 2005 APSA Annual Conference, September 1–4 2005, Panel 44–17.

5. See, for instance, Robert Conquest, 'In Defense of Kremlinology', in Walter Laquer (ed.), *The State of Soviet Studies*, Cambridge Massachusetts: The M.I.T. Press 1965, pp. 124–134; Alex Nove, 'The Uses and Abuses of Kremlinology', in Laquer, *The State of Soviet Studies*, pp. 135–143; and for a very critical view, see Arnold L. Horelick, A. Ross and John D. Steinbruner, *The Study of Soviet Foreign Policy: Decision-Theory-Related Approaches*, London: Sage Publications 1975, p. 36ff.
6. Carl Friedrich and Zbigniev Brzezinsky, *Totalitarian Dictatorship and Autocracy*, Cambridge, Mass.: Harvard University Press 1956.
7. Daniel Bell, 'Ten Theories in Search of Reality: The Prediction of Soviet Behavior', in Vernon V. Aspaturian (ed.), *Process and Power in Soviet Foreign Policy*, Boston: Little, Brown and Company 1971, pp. 289–323 (Reprinted from World Politics, April 1958).
8. Zbigniew K. Brzezinski and Samuel B. Huntington, *Political Power: USA/USSR. Similarities and Contrasts, Convergence or Evolution?* England: Penguin Books 1977, originally published in 1964. See especially Chapter 2 and Conclusions.
9. Zbigniew K. Brzezinski, 'The Soviet Political System: Transformation or Degeneration?', *Problems of Communism*, January/February 1966, pp. 1–15.
10. Gordon H. Skilling and Franklyn Griffiths (eds), *Interest Groups in Soviet Politics*, Princeton: Princeton University Press 1971.
11. For a review, see William E. Odom, 'Soviet Politics and After: Old and New Concepts', *World Politics* Vol. 45, No. 1, October 1992, pp. 66–98.
12. V. Khoros, 'Grazhdanskoe obshchestvo: kak ono formiruetsya (i sformiruetsya li) v post-sovetskoy Rossii?', *Mezhdunarodnaya Ekonomika i Mezhdunarodnye Otnosheniya* 5//1997, pp. 85–98, here p. 96.
13. V.V. Dam'e (1994), 'Ekologicheskie dvizheniya i partii "zelenykh" v byvshem SSSR i Rossii', in V.P. Lyubin (ed.), *Politicheskie partii i dvizheniya v Rossii i na Zapade: protsess formirovaniya*. Metody issledovaniya, Moscow: RAU INION 1994, pp. 96–110.
14. L.P. Borisov, *Politologiya. Uchebnoe posobie*, Moscow: Izdatel'stvo Belye alvy 1996.
15. A.A. Ignat'ev and B.V. Mikhailev, 'Grazhdanskoe obshchestvo i perspektivy demokratii v Rossii', in B.V.Mikhailev (ed.) *Grazhdanskoe obshchestvo i perspektivy demokratii v Rossii*, Moskva: Rossiyskiy Nauchny Fond 1994, pp. 3–30.
16. Alexander Kotrikin, 'Some Thoughts on Youth Organisations in St. Petersburg', in *NGO's in St. Petersburg:. Framework, Features, Projects and Legal Background. A Handbook*. Bureau for Information and Communication of NGOs, St. Petersburg and euroCom Gesellschaft für europäische Kommunikation e.V., Berlin. St. Petersburg, January 1996, pp. 83–87, here p. 84.
17. David Kotz and Fred Weir, *Revolution from Above: The Demise of the Soviet System*, London and New York: Routledge 1997.
18. Jim Butterfield and Marcia Weigle, 'Unofficial Social Groups and Regime Response in the Soviet Union', in Judith B. Sedaits and Jim Butterfield (eds), *Perestroika from Below: Social Movements in the Soviet Union*, Boulder, San Francisco, Oxford: Westview Press 1991.
19. E. Zdravomyslova, 'Opportunities and Framing in the Transition to Democracy: The Case of Russia', in D. McAdam *et al.* (eds), *Comparative Perspectives on Social Movements: Political Opportunities, Mobilizing Structures,*

and Cultural Framings, Cambridge: Cambridge University Press 1996, pp. 122–137. See also A. Duka, N. Kornev, V. Voronkov and E. Zdravomyslova, 'Round table on Russian Sociology: The Protest Cycle of Perestroika: the Case of Leningrad', *International Sociology*, 1995 Vol. 10, No. 1, pp. 83–99.
20. Zdravvomyslova 'Opportunities and Framing in the Transition to Democracy'; see also Sedaits and Butterfield, *Perestroika from Below*.
21. D.V. Olshansky and O.G. Kharitonova, 'Perestroika kak neudachnaya popytka politicheskoy modernizatsii', *Vestnik Moskovskogo Universiteta*, Serija 12, politicheskie nauki 1995, No. 6, pp. 28–36.
22. Sylvia Chan, *Liberalism, Democracy and Development*, Cambridge: Cambridge University Press 2002.
23. Samuel P. Huntington, *The Third Wave: Democratisation in the Late Twentieth Century*, Norman: University of Oklahoma Press 1991, pp. 271–273.
24. See, for instance, Mark J. Gasiorowski and Timothy J. Power, 'The Structural Determinants of Democratic Consolidation: Evidence from the Third World', *Comparative Political Studies*, Vol. 31 (1998), No. 6, 740–771.
25. M. Steven Fish, *Democracy Derailed in Russia: The Failure of Open Politics*, Cambridge: Cambridge University Press 2005, p. 103.
26. Fish, *Democracy Derailed in Russia*, pp. 114–138.
27. See the discussion in Chan, *Liberalism, Democracy and Development*.
28. V. Khoros et al., *Grazhdanskoe obshchestvo. Mirovoy opyt i problemy Rossii.* IMEMO, Moskva: Editorial URSS 1998, pp. 51–57.
29. G.F. Slesareva, 'Glava XIII: Grazhdanskoe obshchestvo', in G.V. Polunina (ed.) *Politologiya. Uchebnoe posobie dlya vysshikh uchebnykh zavedeniy*, Moscow: Akalis 1996, pp. 154–177; K.S. Gadzhiev, *Politicheskaya nauka*, Moscow: Mezhdunarodnye otnosheniya 1995, pp. 73, 75.
30. Fish, *Democracy Derailed in Russia*, p. 192.
31. See Heikki Patomäki and Christer Pursiainen, 'Western Models and the Russian Idea: Beyond Inside/Outside in the Discourses on Civil Society', *Millennium: Journal of International Studies*, London School of Economics, vol. 28, No. 1 (1999), pp. 53–77.
32. Gadzhiev, *Politicheskaya nauka*, p. 189.
33. Robert A. Dahl, 'Development and Democratic Culture', in Larry Diamond, Marc F. Plattner, Yun-han Chu and Hung-mao Tien (eds), *Consolidating the Third Wave Democracies: Themes and Perspectives*, Baltimore and London: The Johns Hopkins University Press 1998, pp. 34–39.
34. Michael McFaul, *Russia's Unfinished Revolution: Political Change from Gorbachev to Putin*, Ithaca and London: Cornell University Press 2001, p. 11.
35. McFaul, *Russia's Unfinished Revolution*, p. 343.
36. Kathryn Stoner-Weiss, 'Resistance to the Central State in the Periphery', in Timothy J. Colton and Stephen Holmes (eds), *The State After Communism: Governance in the New Russia,* Lanham: Rowman & Littlefield Publishers, Inc. 2006, pp. 87–119, here p. 114; see also Kathryn Stoner-Weiss, 'The Limited Reach of Russia's Party System: Underinstitutionalization in Dual Transitions', *Politics Society Vol. 29 No. 3, September* 2001, pp. 385–414.
37. Dahl, 'Development and Democratic Culture', p. 38.
38. Victor Sergeyev and Nikolai Biryukov, *Russia's Road to Democracy: Parliament, Communism and Traditional Culture*, Aldershot: Edward Elgar 1993, pp. 207, 208.

39. Nikolai N. Petro, *The Rebirth of Russian Democracy: An Interpretation of Political Culture*, Cambridge, MA: Harward University Press 1993.
40. Harry Eckstein, 'Russia and the Conditions of Democracy', in Harry Eckstein, Frederic J. Fleron, Erik P. Hoffmann and William M. Reisinger (eds), *Can Democracy Take Root in Post-Soviet Russia?* Lanham: Rowman Littlefield 1998, pp. 349–381, here p.372.
41. Ivan Krastev, 'Paradoxes of the New Authoritarianism,' *Journal of Democracy* Volume 22, Number 2, April 2011, pp. 5–16, here p. 8.
42. Fish, *Democracy Derailed in Russia,* pp.108–112.
43. Vladimir Petukhov and Andrei Ryabov, 'Public Attitudes About Democracy', in Michael McFaul, Nikolai Petrov and Andrei Ryabov, *Between Dictatorship and Democracy: Russian Post-Communist Political Reform*, Washington, DC: Carnegie Endowment for International Peace 2004, pp. 269–291.
44. These polls and surveys are regularly made by major sociological survey institutions, see, for instance: FOM: Public Opinion Foundation, available at: http://english.fom.ru/; also: 'Views on Elections', available at: http://bd.english.fom.ru/report/map/dominant/edom0733/edomt0733_2/ed073320.
45. Andrew Buck, 'Network Mobilization and the Origins of the Putin Coalition', *Journal of Communist Studies and Transition Politics*, 26:4, 2010, pp. 445–470.
46. Michele Micheletti, *Civil Society and State Relations in Sweden*, Aldershot: Avebury 1995, p. 5.
47. John W. Harbeson, 'Civil Society and Political Renaissance in Africa', in John W. Harbeson et al. (eds), *Civil Society and the State in Africa*, Boulder and London: Lynne Rienner Publishers, Inc. 1994, pp. 1–29.
48. I.M. Model', B.C. Model', Vlast' i grazhdanskoe obschschestvo Rossii, ot sotsial'nogo vzaimodeystviya – k sotsial'nomu partnerstvu, Ekaterinburg: UrO RAN 1998, pp. 30-36.
49. The official tax register of the Russian Federation, as of 27 July 2005 according to the official webpage http://www.nalog.ru/index.php?topic=reg_ur_lic (no longer available).
50. *OPFR: O sostojanii grazhdanskogo obshchestva v Rossiiskoi Federacii*, Moscow: Obshchestvennaia palata Rossijskoi Federacii 2008; E. Belov, 'Kolichestvo NKO: otsutstvie nadezhnoj statistiki', to be found at: http://www.socpolitika.ru/rus/ngo/database/document11078.shtml; 'Skol'ko v Rossii NKO?', to be found at: http://www.hse.ru/news/11174012.html.
51. Ibid.
52. Butterfield and Weigle, 'Unofficial Social Groups and Regime Response in the Soviet Union'.
53. Georgy Satarov, 'Russia's government launches dialogue on civil society issues', *The Russia Journal*, Issue No.24 (117), 22 June 2001.
54. Alexander Verkhovsky, 'Operation Civic Forum', *(Un)Civil Societies*, 1 August 2001, Volume 2, Number 30, Radio Free Europe Radio Liberty report series.
55. See, for instance, *Moscow Times*, 10 December 2004.
56. *Moscow Times*, 28 June 2004.
57. R.W. Orttung, 'Russia,' in *Nations in Transit*, Freedom house 2010. Available in http://freedomhouse.eu/images/Reports/NIT-2010-Russia-final.pdf
58. See, for instance: Arend Lijphart, *Patterns of Democracy: Government Forms and Performance in Thirty-Six Countries*, New Haven and London: Yale University Press 1999.

59. Robert A. Dahl, *Polyarchy: Participation and Opposition*, New Haven and London: Yale University Press 1971. However, it should be stated that even Dahl considered that no large system in the real world is fully democratized and therefore used the concept of "polyarchy" instead. Moreover, Dahl's *Polyarchy* is actually a book on democratisation rather than democracy and he makes quite clear what it is realistic to expect from a country moving from authoritarian rule towards democracy. If one looks at his "seven conditions" favouring or not favouring development towards a polyarchy – that is, basically the same structural factors discussed above – one can conclude that the starting point for political change in Russia was not favourable. Dahl's words about this kind of a country go as follows: "In a country with a highly unfavorable profile, the immediate introduction of full polyarchy would be an utopian objective; for even if the existing hegemony were overturned or fell into dissolution and thus enabled a group of innovators to adopt a constitution prescribing the institutions of polyarchy, that constitution could hardly be expected to be effective, and the institutions it prescribed would be empty or ephemeral." Dahl, *Polyarchy*, pp. 203, 217.
60. See, for instance, Philippe C. Schmitter and Terry Lyn Karl, 'What Democracy is…and is Not', in Larry Diamond and March F. Plattner (eds), *The Global Resurgence of Democracy*, Baltimore: John Hopkins University Press 1993.
61. See Patomäki and Pursiainen, 'Western Models and the Russian Idea'.
62. Lilia Shvetsova, *Russia – Lost in Transition: The Yeltsin and Putin Legacies*, Washington DC: Carnegie Endowment for International Peace 2007.
63. Richard Sakwa, 'Two Camps? The Struggle to Understand Contemporary Russia', *Comparative Politics*, July 2008, pp. 481–499.
64. Michael McFaul and Kathryn Stoner-Weiss, 'The Myth of the Authoritarian Model: How Putin's Crackdown Holds Russia Back', *Foreign Affairs*, January/February 2008, Volume 87, Number 1.
65. Vitali Silitski, 'Tools of Autocracy', *Journal of Democracy*, Volume 20, Number 2, April 2009.
66. Andrei Illarianov, 'The Authoritarian Model of Governance', *Kommersant*, April 2, 2007, English version available at http://www.robertamsterdam.com/2007/04/andrei_illarionov_the_authorit.htm.
67. Lilia Shvetsova, 'The Return of Personalized Power', *Journal of Democracy*, Volume 20, Number 2, April 2009, pp. 61–65.
68. Richard Sakwa, *Russian Politics and Society*, 4th edition, London and New York: Routledge 2008(a), p. 469.
69. Richard Sakwa, 'Putin's Leadership: Character and Consequences', *Europe-Asia Studies*, Vol. 60, No. 6, August 2008(b), pp. 879–897.
70. Krastev, *op. cit.*, p. 8.
71. Ibid.
72. For instance, Ian Bremmer and Samuel Charap, 'The Siloviki in Putin's Russia: Who They Are and What They Want', *The Washington Quarterly*, Volume 30, Number 1, Winter 2006–07, pp.83–92; Andrei Illarionov, 'The *siloviki* in Charge', *Journal of Democracy Volume 20,* Number 2, April 2009, pp. 69–72.
73. Robert G. Moser, *Unexpected Outcomes: Electoral Systems, Political Parties, and Representation in Russia*, Pittsburgh: University of Pittsburgh Press 2001;

Zoltan Barany and Robert G. Moser (eds), *Russian Politics: Challenges of Democratisation*, New York: Cambridge University Press 2001.

74. Anders Åslund, *Russia's Capitalist revolution. Why Market Reform Succeeded and Democracy Failed?* Washington D.C.: Peterson Institute For International Economics 2007, p. 6.
75. *The Guardian*, for instance, quoted the President of the United States on 5 October 1993: "'It is clear that the opposition forces started the conflict, and President Yeltsin had no other alternative but to try to restore order,' the US president, Bill Clinton, said. 'The US supported Yeltsin because he is Russia's democratically-elected leader,' he said. 'I have no reason to doubt the personal commitment that President Yeltsin made to let the Russian people decide their own future in elections.'" http://www.guardian.co.uk /world/1993/oct/05/russia.davidhearst.
76. Gasiorowski and Power 1998, 'The Structural Determinants of Democratic Consolidation, p. 766.
77. Fish 2005, *Democracy Derailed in Russia*, pp. 224*ff.*
78. Eugene Huskey, 'Elite recruitment and state–society relations in technocratic authoritarian regimes: The Russian case', *Communist and Post-Communist Studies* 43 (2010), pp. 363–372.
79. The list could be endless, but for examples, see: Yitzhak M. Brudny, 'Continuity or Change in Russian Electoral Patterns? The December 1999–March 2000 Election Cycle', in Archie Brown (ed.), *Contemporary Russian Politics: A Reader*, New York: Oxford University Press 2001, pp. 154–178; Peter Ordershook, 'Institutions and Incentives', in Brown, *Contemporary Russian Politics*, pp. 17–28; Richard Rose, 'How Floating Parties Frustrate Democratic Accountability: A Supply-Side View of Russia's Elections', in Brown, *Contemporary Russian Politics*, pp. 215–223; Moser, *Russian Politics*; Zoltan Barany and Robert G. Moser (eds), *Russian Politics: Challenges of Democratisation*, New York: Cambridge University Press 2001; Stoner-Weiss, 'The Limited Reach of Russia's Party System; Michael McFaul, 'Political Parties', in McFaul et al., *Between Dictatorship and Democracy*, pp. 105–134.
80. Hans Oversloot and Ruben Verheul, 'Managing Democracy: Political Parties and the State in Russia', *Journal of Communist Studies & Transition Politics*, September 2006, Vol. 22 Issue 3, pp. 383–405.
81. Stephen White and Valentina Feklyunina, 'Russia's Authoritarian Elections: The View from Below', *Europe-Asia Studies*, 63:4, 2011 pp. 579–602.
82. Richard Sakwa, *Russian Politics and Society*, 4th edition, London and New York: Routledge 2008, pp. 158–159.
83. Dahl, *Polyarchy*, p. 224.
84. For the law and its amendments, see http://www.cikrf.ru/newsite/law /fz/2001_95fz.jsp.
85. For the Ministry of Justice list of the registered parties, their organisation and financial arrangements, as well as information on parties whose registration has been cancelled, and so forth, see http://minjust.lgg.ru/ru /activity/nko/partii/.
86. Robert G. Moser, 'The Impact of Parliamentary Electoral Systems in Russia', in Brown, *Contemporary Russian Politics*, pp. 195–207, here pp. 204, 205.

87. See, for instance, Stephen White and Ol'ga Kryshtanovskaya, 'Changing the Russian Electoral System: Inside the Black Box', *Europe-Asia Studies*, 63:4, 2011, pp. 557–578, here pp. 563–564.
88. For an effort to provide a comprehensive ideological picture, see Christer Pursiainen and Heikki Patomäki, 'The state and Society in Contemporary Russian Political Thought', in Egle Rindzeviciute (ed.), *Contemporary Change in Russia: In from the Margins?*, Baltic and East European Studies 3, Huddinge, Sweden: Södertörns Högskola 2004, pp. 55–93.
89. See, for example, Laura Petrone, 'Institutionalizing Pluralism in Russia: A New Authoritarianism?', *Journal of Communist Studies and Transition Politics*, 27:2, pp. 166–194.
90. Huntington, *The Third Wave*, pp. 266–267.
91. Michael McFaul and Nikolai Petrov, 'Elections', in Michael McFaul, Nikolai Petrov and Andrei Ryabov, *Between Dictatorship and Democracy: Russian Post-Communist Political Reform*, Washington, DC: Carnegie Endowment for International Peace 2004, pp. 23–55, here pp. 24, 55.
92. Stephen White, 'Elections Russian-Style', *Europe-Asia Studies*, 63:4, 2011, pp. 531–556, here pp. 535–538.
93. Sakwa, *Russian Politics and Society*, pp. 154, 160.
94. Vladimir Putin, *Speech at Expanded Meeting of the State Council on Russia's Development Strategy through to 2020,* 8 February 2008, available in English at http://archive.kremlin.ru/eng/speeches/2008/02/08/1137_type82912type82913_159643.shtm.
95. First Deputy Chief of Staff of the Presidential Executive Office Vladislav Surkov, 'Russian Political Culture: The View from Utopia', *Russian Social Science Review*, vol. 49, no. 6, November-December 2008, pp. 81–97, here pp. 83, 84.
96. Dmitry Medvedev, *Go Russia!*, 10 September 2009, available in English from the official Kremlin site: http://eng.kremlin.ru/news/298.
97. 'Medvedev Makes Dig at United Russia', *The St. Petersburg Times*, 26 November 2010.
98. Tom Parfitt, 'Russian Liberal Opposition Party Barred from Elections,' *Guardian* 22 June 2011.
99. David White, 'Dominant Party Systems: a Framework for Conceptualizing Opposition Strategies in Russia', *Democratization*, 18:3, 2011, pp. 655–681, here p. 675.
100. Henry E. Hale, *Why Not Parties in Russia: Democracy, Federalism, and the State*, Cambridge: Cambridge University Press 2008, p. 243.
101. John F. Young and Gary N. Wilson, 'The View from Below: Local Government and Putin's Reforms', *Europe-Asia Studies*, Vol. 59, No. 7, November 2007, pp. 1071–1088.
102. Stoner-Weiss 2001, op. cit., pp. 386–387. For details, see also Hale, *Why Not Parties in Russia*, p. 133*ff*.
103. David Dusseault, *Elite Bargaining and the Evolution of Centre Periphery Relations in Post-Soviet Russia: A Comparative Analysis,* Helsinki: University of Helsinki 2010.
104. Vladimir Putin, *Speech at Expanded Meeting of the State Council on Russia's Development Strategy through to 2020,* 8 February 2008, available in English at http://archive.kremlin.ru/eng/speeches/2008/02/08/1137_type82912type82913_159643.shtml.

105. Andrey Makarychev, *New Challenges to Russian Federalism*, PONARS Eurasia Policy Memo No. 75, Nizhny Novgorod Civil Service Academy, September 2009, available at http://www.gwu.edu/~ieresgwu/assets/docs/pepm_075.pdf.
106. As formulated by Makarychev, *New Challenges to Russian Federalism.*
107. Samuel Huntington, *The Third Wave: Democratisation in the late Twentieth Century*, Norman: University of Oklahoma Press 1992.
108. Terry Lynn Karl, 'Dilemmas of Democratisation in Latin America,' *Comparative Politics* 23 (October 1990), 23, pp. 1–21; Michael Bratton and Nicolas Van de Walle, 'Neopatrimonial Regimes and Political Transitions in Africa' *World Politics*, 46, July 1994, pp. 453–89; Juan Linz and Alfred Stepan, *Problems of Democratic Transition and Consolidation*, Baltimore and London: The Johns Hopkins University Press 1996, pp. 55–65.
109. The suppression of civil society was much less extreme and the legitimacy of the old communist regime was much weaker in countries in Eastern Europe where communism was imposed by the Soviet military. Transitions in these countries could take place via a negotiated process.
110. See Michael McFaul, 'The Fourth Wave of Democracy and Dictatorship', *World Politics* Vol. 54, No. 2 (Jan. 2002), pp. 212–244.
111. For a masterful analysis of the political destructiveness of the Cultural Revolution, see Roderick MacFarquhar and Michael Schoenhals, *Mao's Last Revolution*, Cambridge, Mass: Harvard University Press 2006.
112. Zhao Ziyang detailed the fierce struggle over policy during the 1980s in his memoir, *Prisoner of the State*, New York: Simon and Schuster, 2008; also see Richard Baum, 'The Road to Tiananmen', in Roderick MacFarquhar (ed.), *The Politics of China: The Eras of Mao and Deng*, New York: Cambridge University Press 1997, pp. 340–471.
113. The liberal wing was seriously weakened in January 1987 when its leading figure, Hu Yaobang, was dismissed as the CCP's general secretary. But the wholesale purge of the liberals at the top did not occur until after the Tiananmen crackdown.
114. Joseph Fewsmith, *China Since Tiananmen: From Deng Xiaoping to Hu Jintao*, New York: Cambridge University Press 2008.
115. Seymour Martin Lipset, 'Some Social Requisites of Democracy: Economic Development and Political Legitimacy', *The American Political Science Review* Vol. 53, No. 1 (March 1959), pp. 69–105.
116. Adam Pzreworski et al., *Democracy and Development: Political Institutions and Well-Being in the World, 1950–1990*, New York: Cambridge University Press 2000.
117. Yingyi Qian and Chenggang Xu, 'The m-form hierarchy and China's economic reform', *European Economic Review* 37 (1993), pp. 541–548.
118. Chen, Jiandong, Hou, Wenxuan and Jin, Shenwu, *A Review of the Chinese Gini Coefficient from 1978 to 2005*, 16 January 2008, available at SSRN: http://ssrn.com/abstract=1328998.
119. *Statistical Yearbook of China 1990*, p. 290.
120. Yasheng Huang made this argument in *Capitalism with Chinese Characteristics: Entrepreneurship and the State*, New York: Cambridge University Press 2008.
121. Suisheng Zhao, 'Deng Xiaoping's Southern Tour: Elite Politics in Post-Tiananmen China', *Asian Survey*, Vol. 33, No. 8, August 1993, pp. 739–756.

122. Minxin Pei, 'Chinese Civic Associations: An Empirical Analysis', *Modern China, 24 (*1998), pp. 285–318.
123. Jialin Zhang, 'China's Response to the Downfall of Communism in Eastern Europe and the Soviet Union', Sanford: Hoover Institution 1994.
124. Other scholars have explored the theme of capitalism without democracy. See Kellee Tsai, *Capitalism without Democracy: The Private Sector in Contemporary China*, Ithaca, NY: Cornell University Press 2007; Bruce Dickson, *Integrating Wealth and Power in China: The Communist Party's Embrace of the Private Sector*, New York: Cambridge University Press 2007.
125. Murray Scot Tanner, *The Politics of Law-making in Post-Mao China: Institutions, Processes, and Democratic Prospects*, New York: Oxford University Press 1999; Young Nam Cho, *The Politics of Lawmaking in Chinese Local People's Congresses*, New York: Cambridge University Press 2006.
126. Kevin J. O'Brien, *Reform Without Liberalization: China's National People's Congress and the Politics of Institutional Change*, New York: Cambridge University Press 1990.
127. Kevin J. O'Brien, 'Agents and Remonstrators: Role Accumulation by Chinese People's Congress Deputies', *The China Quarterly*, 138, 1994, pp. 359–380.
128. There is a vast literature on village elections and local political reform in China. The most comprehensive survey is Larry Diamond and Ramon H Meyers (eds), *Elections and Democracy in Greater China*, New York: Oxford University Press 2000. Another excellent survey is Elizabeth Perry and Merle Goldman (eds), *Grassroots Political Reform in Contemporary China*, Cambridge, Mass: Harvard University Press 2007.
129. David Zweig and Chung Siu Fung, 'Elections, Democratic Values, and Economic Development in Rural China', *The China Journal*, vol. 16, no. 50 (2007), pp. 25–46; Kevin J. O'Brien and Rongbin Han, 'Path to Democracy? Assessing Village Elections in China', *The China Journal*, vol. 18, no. 60 (2009), pp. 359–378.
130. Dong Lisheng, 'Direct Township Elections in China: latest developments and prospects', *The China Journal*, vol. 15, no. 48 (2006), pp. 503–516.
131. Tianjian Shi, *Political Participation in Beijing*, Cambridge: Harvard University Press 1997; Yongshun Cai, 'Managed Political Participation in China', *Political Science Quarterly*, vol. 119, no. 3 (2004), pp. 425–451.
132. Yu Jianrong, "Xinfang zhidu diaocha ji gaige silu" [An investigation of the petitioning system and thoughts on its reform], Zhongguo Shehui Xingshi Fenxi **yu** Yuce, 2005 (Analysis and Forecast of China's Social Situation in 2005), Beijing: Shehui kexue chubanshe 2005.
133. Kevin J. O'Brien and Lianjiang Li, 'Suing the Local State: Administrative Litigation in Rural China', *The China Journal*, No. 51 (2004), pp. 75–96; Minxin Pei, 'Citizens v. Mandarins: Administrative Litigation in China', *The China Quarterly*, No. 152 (1997), pp. 832–862.
134. Guobin Yang, *The Power of the Internet in China: Citizen Activism Online*, New York: Columbia University Press 2009.
135. Kevin O'Brien and Lianjiang Li, *Rightful Resistance in Rural China*, New York: Cambridge University Press 2007; Ching Kwan Lee, *Against the Law: Labor Protests in China's Rustbelt and Sunbelt*, Berkeley: Calif.: University of California Press 2007; Kevin O'Brien (ed.), *Popular Protest in China*, Cambridge, MA: Harvard University Press 2008.

136. Sebastian Heilmann, 'Regulatory Innovation by Leninist Means: Communist Party Supervision in China's Financial Industry', *The China Quarterly*, 181 (2005), pp. 1–21; Kjeld Erik Brødsgaard, 'Institutional Reform and the *Bianzhi* System in China', *The China Quarterly*, No. 170 (2002), pp. 361–386; Dali Yang, *Remaking the Chinese Leviathan: Market Transition and the Politics of Governance in China*, Stanford: Stanford University Press 2004.
137. See Kevin O'Brien (ed.), *Popular Protest in China*, Cambridge, MA: Harvard University Press 2008.
138. Minxin Pei, *China's Trapped Transition: The Limits of Developmental Autocracy*, Cambridge, MA: Harvard University Press, 2006; Yan Sun, *Corruption and Market in Contemporary China*, Ithaca, NY: Cornell University Press 2005; Andrew Wederman, 'The Intensification of Corruption in China', *The China Quarterly*, 180 (2004), pp. 895–921.
139. Andrew Nathan, 'Authoritarian Resilience', *Journal of Democracy*, vol. 14, no. 1, (January 2003), pp. 6–17.
140. Andre Lalibert and Marc Lanteigne, *The Chinese Party-State in the 21st Century: Adaptation and the Reinvention of Legitimacy*, London: Routledge 2007; David Shambaugh, *China's Communist Party: Atrophy and Adaptation*, Berkeley, CA: University of California Press 2008.
141. Jonathan Unger and Anita Chan, 'China, Corporatism, and the East Asian Model', *The Australian Journal of Chinese Affairs*, No. 33 (January 1995), pp. 29–53.
142. Andrew Mertha, *China's Water Warriors: Citizen Action and Policy Change*, Ithaca, NY: Cornell University Press 2008; Guobin Yang, 'Environmental NGOs and Institutional Dynamics in China', *The China Quarterly* 181 (2005), pp. 46–66.
143. Jonathan Unger (ed), *Associations and the Chinese State: Contested Spaces*, Armonk, New York: M E Sharpe 2008; You-Tien Hsing and Ching Kwan Lee (eds), *Reclaiming Chinese Society: The New Social Activism*, London: Routledge 2010.
144. Minxin Pei, 'Chinese Civic Associations: An Empirical Analysis', *Modern China*, vol. 24, no. 3 (1998), pp. 285–318.
145. Pittman Potter, 'Belief in Control: Regulation of Religion in China', *The China Quarterly*, 174 (2003): pp. 317–337; Beatrice Leung, 'China's Religious Freedom Policy: The Art of Managing Religious Activity', *The China Quarterly*, 184 (2005), pp. 894–913.
146. James Tong, 'Anatomy of Regime Repression in China: Timing, Enforcement Institutions, and Target Selection in Banning the Flungong, July 1999', *Asian Survey*, vol. 42, no. 6 (2002), pp. 795–815.
147. Kang Xiaoguang and Han Heng, 'Graduated Controls: The State-Society Relationship in Contemporary China', *Modern China*, vol. 34, no. 1 (2008), pp. 36–55.
148. Debra Davis, Richard Kraus, Elizabeth Perry and Barry Naughton, (eds), *Urban Space in Contemporary China: The potential for Autonomy and Community in Post-Mao China*, New York: Cambridge University Press 1995; William Kirby (ed), *Realms of Freedom in Modern China*, Stanford: Stanford University Press 2003.
149. Nora Sausmikat, 'Generations, Legitimacy, and Political Ideas in China: The End of Polarization or the End of Ideology?', *Asian Survey*, vol. 43, no. 2 (2003), pp. 385–404.

150. James Kung, Yongshun Cai, and Xiulin Sun, 'Rural Cadres and Governance in China: Incentives, Institution and Accountability', *The China Journal*, 60 (2009), pp. 61–78; Pierre Landry, *Decentralized Authoritarianism in China: The Communist Party's Control of Local Elites in the Post-Mao Era*, New York: Cambridge University Press 2008.
151. X. L. Ding, *The Decline of Communism in China: The Legitimacy Crisis, 1977–1989*, New York: Cambridge University Press 2006; Yan Sun, *The Chinese Reassessment of Socialism, 1976–1992*, Princeton, NJ: Princeton University Press 1995.
152. Xueguang Zhou, 'The Institutional Logic of Collusion among Local Governments in China', *Modern China*, vol. 36, no. 1 (2010), pp. 47–78; David S. Goodman, *The New Rich in China: Future Rulers, Present Lives*, London: Routledge, 2008; Xiaobo Lu, 'Booty Socialism, Bureau-Preneurs and the State in Transition: Organizational Corruption in China', *Comparative Politics*, vol. 32, no. 3 (2000), pp. 273–292; Andrew Wedeman, 'Anticorruption Campaigns and the Intensification of Corruption in China', *Journal of Contemporary China*, vol. 14, no. 42 (2005), pp. 93–116; Ting Gong, 'Dangerous Collusion: Corruption as a Collective Venture in Contemporary China', *Communist and Post-communist Studies*, vol. 35, no. 1 (2002), pp. 85–103.
153. The Institute of Sociology at the Chinese Academy of Social Sciences publishes an annual survey of elites trained at the Central Party School in its 中国社会形势预测与分析 series, Beijing: Shehui kexue chubanshe.
154. See Dali Yang, *op. cit.*; Shambaugh, *China's Communist Party.*
155. Minxin Pei, *China's Trapped Transition.*
156. The Institute of Sociology, CASS, 中国社会形势预测与分析, Beijing: Shehui kexue chubanshe, various years.
157. Bruce Dickson, *Red Capitalists in China: The Party, Private Entrepreneurs, and Prospects for Political Change*, New York: Cambridge University Press 2003; Bruce Dickson and Jie Chen, *Allies of the State: China's Private Entrepreneurs and Democratic Change*, Cambridge, MA: Harvard University Press 2010; Gang Guo, 'Party Recruitment of College Students in China', *Journal of Contemporary China*, vol. 14, no. 43 (2005), pp. 371–394.
158. Kenneth Keng, 'China's Unbalanced Economic Growth', *Journal of Contemporary China* vol. 15, no. 46 (2006), pp. 183–214.
159. For instance, the rapid expansion of higher education has created the problem of unemployed college graduates, posing a serious threat to social stability and the party's ability to co-opt social elites. See Limin Bai, 'Graduate Unemployment: Dilemmas and Challenges in China's Move to Mass Higher Education', *The China Quarterly*, 185 (2006), pp. 128–144.

5
Sovereignty or Interdependency?

Sergei Medvedev and Linda Jakobson

After more than two decades of reform, China and Russia have developed new hybrid forms of national capitalism and authoritarianism. Besides the domestic socioeconomic and political challenges, both countries have international ambitions. To be sure, China and Russia share a common denominator in the realm of foreign policy: to manage and, if possible, decrease the impact of US influence upon international affairs. But, putting this commonality aside, the two countries have different goals and conditions, and have adopted different foreign policy strategies to deal with the post-Cold War world order. Russia, seeing its current international standing in decline and being reduced to a mere energy supplier to the world market, is seeking to replay the end of the Cold War and to revive its great power ambitions. China has moved away from its former heavy reliance on bilateral relationships to working within numerous multilateral frameworks. Though this development has been welcomed in the international community, China's more assertive behaviour in the maritime sphere has raised concerns about the implications for regional stability of China's growing power. At the same time, China has not given up on its insistence on respect for sovereignty, nor has China's leadership officially been swayed from the argument that, as a developing country, it must focus on raising the living standards of its own people before taking on more international responsibility.

Starting from this general picture, we ask what are the similarities and differences between these countries in the fields of foreign policy and international relations? To structure this discussion, this chapter scrutinises the approaches of the two countries to the international order (status quo or revisionism), the basis for foreign policy decision-making (ideology or pragmatism), the use of instruments of power (hard versus soft power) and the preferred basis of international relations doctrine (sovereignty or interdependency).

Russia

The evolution of Russia's foreign policy over the past 20 years has been a roller coaster ride. The country has pretended to play such different roles on the world stage: as an ally of the West and its political opponent, as a regional leader, and as a weak, yet ambitious geopolitical giant. Russia's task was particularly difficult because the country had to adapt itself to the changing international situation, while experiencing painful domestic transformation. Under conditions of high uncertainty, Russia could not produce a long-term political strategy; it focused on current problems and opportunities rather than on more fundamental questions about its foreign policy identity, its place and its mission in the world in the twenty-first century. As a result, today Russia is widely acknowledged as an important international actor, but at the same time it is seen by others as a political 'black box', tending to produce somewhat unexpected political outcomes.

Such perplexity arises because of the existence of different foreign and domestic factors, which influence the processes of decision-making in Russia. The list includes the necessity to comply with international obligations, aspirations to be competitive on the world market, ambitions to become one of the 'poles' of the emerging international system, as well as the commitment to preserve state sovereignty, a vested interest in strengthening the political regime, and the activity of lobbyists promoting interests of different domestic groups. The foreign policy of today's Russia is a perfect example of Putnam's 'two-level games',[1] an elaborate interplay between foreign and domestic policy. In this situation, a decision is reached only after protracted deliberation, often carried out behind the public stage.

Russia's position in the international arena is primarily defined by two sets of resources: first, the institutional and military legacy of the USSR, and second, the energy resources, which nourish economic wealth and are used as political leverage in the policy of so-called energy nationalism. However, the significance of the Soviet legacy is clearly decreasing, while the energy lever is highly susceptible to price volatility in world markets. Russia was considerably weakened in the 1990s, when these two factors coincided, and restored its geopolitical position in the 2000s, when high oil prices allowed the implementation of a more ambitious agenda. Russia has alleviated most of the negative geopolitical consequences of the difficult period of transition in the 1990s, and has claimed that other actors should take Russia's foreign policy interests into account. Overall, Russia has pursued a multi-vector foreign policy and has not shied away from conflicts whenever they arose, especially in relations with Western countries.

Over the last 20 years, the country's rapprochement with the West failed at least twice – in the mid-1990s, and again in the mid-2000s – and it returned to its historical role of a 'powerful periphery'. Russia remained highly sensitive to outside critiques of its domestic and foreign policies and continued to portray NATO as a hostile organisation. Russia's foreign policy credo was expressed by (then) President Vladimir Putin in his speech at the 43rd Munich Conference on Security Policy in 2007, when he proclaimed that "Russia is a country with a history that spans more than a thousand years and has practically always used the privilege to carry out an independent foreign policy."[2]

Against this historical background, a number of political and economic developments caused Russia's disappointment with its Western partners. First, Russia's reforms, carried out in accordance with the 'Washington consensus', as discussed in some detail in the preceding chapters, created much more painful consequences than expected, which frustrated Russian society and elites. Second, having lost its geopolitical weight after the breakup of the USSR, Russia had hoped that the West would support it during this difficult period. Instead, the West used the period of Russia's weakness to incorporate the countries of the former Soviet bloc into its zone of influence, eliciting anger and envy in Russia and contributing to the deterioration of the country's relations with the West. Third, the evolving international system in the 2000s was somewhat favourable for the implementation of opportunistic policies. Economic and political failures in the West, from Wall Street to Iraq, the loss of legitimacy of international institutions and regimes, and the rise of non-Western actors all convinced Russia of the idea that the international system was becoming multi-polar, just as the (then) foreign minister Yevgeny Primakov had predicted more than a decade previously.

In fact, Russia was not alone in its desire to raise its international status. Other emerging nations also became more ambitious and self-confident, challenging the balance of power in the international arena: in the mid-2000s the concept of the BRICs (Brazil, Russia, India, and China),[3] invented by the analysts of Goldman Sachs, received a great deal of media attention, and also political traction. The leaders of state and ministers of finance of those four countries met several times between 2008 and 2010, with the aim of establishing an informal club in order to support each other's economic and political aspirations. Their actions are not profoundly anti-Western, but they clearly like emphasising their distinctive political identity.

The economic developments of the past decade have further contributed to a higher profile for those four countries. First, the economic boom of the early 2000s has stimulated the dependence of the West on those emerging economies, namely dependence upon Russia's oil and gas, cheap consumer goods from China, and the skilled workforce of India. Second, during the financial crisis of 2008-09 most developing countries have shown better performance than the European countries and the US. China, Brazil, and India maintained their economic growth at the level of 5-10 per cent, raising hopes for the long-term sustainability of their development.[4] Russia lagged behind them, and was indeed struck quite hard by the crisis, but it still continues to be seen as an attractive investment opportunity by others.

By virtue of its history and geographical location, Russia finds itself at the junction of liberal 'Westernisation' and 'non-Western globalisation'. As was discussed in the preceding chapters in more detail, Russia is also at the heart of the debate about 'authoritarian capitalism' as a means of development, a form of market capitalism without political liberalisation. This term has been used by Azar Gat, Robert Kagan, Sergei Karaganov and other authors,[5] with Kagan proclaiming that

> the return to the international competition of ambitious nations has been accompanied by a return to global ideological competition. More precisely, the two-centuries-old struggle between political liberalism and autocracy has re-emerged as a [...] defining characteristic of the present era.[6]

Obviously Russia, which in the 2000s drifted towards authoritarianism, while receiving high revenues from oil and gas exports, is often mentioned as a country primarily involved in this renewed ideological competition.

Russia was indeed one of the most vocal actors among the 'authoritarian capitalism' countries. Disappointed with the West's passivity in the early 2000s, when it failed to respond to Russia's overtures and proposal for an alliance, Russia subsequently never shied away from openly disagreeing with the West on a number of issues, including the 'colour revolutions' in the post-Soviet countries, NATO expansion, and the deployment of elements of the US anti-ballistic missile system (ABM) in Eastern Europe. The high point of disagreement with the West came in August 2008, with the Russian–Georgian war. In response to Georgia's attack on South Ossetia, a breakaway region in the northern part of Georgia, Russia attacked Georgia, bombing the city of Gori and military targets on the territory of the country.[7] The meaning of this war went far beyond the Russian–Georgian conflict. In fact, Georgia was one of the most anti-Russian countries in the camp of 'new democracies' in the post-Soviet space and had been backed by the US in previous years. Thus, by attacking Georgia in response to its actions in South Ossetia, Russia sent a clear message to the West that further NATO expansion was unacceptable and Russia's concerns with the foreign policies of Western countries were serious.

However, the global financial meltdown and the changes of leadership in Russia and the US in 2008 have lowered the level of tension in the international arena. Countries were forced to focus on domestic problems rather than on international controversies; under these conditions they found limited cooperation to be in everybody's interest and more beneficial than damage limitation or conflict rhetoric. In autumn 2008 Russia's new president, Dmitry Medvedev, proposed the development of a new European Security Treaty in order to prevent any possible future military conflicts in the Euro-Atlantic area, and this proposal is still on the cards[8]. Although Russia's foreign partners seem unwilling to conclude such a treaty, regarding NATO and the OSCE as sufficient instruments for the provision of Euro-Atlantic security, they have not entirely rejected Russia's proposal, and the dialogue on this issue continues. Another attempt at improving the international political climate was a 'reset' in the US–Russia relations, as declared by the new Obama administration in 2009. Both sides tried to concentrate on pragmatic cooperation and to avoid addressing antagonisms, which allowed them to agree terms on the new Strategic Arms Reduction Treaty, which was signed in April 2010.

Russia is an important player, yet it is still an evolving participant in the international arena. After the collapse of the USSR it lost a substantial part of its foreign policy resources and foreign policy identity. An 'inventory' of Russia's foreign policy has been going on for the past two decades, during the course of which the country has sought to define its own identity and its relations with the outside world; this self-seeking is still far from complete. Indeed, Russia today remains as far as ever from a clear-cut domestic and international identity. The nation is currently at the centre of cleavages between *Liberalism* and *Realism* in international relations, between its *institutional affiliations and aspirations*, on the one hand, and its *instincts of sovereignty*, on the other. Finally, Russia also finds itself at the point of global bifurcation between *liberal Westernisation* and various *non-Western variants of modernisation*, 'alternative modernities'. This makes Russian foreign policy an object of political contestation, and further complicates the task of implementing a coherent foreign policy. Therefore, in order to analyse Russia's foreign policy of recent years we should pose the same questions, and posit the same alternatives, that Russia's ruling elite faced during this period. Indeed, this political alternative can be treated as analytical dichotomies, binary oppositions as presented in the introduction to this chapter. Let us discuss each of them in more depth.

Defensive revisionism

One of the main geopolitical consequences of the demise of the USSR was the end of the bipolar international system. The status quo, based on a combination of institutional and political factors, was broken, and since that time actors have been trying to find new foundations for a stable international order. Initially, at the end of the twentieth century, it was presupposed that such a balance could be reached by filling old institutional forms, inherited from the Cold War, with new liberal content. Instead of being reformed, the old post-World War II institutions were reoriented towards 'civilising' and integrating post-communist societies: Russia took a seat of the USSR at the United Nations Security Council; NATO prepared for Eastern enlargement; the International Monetary Fund and the World Bank gained more international weight during the period of large-scale post-socialist economic reforms. In a brief 'unipolar moment' it seemed that Russia and other post-communist countries would quickly complete the tasks of transition and join the developed countries of the West, following which a new liberal status quo in the international system would be reached, the 'End of History'.

In fact, in the 1990s, Russia, then considered a nation 'in transition', followed the emerging 'New World Order',[9] first enthusiastically, and later reluctantly (see the debates on the first wave of NATO enlargement),[10] accepting all its basic postulates: democracy, liberalism, international institutions, and the normative dominance of the West. Another wave of Russia's rapprochement with the West came in the early 2000s, when Russia, led by the pragmatic Vladimir Putin, sought to follow the quickly evolving US-led international order – ultimately acquiescing to NATO's war in Kosovo in 1999, the US War on Terror in 2001 (involving the invasion of Afghanistan, and later Iraq), the abrogation of the ABM

Treaty by the US in 2001, and ultimately NATO enlargement to the Baltic countries in 2004.

However, the period of a 'cooperative Putin' turned out to be short-lived, and since 2003–04 different processes both inside and outside of Russia have pushed the country to start challenging the fragile international consensus: Russia's political regime began its authoritarian drift; the legitimacy of the US as the world leader was weakened after the invasion of Iraq in 2003; and the EU was facing a crisis of integration, caused by the consequences of enlargement and the failure of the first attempt to adopt the European Constitution in 2005. The conflict level within international relations started to rise, and Moscow gradually changed its stance – from a pragmatic alliance with the West to increasingly anti-Western (but also pragmatic) activism aimed at using the uncertainty in international relations to Russia's advantage. The cover page of the *Economist* on 11 December 2004 featured a picture of Vladimir Putin dressed as a boxer and the cover story was titled "The Challenger"; it concluded that "It is time to see Mr. Putin as a challenger, not a friend."[11]

After several years of continued economic growth and international turbulence, in the mid-2000s Russian foreign policy found a new quality and became revisionist. The irony of the situation was that it was not revisionism *per se*, but rather a struggle for the preservation of Russia's current international position and status quo, which in contrast to Russia's geopolitical weakness of the 1990s was perceived as revisionism. In fact, opposing the US attempts to deploy the ABM elements in the Czech Republic and Poland and rebuffing the plans for NATO's enlargement into Ukraine and Georgia, were an attempt to return to the *status quo ante*, and a nostalgia for the days of the Cold War when Russia had a right of veto over strategic decisions on the European continent.

As put by Dmitri Trenin in 2008:

> Moscow is trying to replay the end of the Cold War. This is not to say that the Kremlin seeks to revive the Soviet Union, establish garrisons on the Elbe and the Vistula or re-enter Afghanistan. Moscow seeks an equal footing with its partners East and West and recognition as a power center in the region that stretches from the European Union to China's borders and from the North Pole to the Middle East.[12]

Opinions about the new Russian foreign policy stance were split. Some critics stated that Russia's advances to countries such as Venezuela, Iran, and the Palestinian Authority became yet another manifestation of Russia's perennial anti-systemic tradition, formed by "'the Bolsheviks-outlaws,' who were ready to form blocks with other offended states in order to resist the world leaders of their époque".[13] Meanwhile, others supported these steps as a welcome counterbalance to Western expansionism.

Indeed, in the 2000s Russia has become a revisionist state, but it was revisionism of a special kind: a nostalgic and defensive revisionism of a depressed and defensive geopolitical giant. Memories of the role that the USSR played in the world, and the remaining military and political resources, continue to support Russia's foreign-policy inertia. Though Moscow sometimes may not articulate its interests and prove its competence, it is clear that it has sufficient status to participate in global governance.

Russia's self-assurance during the past decade was mainly supported by the growth of the energy factor in international relations, and the rise of 'energy nationalism' on the world stage. The hike in oil and gas prices in the 2000s permitted Russia's elite to cope with the most critical social problems within the country and to make itself noticed in the international arena. Moscow was quite liberal in the use of its energy weapon against its neighbours – Ukraine, Belarus, and Georgia.

In particular, it should be mentioned that Russia's revisionism has a defensive nature. With these actions Russia tried to stop the process of the expansion of the sphere of Western dominance, whilst being unable to suggest any real alternative projects.

To be true, Moscow's foreign policy moves were sometimes far from diplomatic. As put by Dmitri Trenin:

> The problem is, Moscow's assertive tactics can be misperceived as a strategy of confrontation. In the past, the Soviet Union lost much when what the Kremlin saw as defensive action, from the Berlin blockade to the invasion of Afghanistan, was perceived as aggression by the West and provoked a response that worsened the Soviet Union's international standing. The weak point of Russian foreign policy has traditionally been an inability to explain itself clearly to America and Europe.[14]

A similar situation was almost literally replayed in the 2000s. Indeed, the situation was rather paradoxical: Russia, constantly stressing its adherence to the preservation of the international status quo and to the principles of international law, pursued revisionist policy (or, better put, was imagined as a revisionist country in Western opinion); whilst the

USA, which tried to change the world order to its own liking by using the policy of power, appeared as a status quo country in the international arena. This confusion has further added to Russia's frustration, and to the misunderstandings between Russia and the West.

Pragmatism as an ideology

Soviet foreign policy was ideological at its core. The declaration of commitment to communist ideas classed other states as being either 'foes' or 'friends' of the USSR, making Moscow spend resources on either confrontation or on assistance. In the final analysis, it was this ideological component of the Soviet foreign policy that destroyed the country, leading to excessive spending on the support of cohesion within the socialist block, but producing no real allies in the world.

However, a certain pragmatism also existed in Soviet foreign policy. The ideological confrontation between the Soviet Union and the United States caused the arms race between the two. When the level of armaments produced, and the capacity for mutual overkill, became extremely high, the opponents realised the necessity of negotiations. Shifting relations into a pragmatic field, and searching for technical solutions which were in the interests of both sides became ways to weaken the ideological hostility. Not surprisingly, political scientists remembered this at the end of the 2000s, when Russian–American relations reached their lowest point in the post-Cold War period.[15]

In the logic of the ideological 'zero-sum game', the discrediting of the communist ideology played into the hands of the liberals. As a result, the end of the twentieth century was marked by the triumph of liberal ideology. The Wilsonian liberal discourse claimed to be an uncontested foundation of the 'New World Order', with clear geopolitical and military implications. These were clearly demonstrated during NATO's military operation in Yugoslavia in 1999: "Kosovo was the first war in history that is said to be fought in pursuit of principle, not interest."[16] In an attempt to stop ethnic purges in Kosovo, NATO began bombing Yugoslavia and finally toppled the Milosevic regime.[17]

By contrast with the 'ideological' approach of the West, Russia's foreign policy during the last 20 years has been rather pragmatic. The country faced serious domestic problems and, as put by Sergei Karaganov, 'retreated in panic' from the international arena.[18] 'Damage limitation' was the name of the game for Russia, especially with respect to NATO and EU enlargement, and increasing US unilateralism. Perhaps the only occurrence of the 'ideological' approach in Russian foreign policy happened in the same Kosovo episode in March and April 1999, when NATO's actions provoked massive resentment in Russian society and among the political elite. With regard to the question of Kosovo, Russia has always been committed to a certain vision of the country's mission to support the 'Orthodox brethren' in Serbia, and to oppose action by the United States and NATO in defiance of international law.

Apart from the Kosovo story, throughout the 2000s Russia sought to pursue a pragmatic political course. At the beginning of the decade the country's political elite, driven by Vladimir Putin's trademark 'pragmatism', found it beneficial to align itself with the West. The Russian President was one of the first foreign leaders to speak directly to President Bush after the 9/11 attacks on Washington and New York. In that phone call, he expressed his condolences to the president and the American people and his unequivocal support for whatever response the American president might decide to undertake. As Michel McFaul observed, "He then followed this rhetorical support with concrete policies."[19] Russia actively cooperated with NATO in Afghanistan and still supports this operation. Vladimir Putin also reacted moderately to the US withdrawal from the ABM Treaty in 2001 and to NATO enlargement in 2004, which, back then, seemed to indicate a pragmatic pro-Western shift in Russia's foreign policy. As noted by Dov Lynch:

> The global war on terrorism has represented an opportunity for Moscow to ally itself with the Euro-Atlantic community around a common, and thankfully vague, threat. Russian differences with the West have not gone away; simply, Putin has decided that they are best resolved with Russia comfortably inside the tent rather than with one foot jammed in the doorway.[20]

The period of pragmatic alliance with the West turned out to be short-lived. Soon, Russia stated that it was not going to make any more foreign-policy concessions, treating harshly those neighbours from the 'near abroad' that pursued anti-Russian policies, and was stated that it was considering the possibility of asymmetric response to the threats to its own security. The 'Munich speech' of Vladimir Putin laid down the main principles of Russia's new course, and such events as the gas conflicts with Ukraine in 2005–06, withdrawal from the CFE Treaty in 2007, and the war in Georgia in 2008 became the most important landmarks of a new, assertive, kind of pragmatism.

The reason for the Russian–Ukrainian gas disputes was exactly the de-ideologisation of the relations between the two countries after the 'Orange Revolution' in Ukraine. Earlier, during the presidency of Leonid

Kuchma, Russia had heavily subsidised the gas prices for Ukraine as its supposed ally. As a result of the 2004 'Orange Revolution', Ukraine became more Western-oriented, so a pragmatic conversion to the world market prices on gas was used as a means to punish Ukraine, and to remind it of the power of its eastern neighbour. Russia's withdrawal from the CFE Treaty was also carried out under the slogan "Nothing personal, only business": Russia had to respond to the fact that the majority of its Western counterparts have not ratified the adapted CFE Treaty, while continuing to follow their obligations in accordance with its provisions.[21]

As Timofei Bordachev and Fyodor Lukyanov observed of Russia's new pragmatism:

> Moscow tried moving as far as possible in all fields accessible for expansion. It adopted a new common practice of dropping the dogmatic veneration of all principles it had formerly accepted ... In recent years Russian foreign policy has become hyperactive rather than successful in the strict sense.[22]

Demanding equal treatment, Russia tried to emulate the mode of action of the West: harsh responses to criticism, the use of force where it considered it necessary, decision-making that was dubious from the point of view of international law, and teasing its opponents with military exercises close to their borders (for example, joint military trainings with Venezuela in the Caribbean sea).

Thus Russian foreign-policy pragmatism had two basic tasks: first, the promotion of advantageous conditions for cooperation with the West and other geopolitical centres and, second, guaranteeing the well-being and security of the ruling Russian elite and political regime. In the short-term, Moscow managed to cope with both tasks, but this was mainly due to high oil prices, which compensated for the lack of strategic vision in Russia's foreign policy. Also, because of conflicts with the West, Russia started to pay more attention to other directions for its foreign policy and found new ways of interaction with China, India, and Latin American countries.

The times of 'grand narratives' in Russian foreign policy are probably gone, and Russia is not likely to promote a certain ideology under conditions of limited resources and the necessity of solving many domestic problems. [23] Becoming more self-confident, Russia, according to Alexey Arbatov, chose a down-to-earth 'macho' position, denying any idealism and becoming rudely pragmatic.[24] However, Russia's pragmatism was opportunistic and reactive, which dramatically undermined its effectiveness. Paradoxically, an ideological factor cannot be excluded: indeed, its pragmatism has become its ideology. As observed by Viatcheslav Morozov, the very emphasis on autonomy, control, and sovereignty which the Russian diplomacy is trying to present as a pragmatic shift and a move away from foreign policy driven by ideology becomes desperately ideological in the Marxian sense of the word.[25]

Shortage of soft power

The distinction between soft power and hard power, drawn by Joseph S. Nye Jr., is a rather new concept, emphasising the fact that in the modern world, the soft power of intangible resources, such as culture and political ideals, is often more effective than the hard power of weapons. As described by the author of the concept himself:

> Soft power comes from three main sources: One is the culture of a country – in the case of America, that ranges from Harvard to Hollywood. Second, political values can be very attractive for other countries, from democracy to freedom of speech to opportunity. And the third one is the legitimacy of a country's foreign policy – meaning that if your foreign policy is considered to be legitimate by other nations, you are more persuasive.[26]

Despite being virtually non-operationalised, this concept drew substantial attention for its highlighting of the factors of communication and image. Soft power may play a compensatory role in foreign policy, or may be a kind of 'safety net', minimising the damage of foreign-policy mistakes.

Traditionally, the Russian Empire and the Soviet Union have mostly relied on hard power, supporting its imperative of territorial expansion with military resources. In order to keep control over the vast territory of the country, Russia's elites had to centralise power and control the peripheral territories. In this context, the famous quip from Joseph Stalin about the Pope – "how many divisions does he have?" – may be seen as a Russian foreign policy credo. During Soviet times the country's military expenditure accounted for 15 per cent of its gross domestic product (GDP), and although it had decreased 15 times by the end of the 1990s, the amount of stored armaments, including nuclear weapons, remained high, which allowed Russia to maintain its position as one of the great military powers in times of severe economic depression. During the 2000s, the percentage of defence spending in Russia's

Table 5.1 Military expenditure of Russia

Year	Value (In constant (2008) US $ m.)	Value (As percentage of GDP)
1988	339,100	15.8
1989	314,400	14.2
1990	266,000	12.3
1991	...	...
1992	66,000	5.5
1993	58,300	5.3
1994	56,800	5.9
1995	33,700	4.4
1996	29,700	4.1
1997	33,000	4.5
1998	21,000	3.3
1999	21,800	3.4
2000	29,700	3.7
2001	33,000	4.1
2002	36,600	4.4
2003	39,000	4.3
2004	40,600	3.8
2005	44,200	3.7
2006	48,400	3.6
2007	52,500	3.5
2008	58,300	3.5

Source: The SIPRI Military Expenditure Database http://milexdata.sipri.org/.

Notes: Medvedev is responsible for the parts concerning Russia, whereas Jakobson is responsible for the China-related parts. Medvedev's assistant researcher in the part focusing on Russia has been Igor Tomashov. Jakobson's research assistant in the parts about China has been Ming Tang.

GDP has shrunk even further despite greater military expenditure in absolute figures, enabled by high revenues from the trade of gas and oil. Table 5.1 shows these figures.

The most prominent demonstration of Russia's military might was during the Russian–Georgian war in August 2008, but Russia also has undertaken some other demonstrative actions, including a visit by Russia's fleet and two Tupolev-160 strategic bombers to Venezuela in the autumn of 2008. The TU-160s landed in Venezuela as part of military manoeuvres on 10 September 2008,[27] soon after the war in Georgia, which was seen in Russia as having been provoked by increasing US interference in the post-Soviet space. The visit of Russian warships to Venezuela for joint exercises two months later caused even greater resonance as "the first deployment of this kind in the Caribbean since the Cold war".[28] Russia also tried to deter US ambitions in Eastern Europe, opposing plans to install some elements of the US BMD system in the Czech Republic and Poland and threatening to deploy its Iskander short-range missile systems in the Kaliningrad region near Poland as a response.

Still, Russia also possesses great potential for soft power, inherent in its history and culture. In the course of its history Russia has integrated numerous nationalities into a single nation, which would have been impossible by the use of force alone. The attractiveness of the Soviet model should also not be discarded. In fact, its attractiveness was quite prominent, especially in the 1930s and 1940s, when the USSR seemed to be an alternative to the West, which had been weakened by the Great Depression and discredited by the fascist regimes in Germany and Italy. The Soviet model continued to spread after the end of World War II and then after the dissolution of colonial empires in the 1960s, defining the foreign policy priorities and identities of the new independent countries. Since the collapse of the USSR, the memory of the role it played in the twentieth century, offering an alternative path to modernity, also contributes to Russia's soft power.

Nowadays, Russia has had to reinvent itself in the international arena. It lost a substantial portion of its soft power in the 1990s, when it was a recipient of economic aid and political and cultural norms. In the 2000s it was searching for a balanced international strategy, trying to convert its economic growth and strengthen its geopolitical position into soft power. The home-grown concept of 'sovereign democracy', together with the Western discourse on authoritarian capitalism, formed a conceptual basis for Russia's 'non-democratic' soft power and gave Robert Kagan a reason to speak about the 'league of dictators' united by common views on the methods of governance.[29] In further attempts to build up its soft power, Russia has invested heavily in projects such as hosting the G8 Summit in St. Petersburg in 2006, the organisation of the Eurovision song contest in Moscow in 2009, and preparations for the 2014 Winter Olympics in Sochi, regarding these as good opportunities for promoting an image of Russia as an actively developing and open country.

However, in comparison with the soft power of Western countries, Russia's ability to win hearts and minds abroad is limited. A chain of 'colour revolutions' in the post-Soviet countries was perceived as a geopolitical defeat for Russia, whose neighbours opted for deeper integration into the Euro-Atlantic community. In fact, the events in

Georgia, Ukraine and Kyrgyzstan dealt a serious blow to the Russian political elite, which responded by tightening the political regime at home and by becoming more arrogant on the world stage, as signified by a number of Russia's foreign policy acts: the transfer to market prices in energy relations with Ukraine was interpreted as a 'hard' economic measure, caused by the worsening of political relations; 'the informational response' to the Estonian authorities' removal of the monument to Soviet soldiers in Tallinn resulted a cyber attack on several Estonian websites;[30] and the (in)famous Munich speech of Vladimir Putin aggravated relations between Russia and the West, prompting negative reactions across the globe.

Despite Russia's search for a cohesive international strategy, the main problem with its contemporary foreign policy is the lack of balance: Russian hard power is excessively harsh and its soft power is profoundly weak. As a result, there is little wonder that during recent years Moscow has lost virtually all public relations battles in the international scene. As observed by Sergei Karaganov:

> Things have reached the point of absurdity as Moscow is now stigmatized for expansionism and the policy of pressure when it subsidizes the economies of neighboring countries by selling them energy resources at reduced prices, and then again when it decides to switch to market prices.[31]

Having poignantly perceived criticism from other countries, Russia generally understood that it should counteract on the public level and in the informational sphere in a manner that would correspond to the status of the great power. But, at the same time, Moscow's actual reaction often led to a rise in tension in relations and strengthened negative international attitudes about Russia.

Soft power is in short supply in Russia these days. To begin with, this concept does not sit well with the Kremlin *Weltanschauung*. For Moscow, the idea that other states may cooperate not only on the basis of pragmatic interests, but also on the basis of principles and positive mutual perceptions, seemed quite new and non-compatible with the Realist perception of the world still dominant in Russia's foreign policy quarters. Moreover, Russia's reaction to the concept of soft power was cautious, because it often happened to be a victim of the identity policies of other states. The re-orientation of other countries towards the West, and the search for their own identity, has often happened at the price of demonising Russia. For Estonian, Latvian and Ukrainian elites and societies, Russia has become a constituting Other, and the passionate denial of their Soviet past a means of constructing their contemporary identity.

The concept of soft power stresses the importance for foreign policy of political values and cultural norms which are widespread across several societies. At the same time, soft power cannot be effective without a clear understanding of the reasons for its use and of the image that the country concerned intends to project in the international arena: American soft power supports the global leadership of the US; China's soft power aims at 'damage limitation', seeking to offset the possible negative interpretations of rapid Chinese growth and geopolitical weight by implementing the principles of 'harmonious development'; soft power for small European states supports their recognition as fully-licensed members of the West. Following these arguments, one is left wondering, what are the aims of Russia's soft power? This question remains open while the country is at odds with its foreign-policy identity.

One of the key problems here lies in the fact that Russia, a country with ambitions of being at least a regional leader, lacks an effective social and economic model which may be attractive for other countries. The high popularity of leaders inside the country turns out to be inconvertible into positive attitudes towards them abroad. The same applies to the home-grown concept of 'sovereign democracy', which was invented in the mid-2000s in order to send the West a message not to meddle in Russia's domestic affairs, and it has no export potential. This, in turn, leads to a disturbing dissonance between the growing desire of Russia to participate in global governance and the suspicious attitude in Russia towards the very idea of global governance. As pointed out by Igor Zevelev: "Moscow sometimes looks at its affiliation [with Western clubs] only from the angle of its own status and ability to gain concessions, not from the angle of growing responsibility or search for compromises."[32]

Interdependency of sovereign actors

Looking at the changes in the international system following the end of the Cold War, the 1990s and the 2000s, as different as they may have appeared, were two stages of the same transformation. Indeed, the trend of increasing interdependency between different actors and the trend of re-sovereignisation of states exist side by side. The liberal triumphalism of the 1990s was offset by the rise of international terrorism and 'authoritarian capitalism' in the 2000s; the US aspirations for global domination were counterbalanced by the increased activity of other centres of global power, including Russia, China and the EU; periods of economic growth in the 1990s and 2000s ended with a sudden global financial meltdown at the end of each decade, in 1998 and 2008–09 respectively. Symptomatically, in the wake of the economic crisis of 2008–09, governments across the globe resorted to well-tested protectionism, nationalisation, and increased intervention by the national Central Banks, thus undermining the trend of increasing globalisation and interdependency.

Strengthening its geopolitical influence in the 2000s, Russia insisted on the principle of sovereignty as a critically important element of the international order. This meant the implementation of a revisionist political course in the international arena and the declaration of the unacceptability of foreign interference in domestic affairs. In restoring Russia's 'stateness', the reference point for Russia's leadership was the Soviet Union. As pointed out by Viatcheslav Morozov: "Putin's project as a whole and sovereign democracy as one of its constitutive elements are deeply rooted in the image of the Soviet past as the golden age in the history of Russian statehood."[33] The USSR provided Russia not only with a myth, constituting its identity, but also with resources for concrete actions, for instance, military might and key positions in international organisations.

During the 2000s the Russian leadership and experts used the mantra of sovereignty to provide an ideological basis for Russia's revisionist policies. The situation was ambiguous: on the one side, the West did not have effective mechanisms for returning Russia to the democratic path of development, and on the other side, the level of interdependency was sufficient enough to prevent actors from engaging in open conflict. Yet, despite the vicissitudes of global transformation, the interdependency of major actors remains high: a large-scale disruption of relations is, in any case, impossible, which has been apparent on many occasions, such as the war in Kosovo in 1999 and the war in Ossetia in 2008. Russia cannot engage in diplomatic conflict with the EU, because Europe is its biggest trade partner; the EU is dependent on Russia as its main energy supplier; the US cannot afford to ignore Russia because its cooperation is necessary for solving key problems of US foreign policy, from arms control to Iran; China does not want to sharpen the contradictions with the West on human rights, because it could impede its economic growth; the US is vitally dependent on China in trade and finance, and so on.

In this sense, interdependency, binding together all key actors, has a structural character and leads not to liberal triumphalism, but rather to pragmatic de-ideologised cooperation. They are tied together as political, economic and social units, forming a complex matrix of the global world – but at the same time the system of international relations is eroding. As noted by Timofei Bordachev and Fyodor Lukyanov:

> The international system collides the 'billiard balls' of the interests of major world powers more and more forcefully. The proliferation of anarchy is not a new historical phenomenon at all, but unlike previous historical eras, the erosion of clear international rules, which is taking place right in front of our eyes, is happening against the background of objectively broadening economic interdependence. In the first years of the new century, there were increasingly frequent signs that the international system was entering a 'zone of turbulence'.[34]

One of the biggest political problems of today's international affairs is that *speaking* about structural interdependency has become commonplace but, on the contrary, *promoting* interdependency as mutual respect for the interests of the different actors is not a popular strategy. This general trend was initiated by the United States after the events of 9/11, and since then the principles of interdependency were further undermined by such different phenomena as US unilateralism, Russia's 'sovereign democracy', the 'Beijing consensus',[35] and the rejection of the first draft of the EU constitution by several European states. Interdependency as a principle of foreign policy has come to be perceived as evidence of weakness. The states, seeking to be competitive, perceive interdependency as an instrument of, and not as a final goal of, their foreign policy.

Russia's use of interdependency as an instrument of foreign policy has been particularly evident in the territory of the Commonwealth of Independent States (CIS). Appealing to the Soviet past and regarding itself as a centre of integration, Russia tried to promote the CIS as an alternative to integration with the West. Besides the CIS, cooperation also existed in other formats, such as the Collective Security Treaty Organization (CSTO), created in its current form in 2002, the Eurasian Economic Community (EurAsEC), and the Union State between Russia and Belarus, these latter two both being established in 1996. In July 2010 Russia, Belarus, and Kazakhstan deepened their integration by establishing a new Customs Union.

Russia also admits the importance of interdependency in broader international relations: an interdependency of sovereign actors, as implied in the concept of multi-polarity. Disappointed with the West,

Russia began to develop ties with such rising giants as China and India, as well as regional and anti-Western powers such as Iran and Venezuela. And although Russia's support was hardly critically important for them, it was a notable signal that it was the right time to challenge an international order dominated by leaders from America and Europe. As a result, at the end of the decade the G8 was supplemented by the G20, which proved its usefulness during times of economic crisis.

Russian society perceived the changes in the official position rather favourably, and the percentage of those supporting Russia's cooperation with India and China has grown by 10 per cent during the 2000s,[36] while the percentage of Russians who consider themselves to be European has simultaneously declined.[37] US–Russia relations were undoubtedly at the centre of these changes, which developed in a way reminiscent of a roller coaster: the image of the US in Russia improved in light of the large-scale terrorist attacks on the US in September 2001, deteriorated substantially in the middle of the decade, and improved again after the 'reset' in US–Russia relations by the new Obama administration. The deterioration was severe: in September 2008 around 70 per cent of Russians regarded the US as a hostile country with a bad image.[38]

China

Foreign policy in China is also shaped by domestic political considerations as well as by developments in the international environment. The foreign and domestic strands are "interwoven into a single web and neither strand can be removed without doing fundamental harm to our understanding of the whole".[39] By reversing the Maoist course of perpetual revolution, Deng Xiaoping ushered China into a new age in the late 1970s. Deng's 'Economics in Command' replaced Mao Zedong's 'Politics in Command' as the driving force of China's reform.[40] His insistence that China concentrate all its efforts on modernisation laid the foundation for China's domestic transformation and opening to the outside world. In 1982 Deng expressed China's overriding desire to maintain 'a peaceful international environment' which would allow the implementation of policies to "develop the country and shake off backwardness".[41] At the same time, China's foreign policy development was profoundly influenced by the demise of the Soviet Union and the subsequent emergence of the United States as the world's sole superpower, as well as a process of economic globalisation. Still today, the leaders of China's Communist Party (CCP) suffer from existential anxiety, which in part stems from the collapse of the Communist Party in the Soviet Union. To quote Yuan Peng, Chinese leaders see themselves facing "unrelenting political pressure from the West".[42]

Historic experiences and tradition also inform foreign policy thinking, hence the need to pay "attention to both the enduring and the transient" when assessing China's foreign policy.[43] In China's case, historic undercurrents flow from the 4000 years of China's civilisation and the Chinese elite's traditional notion of China as the Middle Kingdom, the dominant and central power to which other kingdoms and states owed tribute as politically and culturally inferior satellites. Another historical undercurrent is the humiliation that the Chinese suffered at the hands of the Japanese and Westerners during the 'century of shame' from the mid-nineteenth to mid-twentieth century. This culture of national humiliation is kept alive today by a steady flow of new books, films, plays, museum exhibitions, and even theme parks, sponsored by the Chinese Communist Party (CCP), while the government's public education seeks to remind the populace of the CCP's achievements in restoring China's national dignity. This emphasis by the CCP on the century of shame is a "very deliberate celebration of national insecurity", as William Callahan so vividly phrases it.[44] In the words of Jing Men, China has a dual identity: a strange combination of self-superiority and self-inferiority.[45] This dichotomy is still evident despite China's increased power and standing in the international arena.

The Five Principles of Peaceful Coexistence constitute a historical undercurrent as well, forming the framework of Chinese foreign policy for more than five decades. These principles are mutual respect for sovereignty and territorial integrity, mutual non-aggression, mutual non-interference in internal affairs, equality and mutual benefit, and peaceful coexistence. These were first embodied in an agreement signed by China and India in 1954[46] and served as the basic tenets of the Non-aligned Movement. Despite the drastic changes that followed Mao Zedong's death, the Five Principles were incorporated in the CCP constitution in 1982. China continues to regard these principles as the basis for relations with all nations regardless of their social systems or ideology.[47]

The defining goal of China's foreign policy since the country adopted its reform and opening policy in the late 1970s has been to avoid conflict in order to facilitate the concentration of the nation's resources on building up comprehensive national power. Ensuring a peaceful environment along its borders has allowed the Chinese Communist Party to focus on modernisation and economic development, its foremost objectives, which are imperative for regime survival. A recurring theme in nearly all assessments of China's rise by Chinese analysts is that the remarkable success story of the past three decades is anchored in a peaceful and stable international environment: China needs peace to focus on the severe political, economic, and social challenges at home.[48] Continued economic growth and rising living standards constitute a paramount national interest and the basis for CCP legitimacy.

In Chinese official foreign policy doctrine too, peace and development are key themes. To quote a July 2009 study report by Chu Shulong, "the practice and goal of its diplomacy is to create and maintain a peaceful environment in the domestic economic construction, while 'maintaining world peace and promoting co-development' internationally".[49] Economic development encompasses technological and social development. Over the last three decades China's leaders have reiterated that China pursues an independent foreign policy of peace. 'Independent' means that China develops its strategy according to its own understanding and judgement of the international environment and according to the interests of the Chinese people, "free from adhering to or allying with any other country". (One cannot avoid the parallel with Thomas Jefferson's Inaugural Address in 1801: "Peace, commerce, and honest friendship with all nations – entangling alliances with none.")[50] Peace refers to China's pursuit of a foreign policy based on the Five Principles of Peaceful Coexistence. Chu points out that under the current circumstances, this formulation may be too simplistic. He expands upon this by stating:

> China is implementing a strategy that seeks a peaceful environment and peaceful modernisation [...] China's biggest interest today is its domestic economic development and modernisation. All the foreign policies China has implemented since it opened up to the world have been to serve this means. Therefore, to create and maintain a 'peaceful environment' is the essence and goal of China's current foreign policy.[51]

Pragmatism over ideology

Deng Xiaoping's trademark was pragmatism, as the two aphorisms of his era attest: 'seek truth from facts' and 'practice is the sole criterion of truth'. The populist saying attributed to Deng – "it does not matter if it is a white cat or a black cat, as long as it catches mice" – reflects the very essence of his approach to policy-making.[52] Deng condemned the ideological fervour of the Mao era and deemed it more important for Chinese leaders to raise living standards and build comprehensive national strength that could be measured in terms of gross domestic product, levels of technology, and military capabilities rather than the ideological correctness of the population's thoughts.[53] Thus China embarked on an intense pursuit of the four modernisations, articulated by Zhou Enlai in 1975, to raise China's capabilities in agriculture, industry, science and technology, and defence. In a move that proved pivotal for China's extraordinary economic take-off because it brought both overseas Chinese investments and Western know-how into the country, Deng welcomed the help of all Chinese compatriots in building the motherland. By distancing himself from Mao's view that "sitting on the fence will not do" and that all Chinese "must lean either to the side of imperialism or to the side of socialism", Deng opened China's doors to ethnic Chinese around the world regardless of ideological persuasion. Deng proved, in fact, that there was a "third road" which Mao had dismissed.[54] He never relented in his view that the CCP must maintain absolute power and that China's ultimate goal was socialism, but he accepted flexible and pragmatic approaches in order to utilise every possible means to further China's modernisation drive.

In the international arena China ceased to support communist insurgencies and revolutionary movements abroad. It pursued ties with incumbent governments which were based on economic cooperation and were indifferent to ideology. Today, China perceives its economic and security interests as being best served by engagement and cooperation – both through bilateral relations with individual states and through multilateral processes including the active promotion of formal regional institutions.[55] There are numerous other examples of Deng Xiaoping's pragmatic approach in the realm of foreign policy.[56] Beijing not only established diplomatic relations with the United States and Japan in 1978, paving the way for China to reap the benefits of increased trade, technology transfer, and educational exchanges, and later to be in a position to take full advantage of globalisation. Deng also persistently sought to improve relations with the Soviet Union and, following the Soviet collapse, with Russia, despite their glaring contradictions in ideology. His efforts laid the groundwork for the settlement of border disputes in the 1990s and establishment of the strategic Sino–Russian partnership in 1996. Beijing even normalised relations with the Republic of Korea in 1992, the country against which it fought in the Korean War alongside the Democratic People's Republic of Korea.

Yet, ideology has not become obsolete in China's strategic policy formulation. China's official ideology is still Marxism–Leninism–Mao Zedong Thought, though the ideology's name and content have been revised to suit the CCP's needs.[57] Benjamin Schwartz's observation, made 40 years ago, holds true today, that "even as the ideology itself is disintegrating residual elements of ideology continue to shape the world image of communist ruling groups".[58] These elements are most apparent when China holds high – or at least rhetorically upholds – solidarity with the developing world in international affairs. The Maoist view of international politics as a worldwide struggle between imperialism and progressive forces surfaces at a minimum to justify China's actions in impoverished nations. China continues to insist it is a developing nation despite the dramatic increase in its economic, political, and military power. But if 'ideological versus pragmatic' is a criterion used to evaluate China's intent to uphold, remake or reshape the world order, it will be pragmatic considerations – not ideological ones – which will prompt China to act, if it chooses to act at all.

Towards "constructive interference"

In 1984 Harry Harding wrote that "while China has undergone cycles of alignment and isolation, reflecting its ambivalence toward interaction with the West, the centre of gravity of its modern politics is a commitment toward strategic independence and economic self-reliance".[59] Today, China is anything but economically self-reliant, but it is still as committed as it was 15 years ago to ensuring its independence of action. The contradiction between China's staunch view of the need to respect sovereignty and its immense reliance on an increasingly interdependent world is one of Beijing's fundamental foreign policy challenges. For China, sovereignty is sacrosanct. Since the founding of the People's Republic of China the CCP has emphasised that it will never allow a repeat of the Chinese 'century of shame', a time when China was weak and was humiliated by Western powers and Japan. At the same time, China's phenomenal economic rise has benefited from, and been largely dependent on, globalisation. Subsequently Beijing's ascent has been marked by China's rapid integration into the present world order as well as its effective utilisation of world markets, foreign investment, and foreign technology.

Beijing has moved from relying heavily on bilateral relationships to working within numerous multilateral frameworks. China's accession to the WTO in 2001 was a watershed event. "On a secular basis", writes Arthur Kroeber, "China depends profoundly on the existence of a liberal international economic order with free flows of goods and capital, and on the continuous innovations in hard and soft technologies generated by the advanced open economies, principally the US."[60]

Since the 1990s, step by step, China has been compelled to modify its views on sovereignty in order to support the core national interest of economic development. Admittedly, Chinese leaders reject any description of it as a postmodern state: in Robert Cooper's terminology, it remains very much a 'modern state', concerned with sovereignty issues and non-interference by one country in another's internal affairs.[61] Furthermore, Beijing is adamant that it will not make any concessions over external sovereignty in dealing with Taiwan. For this reason, China did not voice support for Russia's military offensive against Georgia in August 2008 despite the Sino–Russian strategic partnership, and even went so far as to ensure that Moscow did not receive support from the Shanghai Cooperation Organization. Furthermore, Beijing has not recognised the independence of Abkhazia and South Ossetia. But Beijing's actual behaviour over the past few decades, like that of most other countries, reveals a pragmatic approach to sovereignty when it is in China's best interests. By joining international organisations, ratifying international treaties, and making concessions to global economic forces, it has substantially adjusted its interpretation of sovereignty. By joining the WTO China has given up some of its economic sovereignty, and it has signed international treaties on human rights, acknowledging – even if not complying with – the notion of universal human rights across territorial boundaries. In Track II settings Chinese scholars readily acknowledge that the changing interpretations of sovereignty have had profound implications within international politics. China has started to accommodate some, if not all, postmodern trends.

Since the 1950's China has officially adhered to the principle of "non-interference in the internal affairs of other countries", one of the Five Principles of Peaceful Coexistence. It is this principle of non-interference that Chinese officials from the top down refer to when justifying China's close ties with governments shunned by Western countries because of grave human rights abuses or when brushing off Western criticism of China's practice of granting development aid with no demands on accountability or transparency. However, there are numerous examples of China accepting a role that *de facto* entails interfering in the affairs of other countries, from China's active participation in recent years in UN peacekeeping operations to Beijing's hosting of the six-party talks on North Korea's nuclear program. As of August 2011, China was a participant in 14 peacekeeping operations in 12 countries.[62] In December 2008,

China dispatched two destroyers and one supply ship to participate in the United Nation's sanctioned anti-piracy operations off the Horn of Africa, the first time in modern history that China has sent naval forces to participate in combat operations beyond its territorial waters in an international mission. As of mid-2011 China had dispatched a total of nine convoys and a hospital ship to the Gulf of Aden.[63] Furthermore, beginning in early 2007, Chinese leaders and diplomats started to take a more active role in international efforts to persuade the Sudanese government to stop the violence in Darfur. When President Hu Jintao met Sudanese President Omar Hassan Ahmed al-Bashir in February 2007 he indicated China's desire to help stabilise Sudan by announcing China's support for a United Nations peacekeeping mission in Darfur.[64] In March 2011 China abstained, but did not use its veto to prevent the United Nations Security Council from passing a resolution approving "all measures necessary" to protect Libyan civilians against Muammar Gaddafi's forces.[65]

China's interpretation of the principle of non-interference is bound to erode further as China's fast-growing economy – and the need for energy, resources, and markets – forces Beijing to engage more deeply with supplier and customer countries. The slaying and kidnapping of Chinese oil workers in Ethiopia and Nigeria in 2007 and in Sudan in 2008, as well as the 2011 evacuation operation of 30,000 Chinese from Libya, involving a People's Liberation Army (PLA) navy frigate, were reminders that China will have to deal with a growing number of non-traditional threats in countries in which it has commercial interests. In private conversation Chinese foreign policy specialists acknowledge that non-interference is no longer practical, tenable, or in line with Chinese national interests.[66]

Deciding how to free China of its 'non-interference trap' and formulate a more activist – yet not overly aggressive – core principle is a major challenge for Chinese foreign policy-makers today. [67] Since 2006 there have been an increasing number of careful formulations in academic journals by Chinese researchers which lay the groundwork for the acceptance of a flexible approach to the non-interference principle.[68] Wang Jisi writes:

> From a diplomatic point of view, non-interference in domestic affairs will still be an important principle. We should, however, note that the stability of other countries has become more and more related to our rights and interests in those countries, including the security of our overseas organisations and civilians. Therefore, China will

> contribute to the construction of a harmonious society of other countries through diversified means of cooperation, consultation, aid, communication and so on.[69]

Commenting on the principle of non-interference at the 2007 China-EU Roundtable in Beijing, one Chinese participant observed that "in Chinese foreign policy practice, when there is a conflict between national interest and principle, national interest will prevail".[70] A senior foreign policy specialist who consults the country's leading policy-makers went a step further in January 2008 by stating in private conversation that China is moving toward a policy of "constructive interference".[71] Analysis by a growing number of non-Chinese researchers supports this line of thinking.[72]

Chinese soft power – more than trade and investments

China's hard power is considerable. Over the past 20 years China has allocated vast resources to significantly upgrade its military capabilities. The People's Liberation Army has not only acquired new weapons systems, but has also professionalised its personnel and increased its capabilities in logistics, mobility, training, communications, intelligence, and other fields. Yet, with the exception of cyber warfare and intercontinental ballistic missiles, China's military has not yet acquired power projection capabilities which would make it a global military power. Rather, it is an increasingly robust regional power.[73] China has concentrated its efforts to ensure that it can defend its core national security interests – territorial integrity and sovereignty – even in the event of conflict with the United States over Taiwan.

China has also invested enormous sums and made strenuous efforts to increase its soft power in the last 20 years. An important diplomatic imperative of China is to assure its neighbours and the rest of the world that its rise will be peaceful and will not cause harm to others. By emphasising equality and multilateralism as the guiding principles of international relations and engaging actively in both regional security mechanisms and international bodies, China strives to alleviate the jitters its neighbours and others might have about its increased military capacity. During the first decade of the twenty-first century increasing flows of trade, investment, tourism, and students between China and its neighbours led some analysts to conclude that China was gaining not only economic clout but also gaining political friends in the region.[74] However, in 2009, 2010 and 2011 China's more assertive behaviour in the South China Sea and East China Sea evoked apprehension and consternation among many Asian elites. In several countries across the region China's maritime actions drove a wedge between business and security communities who hold widely differing views of China's true intentions and their implications. Businessmen speak of the enormous benefits and opportunities that follow from deepening economic engagement with China. Strategic planners voice concerns that a more powerful China will use its military capabilities to enforce its will upon others.

Soft power is sometimes used in conjunction with China when describing the influence (either real or perceived) that China has in other countries because of the investments and business deals made by Chinese companies. However, the economic clout that China wields is not synonymous with soft power. Soft power as defined by Joseph Nye, who injected the term into mainstream debates on international relations, is "the ability to attract others by the legitimacy of one's policies and the values that underlie them".[75] Power is the ability to get others to do what you want. One can rely on coercion (the 'sticks' of hard power), payments ('carrots'), and/or attraction (soft power). According to Nye, the soft power of a country rests primarily on three resources: its culture, its political values, and its foreign policies.[76] Around the world people are indeed increasingly attracted by Chinese culture. As for China's foreign policy, many incumbent leaders very much welcome China's adherence to the principle of non-interference in the internal affairs of another country (whilst many opposition leaders do not). During the George W. Bush presidency in particular, China's official non-meddling approach was positively perceived across continents, in contrast to US foreign policy. But the verdict is still out with regard to the attractiveness of China's political values, because the political system lacks accountability and an independent juridical system, and as result it has bred rampant corruption and acute inequality.

Regardless of whether China's economic sway in Africa, South America, and other Asian countries reflects Beijing's soft power as defined by Nye or simply the skilful use of carrots (payments) in the realm of business, China is getting others to do what it wants: agreeing to Chinese companies' offers to extract resources. Moreover, the immense success of China's economic development over the past three decades is certainly a source of attraction in many countries, and could be a growing source of Chinese soft power. Though China insists it does not want to export its model of development and states that each country should choose its own path, the feat of lifting hundreds of millions of Chinese out of poverty in three decades is seen as an exemplar by many.[77] The degree to which China is genuinely drawing nations into its orbit is still an open question, but there is no doubt that China is becoming more self-confident. In an essay contemplating the importance of the successful Olympics for China, a prominent Communist Party official writes: the "United States' economic problems show the bankruptcy of Western-style democracy, while China's Olympic Games triumph shows the growing 'superiority' of its Communist Party rule".[78]

Moreover, as stated above, China is making huge efforts to increase its soft power in the genuine sense of the term. China's officials "have worked hard since the 1990s to build its reputation as a good global citizen and regional neighbor" in an attempt to dispel anxieties among China's neighbours.[79] China has also invested heavily in new Confucius Institutes,[80] media outlets, and cultural events abroad. At the end of 2010 China had established 322 Confucius Institutes and 369 Confucius Classrooms in 96 countries. In contrast, before March 2006, there were only 54 Confucius Institutes overseas.[81] China is also attracting tens of thousands of overseas students, some of whom the Chinese government provides funding for. As David Shambaugh notes, by training future generations of intellectuals, technicians, and political elites, China is ensuring that many of them will be sensitised to Chinese viewpoints and interests and will have an understanding of Chinese language, culture, history, society, and politics, thus potentially increasing the power of attraction.[82]

A subtle re-shaper

Chinese foreign policy is in a state of flux, a natural consequence of its growing economic, political, and military power. Like their counterparts the world over, Chinese policy-makers are trying to adjust their policies to the changing international environment. In addition, leaders in China must take into account the demands of both the fast-growing economy and China's rapidly transforming society. China needs resources and new export markets in order to sustain economic growth. This imperative is the driving force behind much of China's growing activities worldwide. Chinese society, in turn, is becoming multi-faceted. A growing number of actors seek to influence foreign policy decision-makers. These actors operate both within the traditional confines of the Communist Party, Government, and People's Liberation Army, as well on the margins – for example, provincial leaders, directors of large companies, prominent researchers, intellectuals and media representatives, as well as segments of the online community of netizens. Consequently, a certain degree of pluralism is creeping into foreign policy decision-making. Nearly all foreign policy actors, regardless of whether they belong to the official establishment or operate on the margins, often interpret China's national interests based on their own, sometimes narrowly-defined, perspectives and preferences.[83]

The direction in which China's foreign policy is evolving is the focus of intense debate both within China and among foreign observers. In particular, since the onset of the global financial crisis in 2008, a pivotal question has been whether China is moving away from Deng's prescription that China should keep a low profile in the international arena in order to fully concentrate the nation's efforts on modernisation. This *taoguang yanghui* policy – hiding one's capabilities and biding one's time – was articulated by Deng in the early 1990s and remains the guiding principle of China's foreign policy. However, China's remarkable economic rise is viewed by many Chinese elites as giving Beijing's leaders the prerogative to stand up to the West and Japan more staunchly. There is a growing consensus among both netizens who follow international politics and other foreign policy actors that China should be more active on the international stage and defend its interests more assertively. This stance reflects both genuine (and understandable) pride among the Chinese over the country's remarkable achievements, as well as the government's continued public education emphasising China's 'century of shame'. There are many Chinese who, on the one hand, criticise their government for restricting civil liberties in China and, on the other hand, condemn Western governments' criticism of China's human rights situation, seeing it as an attempt by outsiders to continue to humiliate China. As Zhao Suisheng notes, nationalism is a means for the government to legitimise its rule, but it is also a means for the Chinese people to judge the leadership's performance.[84] On Chinese blogs which focus on international affairs, China's policy responses are routinely bemoaned as weak and China's leaders are admonished not to bow to pressure from industrialised nations. China's officials are aware that dissatisfaction with foreign policy can rapidly transform into citizens questioning the leadership's ability to govern. Hence, in times of crisis, especially when the United States or Japan is involved, the nationalist undercurrent running through society is viewed by Chinese observers as having a constraining effect on China's leaders' actions.[85]

On numerous occasions during 2009, 2010 and 2011 China pursued what it views as its interests and worldview with disregard for the views and sensitivities of Western nations or its Northeast Asian neighbours South Korea and Japan. For example: China opposed binding targets even for developed nations at the Copenhagen climate summit;

Chinese authorities executed a European citizen for the first time in 50 years; China refused to give in to Google's demand to stop censoring its search engine; Chinese authorities sentenced political activist Liu Xiaobo to 10 years in prison; Beijing refused to criticise Pyongyang despite an international investigation concluding that a South Korean navy vessel Choenan was struck by a North Korean torpedo, and again refrained from voicing disapproval when North Korea shelled civilians on Yeonpyeong island; China temporarily suspended exports of rare earths to Japan after Tokyo detained a Chinese fishing boat captain, and so on. Increasingly, Chinese foreign policy experts and officials stress that the West needs to show respect for China's national interests if they expect China to respect the national interests of Western countries. Moreover, this is becoming a prerequisite for securing China's cooperation in solving global problems.

The *quid pro quo* stance that Chinese officials appear to have striven towards since 2009 poses a tremendous challenge for Western governments because China's cooperation is essential on just about every pressing global issue, from enforcing non-proliferation and anti-terrorism measures to reducing drug trafficking and greenhouse gas emissions. Not surprisingly, officials and observers in capitals around the globe are posing questions: is it China's intention to dictate the terms of international engagement and thereby reshape the present world order? If China's economy continues to grow and its political and military power increases, what kind of pressure will China be willing to exert to back its demands that its interests be considered?

But what precisely are China's national interests, or 'core interests' as the Chinese prefer to call them? The top leadership has not articulated a grand strategy. There is no Chinese public document which would comprehensively expound the country's strategic goals and the ways to achieve them. In fact, apart from Taiwan, which China views as an integral part of its territory, there is no single foreign policy issue which China has identified as a core interest.[86] In December 2010 Dai Bingguo, the state councillor in charge of external relations, defined China's core interests as follows: first, China's political stability, namely the stability of the CCP leadership and of the socialist system; second, sovereign security and territorial integrity, and national unification; and third, China's sustainable economic and social development.[87] According to Wang Jisi, "a unique feature of Chinese leaders' understanding of their country's history is their persistent sensitivity to domestic disorder caused by foreign threats".[88] The wording of China's foreign policy objectives are often lacking in specificity. Following the outbreak of the global financial crisis Hu announced that China's diplomacy should "safeguard the interests of sovereignty, security, and development".[89] As China's global reach has expanded, so has the range of issues debated as potential core interests by various foreign policy actors in China.

The jury is still out on whether the more assertive stance China displayed in international affairs during 2009, 2010 and 2011 is a signal of its intention to radically change the world order. How China will use its power in 10 or 15 years time is an open question. To a large extent, Beijing pursues policies that are consistent with international norms and the interests of the US and the EU.[90] As long as the United States or others do not make any movement – perceived or real – toward recognition of a *de jure* independent Taiwan, China does not openly challenge the predominance of the United States as the world's sole superpower in the existing international order.[91] On the contrary, the goal of China's evolving security diplomacy over the past three decades has been to avoid severe conflict with the United States (or any other major power) in order to ensure a peaceful environment for modernisation. Rather, Beijing does its best to thwart US influence whenever possible. During the Bush presidency China skilfully utilised Washington's preoccupation with Iraq and the war on terror and filled the space vacated by the US by expanding and solidifying relations with its Asian neighbours and countries further afield. However, Beijing stays clear of outright antagonism of Washington and even tacitly acknowledges that the US military presence has contributed to peace in the Asia-Pacific region.

Chinese foreign policy officials are aware that to be credible as a rising power – especially one that advocates achieving a "harmonious world"[92] as its foreign policy objective – China cannot be viewed as turning a blind eye to international crises. In explaining China's goal of a "harmonious world", Hu Jintao has said that "China will try to build a stable, friendly and harmonious world of democracy, rule of law, justice and fairness, sincerity, order and harmonious coexistence between man and nature".[93] The term 'responsible stakeholder', put forward by former US Deputy Secretary of State Robert Zoellick in 2005 in a speech about China's international behaviour, has not been endorsed by Chinese officials and researchers. Zoellick said: "It is time to take our policy beyond opening doors to China's membership into the international system. We need to urge China to become a responsible stakeholder in that system."[94] Chinese observers reject Zoellick's underlying insinuation that China is not presently a responsible stakeholder, and furthermore Chinese observers question the right of the US to define the meaning of 'responsible'. To quote Chu Shulong's 2009 report, Zoellick's words were interpreted to mean "if China wants to be a responsible stakeholder, its behaviour patterns, values and even its political systems must all learn from the west and America, a complete transformation is prerequisite".[95]

Yet, in reality, China does want to be seen by outsiders as both responsible and also as a rising power that has a keen interest in and intention to safeguard the wellbeing of the international order. China does indeed care about its international image, and acknowledges that interdependency is not only a reality but also an imperative for China's core national interest: economic development. The distinction here is that China wants to define 'responsible' and reserves the right to decide how to safeguard the world's wellbeing.

Since early 2007 China's credibility has been a recurring theme in internal discussions involving officials, foreign policy advisors, and scholars.[96] Chinese scholars have written about China's image problem in domestic journals, calling on China to "improve its credibility in the international community through enhancing the transparency of its governmental and commercial activities."[97] Ge Zhiguo of Hebei Normal University writes about the "poor behaviour" of Chinese companies in Africa and "their lack of social responsibility", which have not only created obstacles to the "go out" strategy of the enterprises, but "have also hindered the great efforts made by the Chinese government to maintain China-Africa relations".[98] Zhu Feng of Beijing University is quoted by the *Financial Times* as saying that Chinese state-owned companies are "hijacking China's diplomacy".[99]

China will continue to promote a more inclusive approach to international relations. However, that does not mean that it is willing to abide by majority decisions if these go against China's own national interests. China will also continue to call for the establishment of a new architecture of global security on the basis of equality, mutual respect, mutual trust, and benefit. It will also, as Bates Gill notes, continue to "softly balance against the United States at a regional and global level to shape the security environment more on Chinese terms".[100] Hence, China is not a status quo power, but neither is it one that wants to entirely remake the world order. Beijing seeks, in a subtle way, to reshape the world to accommodate its national interests.

Conclusions

This chapter has discussed the foreign policies of Russia and China during the past 20 to 30 years. While the picture is not clear and the future remains open-ended in the realm of these countries' foreign policy approaches, some general tendencies are clearly identifiable. Starting with Russia, one should note that despite the scope and pace of the changes that took place at the end of the twentieth century, Russia is not an entirely 'new' actor in international relations. Underestimating the factor of historical inertia, and the burden of the political, economic, and social legacy of the USSR has been the biggest mistake of those who thought that Russia's transition would be relatively painless. The process of democratic transformation began to malfunction as early as the mid-1990s, and in the 2000s the very concept of transition was called into question. In fact, it turned out that Russia experienced not so much a 'transition', but rather a redistribution of power and property, and the whole process should be addressed as a complex game of elite privatisation, leading to the establishment of a semi-authoritarian bureaucratic regime.

The vision of Russia becoming a 'normal' country was based on the premise that following the collapse of the USSR and the round of painful economic reforms the country has lost resources for expansionism and for the maintenance of its high international status. It seemed that the five-hundred-year "Russian moment in world history"[101] had ended with the voluntary refusal of the political elite to follow the traditional expansionist paradigm of foreign policy.[102] Nowadays one has to admit that this thinking was somewhat idealistic and premature. During 'Putin's (first) decade' of the 2000s, Russia tightened its political regime and, emboldened by the 'oil doping', it has returned to its traditional role of the 'powerful periphery' of Eurasia and of one of the main political opponents and constituent Others of the West. Russia has proclaimed its revisionist aspirations, and has demanded a change of the post-Cold War status quo. Seeking pragmatic benefits from the international situation, it did not hesitate to use the instruments of 'hard power', and it promoted its sovereignty, both domestically and internationally. Russia was constantly present in the international arena, declaring its foreign-policy ambitions and a sovereign opinion on different international issues.

One cannot fail to notice a contradictory, ad hoc nature to Russian foreign policy-making. Pragmatism does not sit well with Russia's defensive, nostalgic revisionism and the antagonistic approach of the Russian elite. Sovereignty these days can no longer be defended or projected by means of hard power alone, and yet Moscow has failed to manage its soft power mechanisms. One can say that Russian foreign policy of the past decade, from Kosovo–1999 to Georgia–2008, has been a foreign policy *by default*, rather than *by design*. Indeed, except for an obvious necessity to sell its oil and gas, at the end of the 2000s Russia still did not have any clear international goals. This is a disturbing and dangerous state of affairs, as Russia's reactive and revisionist foreign policy is finding itself in a strategic deadlock. The lack of a positive agenda in Russia's current foreign policy resembles the state of affairs in Soviet foreign policy 30 years ago, in the early 1980s. This was described by Hannes Adomeit as:

> incapable of or unwilling to embark on fundamental change, the leaders in Moscow adopted the attitude of 'insulted giant.' [...] Faced with this hostile posture and possibly dangerous policies, China and the West moved closer to each other. [...] Moscow still had sufficient power to obstruct and threaten, but no longer actively and constructively to shape world affairs.[103]

Still, Russia is not a main source of threats to the current world order or an obstacle to stabilisation of the international system. Although it sometimes disagrees with the decisions and actions of other countries, in general Russia is bound to the international system strongly enough to be interested in its gradual evolution rather than its radical transformation. This changing attitude is reflected in Russia's official foreign policy documents. For example, while the Foreign Policy Concept of the Russian Federation[104] is based on an assumption that the international system is becoming multi-polar and that Russia should implement a balanced and multi-vector (that is, independent) policy, then a new document from the Ministry for Foreign Affairs, leaked in May 2010, focuses on greater cooperation with Western countries for the purposes of the modernisation of Russia.[105]

Contemporary Russia is looking for more realistic, not only Realist, foreign policy, and for pragmatic cooperation with other countries instead of 'pragmatic' conflicts with them. Looking ahead, in the forthcoming years a sharp change in this foreign policy behaviour seems to be virtually impossible. It is quite probable that Russia will continue its peripheral balancing act between the existing and the emerging geopolitical centres, and will seek to position itself as one of poles of a multi-polar world, especially following the 2008–09 crisis. The contours of the new world are yet to take shape, but it is increasingly likely that through forces as dissimilar as Russia's idiosyncratic ambition and China's rise, this will be a post-Western world.

Turning to China, in a mere two decades China's international role has dramatically expanded; its influence is now evident in every conceivable sphere around the globe. The international activities of Chinese diplomats, officials representing numerous CCP and government agencies, military personnel, businessmen, scientists, and researchers all reflect China's new global activism.[106] Chinese foreign policy-makers are scrambling to accommodate the needs of this diverse group of Chinese actors abroad, many of whom prioritise China's national interests differently. Simultaneously, as a result of the growing number of serious transnational problems and increasing global interconnectedness, China's foreign policy officials are under pressure from other countries to take the demands of the outside world into consideration. Because of the sheer size of its territory, population, economy and armed forces, coupled with its power in the international arena as a permanent veto-wielding member of the United Nations Security Council, China's role is significant on just about every challenging international issue.

Integration into the international order has been essential for the phenomenal economic growth that China has experienced over the past three decades, spurring modernisation faster than either the Chinese or the outside world anticipated. For the last 30 years China's modernisation has greatly depended upon – and continues to depend upon – the existence of a liberal international economic order with free flows of goods and capital. However, the global financial crisis and the resulting economic downturn in developed nations has caused anxiety in Beijing. As a result, Chinese experts and officials have started to contemplate ways to reform some, but not all, of the premises of the present economic order.

Both hard and soft power remain vital, but in the information age soft power has become more compelling than ever before.[107] China recognises this and allocates enormous resources in the diplomatic, cultural, and economic domains to promote an image of a country intent on multilateral problem-solving based on mutual respect and equality. Shaun Breslin notes that a key source of Chinese power is the assumption by others that it either already has – or will soon have – this power and influence, whether in the form of soft or hard power. So, Breslin argues, "alongside the reality of what China has done to date, fears – often well founded – of what China might do and become in the future might play some role in creating the very power that is feared".[108]

China last engaged in warfare in 1979, against Vietnam. For the past 30 years Beijing has not only rhetorically, but also in its actions, demonstrated a wish to rely on means other than the use of force to resolve disputes – except when it comes to insisting on its resolve to deter any move (by force if necessary) toward recognition of *de jure* Taiwanese independence. The unresolved status of Taiwan's political future is clearly the central and only foreseeable issue which could impel Beijing to fall back on hard power.

When addressing the question which this chapter set out to shed light upon – whether China wants to uphold, remake or reshape the present world order – one can conclude that China seeks to incrementally reshape the world order to accommodate its growing economic, political, and military power. China did not participate in designing the "rules of the game", a prerequisite laid out by power transition theorists A.F.K. Organski and Jacek Kugler for status quo states.[109] On the other hand, China has indeed benefited enormously from the "rules of the game" – another prerequisite in Organski's and Kugler 's definition. But China is now in a position to seek adjustment of some of those rules in order to allow it to pursue its national interests more fully. While China's ultimate nature and intentions are ambiguous, it may well be that the sheer scale of its emergence will cause it to become "a strategic competitor to the United States by virtue of the structural imperatives that confront a rising world power determined to secure its ever-expanding interests, irrespective of its leaders' ambitions to pursue a 'peaceful rise'".[110] Moreover, China will not give up on its insistence on respect for sovereignty. Practical considerations will be the driving force in this incremental process, by which China will attempt to modify the rules that guide international interaction, and will use both its soft power and economic clout to do so. Nor will China's leadership officially swerve away from the argument that, as a developing country, China must focus on raising the living standards of its own people and hence must choose its own development path.

Notes

1. Robert D. Putnam, 'Diplomacy and Domestic Politics: The Logic of Two-Level Games', *International Organization,* vol. 42, no. 3, Summer 1988, pp. 427–460.
2. Putin's Prepared Remarks at 43rd Munich Conference on Security Policy, *The Washington Post,* 12 February 2007. Available at http://www.washingtonpost.com/wp-dyn/content/article/2007/02/12/AR2007021200555.html.
3. Dominic Wilson, Roopa Purushothaman, 'Dreaming With BRICs: The Path to 2050', *Global Economics Paper no. 99,* October 2003. Available at http://www2.goldmansachs.com/ideas/brics/book/99-dreaming.pdf.
4. 'BRICs Are Still on Top', *Newsweek,* 7 December 2009. Available at http://www.newsweek.com/2009/12/06/brics-are-still-on-top.html.

5. Azar Gat, 'Vozvrashenye velikikh avtoritarnykh derzhav' [The Return of Authoritarian Great Powers], *Russia in Global Affairs*, no. 4, July–August 2007. Available at http://www.globalaffairs.ru/number/n_9213.Sergei Karaganov, 'A New Epoch of Confrontation', *Russia in Global Affairs*, no. 4, October–December 2007. Available at http://eng.globalaffairs.ru/number/n_9791.
6. Robert Kagan, 'End of Dreams, Return of History', *Policy Review* no. 144, August 2007. Available at http://www.hoover.org/publications/policy-review/article/6136.
7. 'Day-By-Day: Georgia-Russia Crisis,' *BBC News*. 21 August 2008. Available at http://news.bbc.co.uk/2/hi/europe/7551576.stm
8. Dmitry Medvedev, *Speech at World Policy Conference*, 8 October 2008. Available at http://archive.kremlin.ru/eng/speeches/2008/10/08/2159_type-82912type82914_207457.shtml.
9. Curiously, this phrase has a double meaning, being the *New* World Order, but also the *New World* Order, i.e. *Pax Americana*.
10. Sergei Medvedev, 'NATO Enlargement and Russia: The Post-Madrid Agenda', in Filip Tunjic (ed.), *Stability and Security of Eastern and Southeastern Europe*, Ljubljana: Ministry of Defense 1997, pp. 71–82.
11. See *The Economist*, 11 December 2004. Available at http://wenku.baidu.com/view/84e31e160b4e767f5acfceab.html.
12. Dmitri Trenin, *Russia's Coercive Diplomacy*, Carnegie Moscow Center's Briefing, January 2008. Available at http://www.carnegie.ru/en/pubs/briefings/PB%20_Jan_10_1_2008_Eng_web.pdf.
13. Dmitry Trenin, 'Integraciya i identichnost': *Rossiya kak "novyi Zapad"* [Integration and Identity: Russia as a "new West"], Moscow: Izd-vo Evropa 2006, p. 178.
14. Trenin, *Russia's Coercive Diplomacy.*
15. Rose Gottemoeller, *Russian-American Security Relations after Georgia*, Carnegie Moscow Center's Briefing, October 2008. Available at http://www.carnegie.ru/en/pubs/briefings/russia_us_security_relations_after_georgia.pdf.
16. Sergei Medvedev, *Kosovo: A European Fin-De-Siecle*. Available at http://www.ctheory.net/articles.aspx?id=117.
17. *NATO Strikes: The First Week*. Available at http://news.bbc.co.uk/2/hi/special_report/1998/kosovo/312003.stm.
18. Sergei Karaganov, *Ponyat' menyayushiisya mir* (Understanding Changing World), EJ. 4 March 2008. Available at http://www.ej.ru/?a=note&id=7841.
19. Michael McFaul, *US-Russia Relations After September 11, 2001*. Available at http://www.carnegieendowment.org/publications/index.cfm?fa=view&id=840.
20. Dov Lynch, *Anchoring in Troubled Seas*. Paper presented at the conference on 'Reassessing the Transatlantic Partnership', Instituto Affari Internazionali, Rome, 19–20 July 2002.
21. 'Russia Suspends Arms Control Pact', *BBC News*. 14 July 2007. Available at http://news.bbc.co.uk/2/hi/6898690.stm.
22. Timofei Bordachev and Fyodor Lukyanov, 'A Time to Cast Stones', *Russia in Global Affairs* no. 2, April–June 2008. Available at http://eng.globalaffairs.ru/number/n_10937.
23. Viatcheslav Morozov, 'Sovereignty and Democracy in Contemporary Russia: A Modern Subject Faces the Postmodern World', *Journal of International Relations and Development*, November 2008, pp. 152–180, here pp. 167–168.

24. A. Arbatov, 'Don't Throw Stones in a Glass House', *Russia in Global Affairs*, no.3, July–September 2008. Available at http://eng.globalaffairs.ru/number/n_11289.
25. Morozov, 'Sovereignty and Democracy in Contemporary Russia'.
26. J. Nye, 'It Is Pointless to Talk to Al-Qaida', *Spiegel Online International* 17 August 2009. Available at http://www.spiegel.de/international/world/0,1518,643189,00.html.
27. 'Russian Bombers Land in Venezuela', *BBC News* 11 September 2008. Available at http://news.bbc.co.uk/2/hi/7609577.stm.
28. 'Venezela Welcomes Russian Ships', *BBC News* 25 November 2008. Available at http://news.bbc.co.uk/2/hi/7747793.stm.
29. Robert Kagan, *League of Dictators?*. Available at // http://www.washingtonpost.com/wp-dyn/content/article/2006/04/28/AR2006042801987.html
30. Phillip Mueller *et al.*, *Security 2.0: The Estonian-Russian Cyberwar of 2007*, Willy Brandt School of Public Policy, 29 December 2008. Available at http://www.globalize.de/security-20/.
31. Sergei Karaganov, 'A New Epoch of Confrontation', *Russia in Global Affairs* no. 4, October–December 2007. Available at http://eng.globalaffairs.ru/number/n_9791.
32. Igor Zevelev and Mikhail Troitsky, 'Russia and China in the Mirror of U.S. Policies', *Russia in Global Affairs* no. 4, October–December 2007. Available at http://eng.globalaffairs.ru/number/n_9778.
33. Morozov, 'Sovereignty and Democracy in Contemporary Russia', pp 158–159.
34. Bordachev and Lukyanov, 'A Time to Cast Stones'.
35. Joshua Cooper Ramo, *The Beijing Consensus*, The Foreign Policy Center, 5 November 2004. Available at http://fpc.org.uk/fsblob/244.pdf.
36. *International Security – Trends*, Center for the Study of Public Policy at the University of Aberdeen. Available at http://www.russiavotes.org/security/security_trends.php#443.
37. *International Security*. Center for the Study of Public Policy at the University of Aberdeen. Available at http://www.russiavotes.org/security/security_russia_place.php#nrb2.
38. Ibid.
39. Michael H. Hunt, 'Constructing a History of Chinese Communist Party Foreign Relations', *The Cold War in Asia*, Woodrow Wilson Center for International Scholars, Issues 6–7, Winter 1995–1996, p. 132.
40. See, for example, Emmanuel C.Y. Hsü, *The Rise of Modern China*, New York: Oxford University Press, p. 777; Li Xing, "From 'Politics in Command' to 'Economics in Command'. A Discourse Analysis of China's transformation", *Copenhagen Journal of Asian Studies*, no. 18, 2003, pp. 65–87.
41. Deng Xiaoping, 'China's Foreign Policy', 21 August 1982 in People's Daily (ed.), *Selected works of Deng Xiaoping, Volume II (1975–1982)*, Beijing: Foreign Languages Press, 1984.
42. Yuan Peng's comments in Nina Hachigian and Yuan Peng, 'The US-China Expectations Gap: An Exchange', *Survival*, 21 July 2011.
43. Harry Harding, 'China's Changing Roles in the Contemporary World' in Harry Harding (ed.), *China's Foreign Relations in the 1980s*, New Haven and London: Yale University Press 1984 p. 179.

44. William A. Callahan, 'National Insecurities: Humiliation, Salvation and Chinese Nationalism', *Alternatives* 29, 2004, p. 199.
45. Jing Men, 'China's Peaceful Rise?', *Studia Diplomatica*, vol. 56, no. 6, 2003, p. 17.
46. Agreement between the Republic of India and the People's Republic of China on Trade and Intercourse between Tibet Region of China and India, 29 April 1954.
47. Robert L. Worden, Andrea Matles Savada and Ronald E. Dolan (eds) *China: A Country Study*, Washington: GPO for the Library of Congress, 1987; see also Ministry of Foreign Affairs of PRC, 'China's Initiation of the Five Principles of Peaceful Co-Existence', 17 November 2000. Available at http://www.mfa.gov.cn/eng/ziliao/3602/3604/t18053.htm.
48. For overviews by Chinese observers of China's evolving foreign policy, see, for example, Zheng Bijian, 'China's Peaceful Rise to Great Power Status', *Foreign Affairs*, September–October 2005, vol. 84, no. 5, pp. 18–24; Wang Jisi, 'China's Search for Stability with America', *Foreign Affairs*, September–October 2005, vol. 84, no. 5, pp. 39–48; Xu Bu, 'Achievement and Experience of New China's Diplomacy', *Foreign Affairs Journal*, Beijing: China Foreign Affairs University, no. 93, 2009, pp. 1–16.
49. Chu Shulong *et al.*, *The Rise of China's Power and International Role*, Beijing: Institute of International Strategic and Development Studies, Tsinghua University, June 2009, p. 12.
50. The Papers of Thomas Jefferson. First Inaugural Address. Princeton University. Available at http://www.princeton.edu/~tjpapers/inaugural/inednote.html.
51. *Ibid.*, pp. 24–25.
52. Deng Xiaoping, 'Restore Agricultural Production', 7 July 1962, in People's Daily (ed.), *Selected Works of Deng Xiaoping, Volume I (1938–1965)*, Beijing: Foreign Languages Press 1991.
53. Deng Xiaoping, 'We Shall Concentrate on Economic Development', in People's Daily (ed.), *Selected Works of Deng Xiaoping, Volume III (1982–1992)*, Beijing: Foreign Languages Press 1994.
54. Samuel S. Kim and Lowell Dittmer, 'Whither China's Quest for National Identity?', in Dittmer and Kim (eds) *China's Quest for National Identity*, Ithaca: Cornell University Press, 1993, pp. 258–9. The quotes are from *Selected Works of Mao Tse-tung*, Beijing: Foreign Languages Press, 1961, vol. 4, p. 415.
55. Shaun Breslin, 'Understanding China's regional rise: interpretations, identities and implications', *International Affairs* 85: 4, 2009, p. 817.
56. See, for example, Fang Lexian, *Is China's Foreign Policy Becoming Less Ideological?*, paper presented at workshop 'Regional Governance: Greater China in the 21st Century', University of Durham, UK, 24–25 October 2003. Available at http://www.dur.ac.uk/resources/china.studies/ischinasforeignpolicybecominglessideological.pdf; Ming Zhang, 'The new mission of the Chinese Communist Party', *Journal of Communist Studies and Transition Politics*, vol. 13, issue 4, December 1997, pp. 79–98.
57. The words 'Deng Xiaoping Theory and the important thought of Three Represents', as well as the 'Scientific Outlook on Development', have been added on to Marxism–Leninism and Mao Zedong Thought. See 'Full Text of

Constitution of Communist Party of China', 21 October 2007, available at http://news.xinhuanet.com/english/2007-10/25/content_6944738.htm.

58. Steven I. Levine, 'Perception and Ideology in Chinese Foreign Policy', in Thomas W. Robinson and David Shambaugh (eds), *Chinese Foreign Policy: Theory and Practice*, New York: Oxford Books 1994, p. 32; Levine refers to Benjamin Schwartz, *Communism and China: Ideology in Flux*, Atheneum 1970, p. 71.
59. Harry Harding, 'China's Changing Roles in the Contemporary World', in Harry Harding (ed.), *China's Foreign Relations in the 1980s*, New Haven and London: Yale University Press 1984, p. 179.
60. Arthur Kroeber, 'Seismic shift: Economics give way to politics', *China Insight*, Beijing: GaveKal-Dragonomics,13 February 2008, p. 6.
61. Robert Cooper, 'The Post Modern State', in Mark Leonard (ed.) *Re-Ordering the World: The Long-term Implications of September 11th*, London: Foreign Policy Centre 2002.
62. UN Peacekeeping, 2011, 'UN Mission's Summary detailed by Country', United Nations Peacekeeping Operation, pp. 7–8, http://www.un.org/en/peacekeeping/contributors/2011/may11_3.pdf; see also Bates Gill and Chin Hao Huang, *China's Expanding Role in Peacekeeping*, SIPRI Policy Paper no. 25, Stockholm International Peace Research Institute, November 2009.
63. Ministry of National Defense of PRC. Available at http://news.mod.gov.cn/action/hh.htm.
64. Chen Hegao and Liu Yunfei, '胡锦涛同苏丹总统巴希尔会谈' [Hu Jintao meets Sudanese President Bashir], Xinhuanet, 2 February 2007. Available at http://news.xinhuanet.com/world/2007-02/02/content_5688877.htm.
65. Security Council SC/10200, 'Security Council approves 'no-fly zone' over Libya, authorizing 'all measures necessary' to protect civilians, by vote of 10 in favour and with 5 abstentions', 17 March 2011, available at http://www.un.org/News/Press/docs/2011/sc10200.doc.htm.
66. Linda Jakobson, 'The burden of 'non-interference', *China Economic Quarterly*, vol. Q2, 2007.
67. *Ibid.*
68. Zeng Aiping, '探讨21世纪中非关系 把握中国非洲学发展机遇—中国非洲史研究会第八届年会暨学术讨论会' [Discussing China-Africa relations in the 21st century, grasping the opportunity to develop China's Africa studies – China African the 8th seminar], *Xiya Feizhou*, vol. 1, 2008; Wang Jisi, '关于构筑中国国际战略的几点看法' [Few ideas on establishing China's international strategy], *Guoji Zhengzhi Yanjiu*, vol. 4, 2007; Wang Yingying, '非洲新形势与中非关系' [New Situation in Africa and Sino–African Relations], *Guoji Wenti Yanjiu*, vol. 2, 2004.
69. Wang Jisi, '和谐世界:中国外交新理念' [Harmonious world: new concept of China's diplomacy], *Zhongguo Dangzheng Ganbu Luntan*, vol. 7, 2007.
70. Comment by Chinese researcher at the China-EU Roundtable held at the China Institute of Strategic Studies in Beijing, 28 June 2007.
71. Author's meeting in Shanghai, 17 January 2008.
72. See, for example, Bates Gill, *Rising Star, China's New Security Diplomacy*, rev. ed. Washington DC: Brookings Institution Press 2010, pp. 113–116; Stephanie Kleine-Ahlbrandt and Andrew Small, 'China's New Dictatorship Diplomacy: Is

Beijing Parting with Pariahs?', *Foreign Affairs*, January–February 2008, p. 46.; Bates, Gill, Huang Chin-hao and J. Stephen Morrison, 'China's Expanding Role in Africa: Implications for the United States', Washington, DC: Center for Strategic International Studies, CSIS Report, January 2007; Jiang Wenran, 'Beijing's "New Thinking" on Energy Security', *China Brief*, Jamestown Foundation, vol. 6 (5), 12 April 2006.

73. For example, David Shambaugh, *Charting China's Future 2010–2015*. Forthcoming.
74. For example, Joshua Kurlantzick, 'China's Charm Offensive in Southeast Asia', *Current History* 2006; Samuel C.Y. Ku, 'China's Changing Political Economy with Southeast Asia: Starting a New Page of Accord', *Asian Perspective*, vol. 30, no. 4, 2006.
75. Joseph S. Nye, 'The Decline of American Soft Power', *Foreign Affairs*, May–June 2004. Nye injected the term 'soft power' into mainstream international relations debates with his book: *Soft Power: The Means to Success in World Politics*, New York: Public Affairs 2004.
76. Joseph S. Nye's comments in 'The Rise of China's Soft Power', transcript of panel discussion at Kennedy School of Government, Harvard University, Cambridge, MA, 19 April 2006. Available at http://www.iop.harvard.edu/JFKJrForumArchive/transcripts/04192006_The_Rise_of_Chinas_Soft_Power.pdf; see also Joseph S. Nye, 'Think again: Soft power', *Yale Global Online*, 2006. Available at http://yaleglobal.yale.edu/content/think-again-soft-power.
77. Bates Gill and Huang Yanzhong, 'Sources and limits of Chinese "soft power"', *Survival* 48: 2, 2006, pp 19–21.
78. The essay was re-published in the Communist Party's principal *Renmin Ribao* (People's Daily) and written by Mei Ninghua, the chief publisher of another major Party newspaper Beijing Daily: Mei, Ninghua, '对现代国家制度的新思考——从奥运成功举办看我国政治体制的优势' [A new perspective on modern structure of states – Looking at the superiority of my country's government structure from the viewpoint of the Olympic success], *Beijing Ribao* 22 September 2008. Available at http://news.xinhuanet.com/politics/2008-09/22/content_10090725.htm.
79. Zhang Yunling and Tang Shiping, 'China's regional strategy', in D. Shambaugh (ed.), *Power Shift: China and Asia's New Dynamics*, Berkeley: University of California Press, 2005, p. 51.
80. Confucius Institutes operate for the most part at overseas universities, while Confucius Classrooms are set up as Chinese language courses at primary and secondary schools in foreign countries.
81. '汉语言办公室"孔子学院总部"2010年度报告' [Confucius Institute Headquarters 2010 Annual Report], available at http://www.hanban.edu.cn/report/pdf/2010_final.pdf.
82. David Shambaugh, 'Return to the Middle Kingdom: China and Asia in the early Twenty-first Century', in D. Shambaugh (ed.), *Power Shift: China and Asia's New Dynamics*, Berkeley: University of California Press 2005, p. 25.
83. Linda Jakobson and Dean Knox, *New Foreign Policy Actors in China*, SIPRI Policy Paper, Stockholm: Stockholm International Peace Research Institute, 26/2010.

84. Zhao Suisheng, 'Chinese Foreign Policy under Hu Jintao: The Struggle between Low-Profile Policy and Diplomatic Activism', *The Hague Journal of Diplomacy* 5 (2010), p. 363.
85. Jakobson and Knox, *New Foreign Policy Actors in China*.
86. Wang Jisi, 'China's Search for a Grand Strategy', *Foreign Affairs*, vol. 90, issue 2, March–April 2011.
87. Dai Bingguo, 'We Must Stick to the Path of Peaceful Development', Ministry of Foreign Affairs of the People's Republic of China, 6 December 2010, available at: http://songkhla.chineseconsulate.org/eng/xwdt/t777848.htm. See also Da Wei, 'Why Should China Declare Its Core Interests?', *Huanqiu Shibao Online*, 28 July 2010.
88. Wang Jisi, 'China's Search for a Grand Strategy', *Foreign Affairs*, vol. 90, issue 2, March–April 2011.
89. Hu Jintao's speech available at http://news.xinhuanet.com/politics/2009-07/20/content_11740850_1.htm.
90. Bates Gill, *Rising Star*, Washington DC: The Brookings Institution 2007, p. 2.
91. Hiski Haukkala and Linda Jakobson, 'The Myth of a Sino-Russian Challenge to the West', *International Spectator*, vol. 44, no. 3, September 2009, pp. 59–76.
92. Hu Jintao, *Build Towards a Harmonious World of Lasting Peace and Common Prosperity*, speech at the United Nations Summit, New York, 15 September 2005.
93. Hu Jintao, *Build a Harmonious World of Enduring Peace and Common Prosperity*, speech at the CEO Summit of the Asia-Pacific Economic Cooperation (APEC) in Hanoi, Vietnam, 17 November 2006.
94. Robert B. Zoellick, *Whither China: From Membership to Responsibility*, remarks at the National Committee on US–China relations, New York, 21 September 2005.
95. Chu Shulong *et al.*, *The Rise of China's Power and International Role*, Beijing: Institute of International Strategic and Development Studies, Tsinghua University, June 2009, p. 21.
96. Author's conversations with officials at the Ministry of Foreign Affairs of the PRC and Chinese researchers at universities and research institutes in Beijing in October and November 2007.
97. Zha Daojiong, '从国际关系角度看中国的能源安全' [China's Energy Security: A Perspective on International Relations], *国际经济评论* [*International Economic Review*], vol. 11–12, 2005.
98. Ge Zhiguo, '中国'和谐世界'外交理念的践行—近年来中非关系论析' [The Practice of China's Diplomatic Concept of "Harmonious World"—Analysis of Sino–Africa Relations in Recent Years], *高校社科动态* [*Social Sciences Perspectives in Higher Education*], vol.3, 2007.
99. Richard McGregor 'Chinese diplomacy "hijacked" by companies', *Financial Times*, 17 March 2008.
100. Bates Gill, *Rising Star, China's New Security Diplomacy*, rev. ed. Washington DC: Brookings Institution Press 2010, p. 68.
101. Marshall Poe, *The Russian Moment in World History*, Princeton and Oxford: Princeton University Press 2006.
102. Sergei Medvedev, *Rethinking the National Interest: Putin's Turn in Russian Foreign Policy*, Marshall Center Papers. No. 6, August 2004. Available at

http://www.marshallcenter.org/mcpublicweb/MCDocs/files/College/F_Publications/mcPapers/mc-paper_6-en.pdf.

103. Hannes Adomeit, 'Russia as a "great power" in World Affairs: Images and Reality', *International Affairs* (London), Vol. 71, no. 1. January 1995, p. 41.
104. *The Foreign Concept of the Russian Federation*, 12 July 2008. Available at http://www.mid.ru/ns-osndoc.nsf/0e9272befa34209743256c630042d1aa/cef95560654d4ca5c32574960036cddb?OpenDocument.
105. Nikolaus von Twickel, 'Leaked Paper Calls for Friendlier Foreign Policy', *The Moscow Times* 13 May 2010. Available at http://www.themoscowtimes.com/news/article/leaked-paper-calls-for-friendlier-foreign-policy/405884.html.
106. Phillip C. Saunders, *China's Global Activism: Strategy, Drivers and Tools*, Washington DC: National Defence University Press 2006, pp. 6–9; Bates Gill, Chin Hao Huang and J. Stephen Morrison, *China's Expanding Role in Africa: Implications for the United States*, Washington, DC: Center for Strategic International Studies, CSIS Report, January 2007, pp. 16–18.
107. Joseph S. Nye, 'Redefining the National Interest', *Foreign Affairs*, vol. 8, issue 4, July–Aug 1999. Available at http://www.mtholyoke.edu/~jwestern/ir317/joseph_s_nye_jr.htm.
108. Shaun Breslin, 'Understanding China's Regional Rise: Interpretations, Identities and Implications', *International Affairs* 85: 4, 2009, p. 818.
109. A.F.K. Organski and Jacek Kugler, *The War Ledger*, Chicago: Chicago University Press 1980.
110. Daniel Twining, *As Asia Rises*, Washington DC: German Marshall Fund of the United States 2010, p. 25.

6
Conclusions

Christer Pursiainen

Over the past two decades, Russia and China have both experienced extensive socioeconomic and political transformation, as well as foreign policy reorientation. However, this transformation has not followed one pattern, but rather has taken two specific routes. In this book we have discussed these routes and provided arguments on why Russia and China have chosen such different paths for their post-communist transitions. We have discussed in some detail questions such as how have their strategies differed, and how have they been interrelated, at what junctures were the crucial choices made, how do their current systems resemble each other, and where do they differ? Perhaps even more importantly, we have outlined our understanding about what the strategic choices are that have yet to be made by Russia and China, what the alternatives are, how they are constructed and what the internal and external settings are which constrain the choices between different policy lines. Let us restate our starting points and summarise our findings here.

In Chapter 1 we presented the overall theoretical and methodological approaches. Generally speaking, our comparison of the post-communist developments of Russia and China includes two elements. First, we decided to compare these developments from the perspective of three interrelated arenas of social change: socioeconomic systems, political systems, and international roles. In this multidisciplinary spirit, our analysis combined several theoretical and methodological perspectives, derived particularly from Sociology, Political Science, and International Relations. While the respective chapters on these three dimensions function as separate comparative treatments in their own right, brought together, we argue, we receive a more coherent, holistic picture of the post-communist developments in these two countries.

Second, from the very beginning we adopted the approach that we are not aiming at explanations based on any single factor- or single level-theory. We are not claiming that historical legacy, or oil, or bad management and greed, can explain why Russia did not democratise, nor do we argue that China's modernisation path was predetermined by its socioeconomic development level. Instead, we emphasise the importance of the interplay of structures and agents, processes and individuals, culture and institutions, and identities and interests, in order to understand the transformations of Russia and China. Perhaps the most important feature of this approach is that it allows and even encourages us to think in terms of the open-endedness of the developments. In our analysis both structure and agency are in flux, and even if structures limit and condition actions and choices, at the same time they are objects of those very choices. Chapter 2 provided the historical background, claiming that for centuries both Russia and China have sought effective strategies to 'catch up' with the West. Thus, it is claimed, this pressure from the West is in a way the main exogenous structural factor affecting the endogenous modernisation processes in both countries. Russia and China have been positioned in this competition as underachievers or latecomers. With the combination of economic, political and military pressure it is natural that Russia and China themselves have often built their own identities on the basis of this perceived defensive position, and their search for modernisation has been characterised by a search for different types of catching-up strategies compared to the West. The communist project put both of these countries into a situation where they, instead of the capitalist West, were supposed or imagined to lead and set the standards of modernisation. As it turned out, the communist modernisation strategy was only a short-term success story. In the longer term it was more the creation of an illusion than a solution, and it ended in chaos. China was the first to understand the failure, and adopted a new modernisation strategy in 1979; the Soviet Union, with its inertia of 70 years of communist-forced, top-down modernisation started its reforms around 10 years later.

Chapter 3 focused on *socioeconomic modernisation*, which is perhaps the deepest dimension of change discussed in this book as it is visible to every citizen in the respective countries in very real terms. Both countries face the challenge of developing a new socioeconomic model and a new social contract between the state and society. This chapter asked: will the new model be based on the idea of the 'power of the market place', namely a privatised social welfare system with, perhaps, a strong third sector taking care of many of the previous responsibilities of the state? Or will a new welfare state be developed upon the ruins of the old 'socialist welfare state', thus developing a new and perhaps more equal state-led system of welfare?

The analysis of these issues is rooted in class structures. In China as well as in Russia, the economic transition towards market-based societies, including elite and mass privatisation, has fundamentally transformed social structures. In both countries the transition has created a new capitalist class as well as small employers' and petty bourgeois social classes. However, the privatisation process looks very different in these two countries. Russia's privatisation process started with the so-called spontaneous privatisation, which allowed the old managerial elite to capture most of the property subject to privatisation. Fearing the comeback of communism, the reformist government adopted a new approach and created a new entrepreneurial class of capitalists: the oligarchs. They took over control of the largest natural resources and related production facilities and created financial institutions to manage this stage of privatisation, quickly accumulating huge private wealth. The third – and so far, final – phase of privatisation is characterised by a partial re-nationalisation or bureaucratisation of property, where strategic parts of the Russian economy have been put into the control of hand-picked members of the political elite. The Chinese privatisation started in the countryside and then spread to other sectors in a step-by-step fashion. However, by the 1990s a capitalist class had formed. The chapter argues that before the late 1990s there were, to some extent, conflicts between political elites and the new economic elites, but since then an 'elite consensus' has been reached. This gave the state the role of arbitrator of conflicts of interest between the new capitalist and upper classes versus the majority of the population. In any case, both in Russia and China, the privatisation process has led to the re-emergence of the capitalist and middle-class entrepreneurial classes, and the former is particularly closely connected to or intertwined with the state.

As to the emerging post-communist class structure, in Russia the new wage-labouring middle-class positions have grown during the post-Yeltsin regimes, after having declined during the first ten years of transition. The working class has lost its celebrated status, but in economic terms its situation has improved over the last ten years. China has been doing much better in relative terms, however. Nevertheless, the most important issue that distinguishes China from Russia is that for China the post-communist transition meant not only transforming from a planned economy to a market economy, but also transforming from an agricultural society to an industrialised society. The most dramatic change in the social structure of China during the transition period is the migration of huge numbers of peasants into the cities, part of the urbanisation and industrialisation trends, followed by their occupational transformation from farmers into the working class or other social classes.

However, social inequality as measured by the Gini coefficient has grown in both countries, especially in terms of regional or urban–rural disparities. There is no strong welfare sector in either country. Trade unions are relatively weak in promoting the interests of the working class in the formation of welfare regimes. The upper and middle classes are inclined towards a liberal model of the welfare states. In Russia, one can identify a tendency towards building a liberal model of welfare system based on the power of the market place and self-financed private sector. But in China, a country more fearful of the social and political consequences of extreme inequality on stability, policy is shifting from an initially liberal approach towards a more socially acceptable and state-centred 'European model', though naturally with its own unique features.

Chapter 4 was about *political modernisation*. The main issue for the political system in both countries is the choice between authoritarianism and democracy. Russia has undergone a major political transformation and established formally democratic political institutions; however, they remain characterised by the legacy of the old system and the emergence of some new authoritarian trends. Democratic institutions do not work in the liberal fashion: the government cannot be seen as truly accountable and representative of the society. The link between the state and civil society is weak or controlled by the state. Russia is, in a way, pluralistic, but not truly democratic in the Western sense. China, still a one-party state, has experienced some small-scale local-level democratisation, which has not bestowed political freedom as such, but has rather used the ballot box as a weapon against corruption in local administrations. Some 'intra-party' democracy issues have been discussed, as though a substitute to democracy at large, but this has not developed into a detailed strategy. A combination of regime learning and adaptation has enabled the Chinese Communist Party to develop an effective survival strategy. As a result of its effective adaptation, China has seen the emergence of a unique hybrid capitalist–authoritarian order. In some important ways, this order is similar to that of post-Soviet Russia: in both countries, elite-based political coalitions control power; the state wields decisive influence in the economy through the direct control of the largest corporations and the financial system; the leading economic elites of both countries have, to various extent, entered into an alliance with global capitalism; and selective repression and different co-opting strategies are used to defend the regime's political monopoly.

The experiences of both countries show that that economic progress and globalisation do not necessarily lead to political modernisation in the form of democratisation. Instead, economic modernisation, or the necessity for it, may force the ruling elites to opt for strategic choices that are intended to preserve their political monopoly. These choices can lead to the adoption of policies and institutional changes that forge a close link between capital and political power. In Russia, in particular, this link has been given many names, such as 'bureaucratic capitalism', 'oligarchic capitalism', or 'crony capitalism'. Once formed, this link is hard to break because of the overwhelming advantage that this elite capital–power coalition possesses vis-à-vis societal forces that want to challenge its dominance.

It is concluded in this chapter that, in the case of both countries, a kind of an elite equilibrium has been achieved and there seems to exist no forces powerful enough within the current elites, or potential alternative elites, who would be able to propose alternative political systems in the short term. The societal level, on the other hand, despite the mass protests in Russia, is too weakly organised into interest groups and too fragmented or marginalised politically to put forward alternative cohesive modernisation strategies. However, when it comes to the stability of the current systems, the chapter notes that this capital–power alliance may not be durable despite its apparent resilience, due to the self-degenerative nature of capitalist authoritarianism; corruption, opportunism, and inefficiency permeates the system, weakening it from within and making it more vulnerable to exogenous shocks and endogenous societal revolts. These kinds of shocks can perhaps be avoided if preventive survival and adaptation strategies grow from within the elites. In this sense, China's leadership seems paradoxically to have been, and to continue to be, much more sensitive than its Russian counterpart in reading the early warning signs of instability.

Chapter 5 dealt with the *international roles* of China and Russia. The chapter asks whether their international strategies will be based on defending autonomy and sovereignty, or whether they will decide to participate in (or are drawn to) developments which institutionalise growing interdependency and norm-based cooperation between them and the outside world? The chapter states that Russia's current foreign policy is profoundly controversial, and demonstrates how Russia seeks to replay the end of the Cold War and revive at least some of its great power ambitions. Its foreign policy is characterised by 'nostalgic revisionism', with an inclination towards sovereignty understood as independence from international institutions and regimes, and towards displays of traditional hard power. Russia has not really managed to adapt its foreign policy to the post-modern world, where sovereignty can no longer be defended or projected by means of hard power alone. However, Russia also professes pragmatism, largely defined by the economic interests of the various elites, who are vitally dependent on the West. Yet Russia's uneasy combination of pragmatism with revisionism, overall reliance on hard power, and the neglect of soft power instruments seem not to be particularly successful.

China, on the other hand, is scrambling to come to terms with the new international role that comes with its economic power. It has hesitated in deciding whether it should take on more international responsibility or continue to focus on domestic modernisation. In any case, Beijing has moved from its former heavy reliance on bilateral relationships to working within numerous multilateral frameworks. Compared to Russia, China's foreign policy appears to be much more effective and better designed. It has also expended a great deal of effort and resources to build up its soft power capacity. Yet China has to find a balance between the changing needs of the country and the rising expectations of the international community. Its own modernisation requires the avoidance of conflicts in order to facilitate concentration of the nation's resources on building up comprehensive national power. If the Chinese Communist Party's focus on modernisation is its paramount objective, and also imperative for regime survival, then its foreign policy must be subordinated to facilitating this modernisation. China's modernisation has greatly depended upon – and it continues to depend upon – the existence of a liberal international economic order with free flows of goods and capital, and consequently China's foreign policy has reflected its reliance on the outside world. To a large extent Beijing has pursued policies that are consistent with international norms and the interests of the US and European Union. At the same time, China has not given up on its insistence on respect for sovereignty. Nor has China's leadership officially been swayed from the argument that, as a developing country, China must focus on raising the living standards of its own people before taking on greater international responsibility.

Taken together, the different dimensions discussed in this book draw a fairly comprehensive picture of the post-communist modernisation paths of Russia and China. There are, naturally, interrelated – and not only separate and isolated – aspects. Within each chapter these interrelationships have been discussed in some detail. It seems clear that historical legacies affect the current modernisation paths in a variety of ways, both in terms of material structures and values. In each country, their legacies have not facilitated a development towards democracy, though they do not necessarily hinder it either. Another interesting linkage is that between the socioeconomic and political systems. Here the Russian and Chinese experiences seem to provide contradictory – though not necessarily incommensurable – lessons. Russia's poor socioeconomic performance and the chaos of the 1990s can be seen as a precondition for why a major part of Russian society was, and seems to remain willing, to adapt to more authoritarian rule. In the Chinese case, on the contrary, its huge socioeconomic performance can be seen as the main source for the legitimacy of the current leadership. A third linkage is between the political systems and the respective country's international role. While it seems clear that the possible democratisation of these countries would have causally important consequences on their international behaviour, this change might not overshadow the traditional balance of power politics of great powers.

Index